JAPANESE WOMAN AND CHILD
Watercolor by Bunzo Watanabe, 1882

JAPAN DAY BY DAY

IN TWO VOLUMES
VOLUME I

JAPAN DAY BY DAY
1877, 1878-79, 1882-83

BY

EDWARD S. MORSE

FORMERLY PROFESSOR IN THE IMPERIAL UNIVERSITY OF TOKYO
MEMBER OF THE JAPAN SOCIETY OF NEW YORK
MEMBER OF THE JAPAN SOCIETY OF LONDON
AUTHOR OF "JAPANESE HOMES AND
THEIR SURROUNDINGS," ETC.

WITH 777 ILLUSTRATIONS FROM SKETCHES
IN THE AUTHOR'S JOURNAL

VOLUME I

BOSTON AND NEW YORK
HOUGHTON MIFFLIN COMPANY
The Riverside Press Cambridge
1917

TO MARGARETTE W. BROOKS

WITHOUT WHOSE EFFICIENT HELP AND UNFLAGGING

INTEREST THE MANUSCRIPT WOULD NEVER

HAVE BEEN READY FOR THE PRESS

THIS WORK IS AFFECTIONATELY

DEDICATED

PREFACE

I FIRST visited Japan solely for the purpose of studying various species of Brachiopods in the Japanese seas. While pursuing my work in a little laboratory established at Enoshima, I was invited by the Educational Department to take the chair of Zoölogy in the Imperial University in Tokyo. During my residence in Japan of nearly four years I kept a daily journal to avoid the duplication of home letters. A portion of my sojourn had ended before records were made of subjects which might afterwards be published. These, however, were special in their nature, such as notes and sketches relating to the dwelling-house and associated features. These memoranda formed the material for my book entitled *Japanese Homes and Their Surroundings*. For this reason scant reference to these subjects is made in the present work, though a few sketches that appeared in that book are reproduced. I made no effort to record or collect data upon subjects in which I was not specially interested. Having little interest in Japanese religions — Buddhist or Shinto — or in Japanese mythology and folklore, no studies were made of these subjects. With no interest in geography, I hardly learned the names of rivers crossed, or regions traversed. The excellent guidebooks of Murray, Satow, and lately the interesting one of Terry, published by Houghton Mifflin Company, render it unnecessary for me even to allude to the countless features of interest in the towns and cities through which I passed, as in these guidebooks these matters have been dealt with to the minutest detail.

Not a day passed that some note or sketch was not made, oftentimes of the most trivial character. I realized the importance of recording matters of interest at the time the observations were made, knowing full well that soon they would become hackneyed and escape recognition. Professor Bliss Perry, in his admirable *Park-Street Papers*, quotes the following extract from a letter Hawthorne wrote to his friend Horatio Bridge, who was just going across the ocean. "Begin to write always before the impression of novelty has worn off from your mind, else you will be apt to think that the peculiarities which at first attracted you are not worth recording; yet these slight peculiarities are the very things that make the most vivid impression upon the reader. Think nothing too trifling to set down, so it be in the smallest degree characteristic. You will be surprised to find, on re-perusing your journal, what an importance and graphic power these little peculiarities assume."

Whatever value these records may possess lies in the fact that when they were made, Japan had within a few years emerged from a peculiar state of civilization which had endured for centuries. Even at that time, however (1877), changes had taken place, such as the modern training of its armies; a widespread system of public schools; government departments of war, treasury, agriculture, telegraph, post, statistics, and other bureaus of modern administration, — all these instrumentalities making a slight impress on the larger cities such as Tokyo and Osaka, sufficiently marked, however,

to cause one to envy those who only a few years before had
seen the people when all the samurai wore the two swords,
when every man wore the queue and every married woman
blackened the teeth. The country towns and villages were
little, if at all, affected by these foreign introductions, and the
greater part of my memoranda and sketches were made in
the country. The extent of territory traversed may be indicated by stating that my travels extended from Otaru nai,
on the west coast of Yezo, north latitude nearly 41°, to the
southernmost end of Satsuma, latitude 31°, mostly overland
by jinrikisha and on horseback. By far the larger mass of notes
and sketches would be similar to records made a thousand
years ago; indeed, so little had the country changed that ex-
tracts from the *Tosa Diary* (translation of Aston) depicts scenes
and conditions resembling those I was daily recording.

Precisely how to present this material, comprising thirty-
five hundred pages of journal, had long perplexed me; in fact,
had it not been for a letter from my friend, Dr. William Stur-
gis Bigelow, with whom I visited Japan for the third time,
the journal would never have been prepared for publication.
I wrote to my friend exultingly that I had a long leave of
absence from the Peabody Museum of Salem, and the Boston
Museum of Fine Arts, in order to finish a number of studies on
Mollusks and Brachiopods, and in return received the following in a letter from Dr. Bigelow: "The only thing I don't like in
your letter is the confession that you are still frittering away
your valuable time on the lower forms of animal life, which
anybody can attend to, instead of devoting it to the highest,
about the manners and customs of which no one is so well

qualified to speak as you. Honestly, now, is n't a Japanese
a higher organism than a worm? Drop your damned Brachiopods. They'll always be there and will inevitably be taken
care of by somebody or other as the years go by, and remember that the Japanese organisms which you and I knew fa-
miliarly forty years ago are vanishing types, many of which
have already disappeared completely from the face of the
earth, and that men of our age are literally the last people
who have seen these organisms alive. For the next genera-
tion the Japanese we knew will be as extinct as Belemnites."
The point he made was overwhelming and unanswerable,
and reluctantly I began the work of preparing the material
for publication. I at first resolved to classify the memoranda
under the headings of a course of twelve lectures on Japan
given before the Lowell Institute of Boston in the winter of
1881–82. These were as follows: 1. Country; people; language.
2. Traits of the people. 3. Houses; food; toilet. 4. Homes and
their surroundings. 5. Children; toys; games. 6. Temples;
theatres; music. 7. City life and health matters. 8. Country
life and natural scenery. 9. Educational matters and students.
10. Industrial occupations. 11. Ceramic and pictorial art.
12. Antiquities.

Some of these subjects have already been dealt with by
others with a wealth of illustration that makes their work
monographic in character. It would have been an endless un-
dertaking to have classified the material after the Lowell Institute course and would have required many new subhead-
ings. Hence I have been reluctantly compelled to present
these journal notes as a continuous record, and the title of

the book, *Japan Day by Day*, suggested independently by Mrs. H. A. Garfield and Lorin F. Deland, Esq., is a simple statement of fact. Much of the material is as light and disjointed as the rambling crowds on the streets which the journal so often depicts. It records, however, many features rarely seen to-day and many that are obsolete. Important subjects of the journal I have already published elsewhere.[1]

With these eliminations certain data were still left for special magazine articles. This material is now included with the rest of the diary. Neither time nor strength permitted me to redraw the hundreds of "thumb-nail" sketches which illustrate the journal, many of which were made under trying circumstances, in jostling crowds, even from bumping jinrikishas. Many of these sketches are rough to the last degree, yet, as an artist friend observed, they possess a certain psychological value which if redrawn they would lose.

I was urged by Mr. J. E. Lodge, of the Boston Museum of Fine Arts, to accompany the name of every Japanese object with the Chinese character, or characters, representing the name. It would have added very greatly to the task of pre-

---

[1] These memoranda have been embodied in various articles, memoirs, and books, as follows: In *Popular Science Monthly*, three articles entitled "Health Matters in Japan"; "Traces of Early Man in Japan," illustrated, and "Dolmens in Japan," illustrated. In the *Youth's Companion* an article on "Kite-flying in Japan," illustrated. In *Harper's Monthly* an article entitled "Old Satsuma," with 11 woodcuts, illustrating 49 objects. A book entitled *Japanese Homes and Their Surroundings*, with 307 figures. *Shell Mounds of Omori*, published by the Imperial University of Tokyo, with 18 folded lithographic plates, containing 267 figures. My notes on Japanese pottery formed a quarto volume of 364 pages with 68 photogravure plates and 1545 potter's marks in the text, published by the Boston Museum of Fine Arts. My Brachiopod work, which first led me to Japan, was published by the Boston Society of Natural History. This formed a quarto volume of 86 pages with 23 lithographic plates.

paring the manuscript for the press, and realizing that the few readers who cared for the Chinese ideographs would have in their possession, or could readily find access to, Hepburn's *Japanese and English Dictionary*, where the equivalent characters might be found, I have reluctantly declined to follow this excellent suggestion. It may be added that a good font of Chinese characters would be difficult to find in this country. One would have to send to Brill, of Leyden, to secure the type. The long ŏ has been omitted for similar reasons.

In the journal many statements are broadly made; as, for example, when I speak of the honesty of the Japanese I do not imply by these general statements that petty thefts are not known; the fact that one sees policemen and that jails and prisons exist, indicates that infractions of the law occur. As for the proverbial dishonesty of bric-à-brac dealers, where in the wide world could one find an honest example? When I declare that the Japanese do not swear, I base the statement on the fact that the Japanese have no "swear words." They have deities and saints enough, but their names are never invoked, or damned, as in Spain, where odious epithets are coupled with the names San Pedro, San Juan, and other apostles.

In regard to the many errors that are sure to be found, I can only say that the best authorities were consulted, and in the forty years that have elapsed since these records were made new light may have been shed; thus Mr. Tomita writes me that Fuji, in Fujiyama, is a word of Ainu origin, meaning volcano.

Among the earlier friends I made in Japan and to whom I am much indebted were Dr. Hideyoshi Takamine, Director

of the Female Normal School, and his friends, Tsunijiro Miyaoka and Seiken Takenaka. Mr. Miyaoka has since become
a distinguished lawyer. He was formerly in the diplomatic
service, having been councillor in the Japanese embassies at
Berlin and Washington. When a little boy nine years old he
was a playmate of my own boy of the same age. He was at my
house very often, and from him and his brother I got innumerable items of information relating to proverbs, superstitions,
games, manners, and customs. My grateful acknowledgments
are due also to my special students with whom I was intimately associated in the laboratory. To Dr. Kato, Director
of the Imperial University, and to the Vice-Director, Dr.
Hamao, and to Dr. Hattori; Count Tachibana, Director of
the Nobles' School, and to the hosts of Japanese students
and friends, teachers of tea ceremony and music, whose names
are mentioned in the preface of *Japanese Homes*, my obligations are due. The patient and courteous answers they made,
often choking with laughter at the apparent absurdity of
some of the questions, enabled me to record many customs
that had not been noted before. Some of my interlocutors had
scant knowledge of English and this with my equally scant
knowledge of Japanese led to many erroneous records at the
outset. It is considered rude to differ in opinion, and when
you think you comprehend the subject your friend amiably
agrees with you!

My thanks are due to Mr. Kojiro Tomita, of the Museum
of Fine Arts, and to Miss Chie Hirano for assistance in various
ways. To my daughter, Mrs. Russell Robb, who was with me in
Japan, I am indebted for reminding me of many incidents and

experiences which I had not recorded, and also to Mr. Russell Robb, who critically read every page of the typewritten manuscript, reducing redundancies, shortening sentences, and in various ways smoothing asperities; and finally, to Miss Margarette W. Brooks, who read and copied my execrable manuscript, and in so doing made the rough smooth and the obscure plain, and who persistently kept me at the work, my obligations are infinite.

E. S. M.

CONTENTS

JAPAN DAY BY DAY

CHAPTER I

OMITTING all details of the voyage from San Francisco and the delights of getting on land after a seventeen days' voyage, the journal will start with the first sight of a native.

It was dark when we dropped anchor at Yokohama. A Japanese boat belonging to the hotel came alongside and into this a number of us got. The boat was a long, clumsy affair sculled from the side by three Japanese, their only clothing consisting of a loin-cloth: little short fellows they were, but immensely strong, for they easily brought down on their naked backs the heavy trunks and other packages. How vigorously they worked sculling us two miles to the shore! And such a peculiar series of grunts they made, keeping time with each other with sounds like *hei hei cha, hei hei cha,* and then varying the chanty, if it were one, putting quite as much energy into the grunts as they did into the sculling. The noise they made sounded like the exhaust of some compound and wheezy engine. I felt a real sympathy for them in seeing the intense energy they gave to each stroke, and they never let up in the entire two miles. The boat was curiously arranged for sculling from the side. A plan shows transverse pieces which rest on the edge of the boat and overlap several inches (fig. 1). A knob in the oar fits into a hole in the

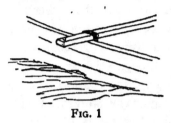

Fig. 1

end of this transverse piece. The oar (fig. 2) is composed of two pieces firmly tied together, heavy and apparently clumsy. One man sculled on one side and two on the other, one of these steering as well. As we neared the shore, one of the boatmen called out, "Jinriki-sha," "Jinrikisha," and was promptly answered by some one

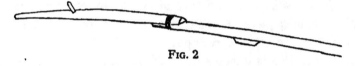

Fig. 2

on shore. It was a call for the two-wheeled vehicle drawn by man power.

Finally the boat grounded, and I jumped out on the shores of Japan tickled enough to yell, which I mildly did. In landing you feel a curious exaltation of accomplishment. The customs officers came sedately down to inspect our baggage, little Japanese fellows with their black hair showing strangely under their uniform caps of pure white. Away we went in the dark, following a street that led by the shore. The hotel was somewhat disturbed by our late arrival, and a few Japanese servants scurried about preparing our rooms. We went to bed excited by the novelty of our situation and so eager to see the morning light that, like boys anticipating the pleasures of a Fourth of July morning, we hardly slept a wink.

Here on my thirty-ninth birthday, what a world of delight

burst upon me as I looked out the hotel window this morning on the frigates of the various nations in the harbor and
the curious native boats and junks, with everything novel
but the ships and the sea. At our corner is a canal which
comes down from the country. Through this narrow channel the quaintest boats were passing, the boatmen singing
their curious chanties as they vigorously worked. People
were going by clothed in the scantiest garments, some carrying wares of various kinds, most of them wearing the rude
wooden clogs, which make a curious, resonant clattering on
the hard road. The clogs were of two types, one consisting
of an oblong piece of wood with two thin pieces fastened

crosswise, the other carved out
of a solid block of wood. A thick
cord is so arranged that the front
part of it comes between the big
toe and the next one to it, as
shown in figure 3, which was
sketched from the foot of a re-

Fig. 3

spectable old woman. The road along which the people
passed, for there were no sidewalks, was curiously marked
by the wooden clogs, and narrow wheels of the jinrikishas.
There are many kinds of clogs and sandals: neat ones made
of straw lying about the stairways, others of the rudest straw
costing less than a cent apiece, worn by the poorest people,
and on the road you often see the discarded ones.

At the entrance of the canal a new sea wall is being built,
and one could watch with interest for hours the curious
human pile-driver. The staging is lashed together with ropes

of straw. The men at their work are nearly naked, and, in one case, with the exception of the loin-cloth, absolutely so. The pile-driver is a curious contrivance. A heavy weight is attached to a long pole which is guided by a workman who sits on a plank of the stage, while others pull ropes which are attached to the weight below and run through pulleys above,

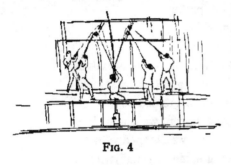

as in figure 4. There were eight men in the circle, but my sketch, for simplicity, shows four. An odd, monotonous chant was sung, and at the end of the stanza all pulled together, and then sud-

FIG. 4

denly letting go, the weight dropped with a thud. It seemed a ridiculous waste of time to sing the chanty, for such it was, without exerting the slightest effort to raise the weight. Nine tenths of the time was devoted to singing!

Immediately after breakfast we started to see the town. Never will these first impressions of wandering through the streets of a Japanese town be effaced: the odd architecture; the quaint open shops, many like the cleanest cabinets; the courtesy of the attendants; the novelty of every minutest object; the curious sounds of the people; the delicious odor of cedar and tea filling the air. About the only familiar features were the ground under our feet and the warm, bright sunshine. At the corner of the hotel a number of jinrikishas were lined up waiting for a fare (fig. 5), and as soon as we started

they called out "Jinrikisha?" We plainly signified that
we did not want one; nevertheless, two of
them followed us; when we stopped, they
stopped, and when we peered into the little
shops and smiled at anything, they smiled.
I wondered at their patience in following us
so far, for we did not intend to hire, prefer-
ring to walk. However, they knew better
than we did what would happen, that in our

FIG. 5

wanderings we should not only get tired, but lose ourselves,
which was precisely what we did, and having become completely exhausted by the novelties which greeted us at every
step, lost, and fatigued by the long tramp, we gladly indicated our intention of riding back. As we stepped into the
frail-looking vehicle I, for one, felt a sense of humiliation in
being dragged by a man and should have felt less embarrassed if I could have got out and exchanged places with
the naked-legged human. But this feeling soon wore away,
and the exhilaration of having a man ahead running like
the old scratch the entire distance to the hotel, without
stopping, was as surprising as most of the experiences of that

FIG. 6

morning. Their charge at the
end of the ride was ten cents,
and for this they had spent an
entire forenoon! The wonderful endurance of these men exceeds belief, for we are told
that they will run for miles in
this way, hour after hour, without apparent fatigue (fig. 6).

In carrying passengers they never walk, but always run with a long, swinging lope, barelegged and barefooted, and, generally, bareheaded, no matter how hot the sun. They have sometimes a band of cloth tied about the head and on the back a short indigo-dyed coat of thin cotton cloth, while about their loins is tied a breech-cloth. They apparently are clad no more warmly in winter. A cool costume, certainly, but odd enough to our eyes. How we enjoyed the ride! Going at full speed through the narrow streets of a town, the peculiarities of the simple dwellings, the people, dress, shops,

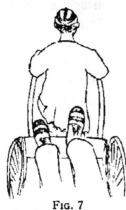

hundreds of women and children, old men and boys, all recalled the various pictures we had seen on fans and which we thought were exaggerations. Jinrikisha riding is a constant delight; a gentle up-and-down oscillation of the vehicle is all the motion perceptible. You really travel at a good speed, your horse never runs away, and when you stop he guards your property. Here is the way my man looked on the first long ride I took (fig. 7). The

FIG. 7

top of the head was shaven and a little waxed queue rested upon the bald area. A white cloth was tied around the head.

Everybody seems to "keep shop." The shop and the room back are wide-open to the street, and as one stops to barter he finds himself rudely looking beyond the stock in trade to the family at supper, or going through their rounds of domestic work, which is reduced to the last expression of simplicity. In nearly every house is a receptacle filled with ashes in which is buried a burning coal. Over this water is heated for the tea and on cold days the hands are warmed, but the chief service seemed the providing of a convenience for the smoker. The pipe and mouthpiece are of metal, the stem a reed of some kind (fig. 8). The tobacco is light-colored, finely

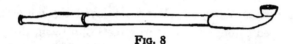

Fig. 8

cut, very dry, and very mild. The bowl will hold a ball of tobacco the size of a small pea, and after filling it and lighting it from the coal one or two whiffs consume it all. Even one smoke will often suffice, though the pipe may be filled a few times for successive smokes. Opportunities to make tea are ever ready, and a common mark of hospitality when you visit a shop is to offer you a cup of tea. It is impossible to describe the appearance of these tiny shops. In some respects they remind you of an open shed with a floor raised from the ground, on the edge of which you sit. The goods, often a pitifully small stock, are arranged on a series of low, step-like shelves, so near that one can reach the objects from where he sits, and beyond, the family in a room back are eating, reading, or sleeping, and if the shop deals in manufactured objects the room behind is devoted to the making of fans, cakes, candy, toys, or whatever may be the articles sold. You get the impression of a lot of children playing baby house. No chairs, table, or other articles of furniture are seen, unless it might be a case of drawers; no chimney, no stove, no attic, no cellar, no door even, only sliding screens. The family sleep on the floor, which, however, consists of mats of uniform length, of six feet by three, fitting tightly as a boy's blocks might fill the bottom of a box. There is a little head-rest for a pillow and heavily quilted comforters cover one at night.

The utter freedom of the people gives a vivid impression of their peculiarities. For instance, you often pass a woman walking in the middle of the street openly nursing her child. Though the country people seem very polite in their repeated bowings, we have seen but little gallantry so far. As an example, we observed a young woman drawing water from a well. These in many towns are at the side of the street. She was interrupted by three men who left their load in the street to get a drink of water, she standing patiently by until they had finished. We supposed, of course, they would draw up a bucket of water for her; but nothing of the kind, — they did not even thank her.

In entering a shop, which in most cases is simply by stepping over a sill on to the hard ground again, men and women leave their clogs behind them. As shown in an earlier sketch the stocking is like a mitten, the big toe separate from the other four toes. By this arrangement one can immediately step out, or rather off, the clog or sandal. A section of an ordinary shop is shown in figure 9. No mat-

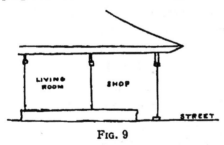

Fig. 9

ter how small the area back of a house or shop, an attempt is made to have some sort of a garden.

One notices with sympathy the painful endurance of a class of men who take the places of horses or bulls in dragging and

FIG. 10

pushing a two-wheeled cart with heavy loads of merchandise (fig. 10). In their efforts they bark or grunt out a series of short sounds and so loudly that they may be heard a considerable distance. The refrain sounded as follows: *Hoida hoi! Hoi saka hoi!* The beads of perspiration pouring down their faces and water dripping from their mouths are evidences of the painful efforts they are making. The duty of the *betto*, or footman, as he has to be literally, since he is rarely allowed to ride, is to run ahead of the carriage to clear the way through the crowds in the streets, for everybody walks in the roadway. In this way men will run as fast as a horse will trot and continue for miles and miles. These bettos dress in black with round, black, bowl-shaped affairs on their heads and long flowing sleeves floating out behind. One is reminded of black demons.

The extensive rice-fields everywhere indicate the enormous amount of labor involved, not only in making them, but in the yearly amount of labor expended in planting-time. The

rice-fields are divided into irregular plots by narrow embankments which form pathways to the plots. In some of the
plots men are at work breaking up the soil (fig. 11); in others
distributing from buckets the liquid manure; while in still

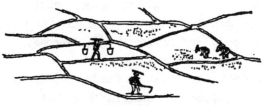

Fig. 11

others the work of transplanting is going on; for every little
rice plant, like a spear of grass, has to be put in place by the
hands, a task that seems incredible, but the whole family join
in the work, old women as well as the children. The smaller
children seem to be in attendance as spectators, carrying on
their backs the babies. This carrying of babies on the backs
one sees everywhere. It is a remarkable sight to see four
women out of five, and five children out of six, lugging babies
upon their backs, oftentimes held in place by the hands of
the holders crossed behind, or the child riding with its legs
astride the carrier. A rare thing is to hear a baby cry, and thus
far I have never seen the slightest sign of impatience on the
part of the mother. I believe Japan is the only nation in the
world that yields so much to the babies, or in which the babies
are so good. I saw one mother shaving a baby's head with a
sharp razor; the baby was crying, but, nevertheless, standing
perfectly still. I contrasted all this behavior again and again,
with that found in certain tenement regions at home.

In the fields and woods I noticed some plants precisely like those at home, while others were most unlike: palmetto, bamboo, and other forms distinctly semi-tropical. At the head of a little valley a body of French marines, with their jaunty hats and bright blue and white trimmed uniforms, were practicing target-shooting, banging away at a lively rate. I saw tea growing for the first time, and whichever way I turned, my eyes met some new object of interest.

We rode across Yokohama in the fascinating jinrikishas on our first visit to Tokyo, the name meaning "Eastern Capital." It is a city of nearly a million inhabitants. Its old name was Yedo, and the older foreign residents still call it Yedo. The train bearing us to Tokyo was made up of first, second, and third class cars; we found the second class cars clean and comfortable. The cars are a triple cross between the English car, the American car, and the American horse-car. The couplings, truck, and bunter-beam are English, the platforms and doors in ends of cars are American, and the seats running lengthwise are like our horse-cars. With what interest we watched the landscape. The rice-fields, stretching for miles on each side of the railroad, are now (June) covered with water, and the people working in them are up to their knees in mud; the new rice, of a light-green color, contrasts vividly with the dark shaded groves. The farmhouses have enormous thatched roofs, on the ridge-poles of which are growing plants with leaves like the iris. At intervals we passed a temple of worship, or a shrine, always in some charming, picturesque place surrounded by trees. The sights were novel and absorbing and the ride of seventeen miles went like a flash.

We were in Tokyo. As the train stopped, the passengers alighted on a cement walk, and the clatter made by the wooden clogs and sandals was somewhat like the sound produced by a troop of horses crossing a bridge — a peculiar resonant or rather musical vibration was mingled with this clatter of sound. Our jinrikisha had an extra man in front with a rope on his shoulders, in fact a tandem team, and off we started at a lively rate. If Yokohama had been interesting, the narrow streets and hum of life in this great city were vastly more so. To ride along so rapidly, to peer into every house, to pass the odd characters, — priests, gentlemen, brightly dressed women, students, school-children, nearly every one bareheaded and all black-haired, and some, if not all, of the lower classes having a loose sort of gown tied about the waist, — was bewildering. My head fairly became confused with the various sights and novelties.

In passing through a large burned district such activity I have never seen. Two types of buildings were going up, the little one-story dwelling-houses and shops of the flimsiest character and the tall, two-story, fireproof buildings, massive and sombre. In building a large fireproof structure the staging is built first and then covered with matting so that the plaster, which they use so freely, shall not dry too quickly. On these a heavy tiled roof is used. This is believed to be of great security in earthquakes, for the inertia of the roof is such that it does not move, while the building itself may be swaying. In balancing a cane on the finger some difficulty is experienced. If a heavy book could be fastened to the top of the cane, it would be much easier to balance it,

and the hand could be moved rapidly back and forth a few
inches without the book moving at all. A solid frame is built,
and then a network of bamboo is interwoven between the
beams like basket-work, and the plaster is applied to both
sides of the network. If the building be first boarded, square
tiles are laid on, sometimes diagonally and sometimes hori-
zontally, and after that the seams are very tastily plastered
with white plaster making a very neat and pretty appear-

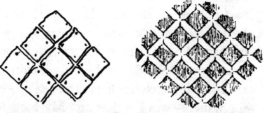

FIG. 12

ance (fig. 12). It is customary for merchants to lay by a
sum of money every year for building purposes in anticipa-
tion of the conflagrations which often ravage large areas;
but the district through which we were going had been for so
long a time exempt from such a calamity that the accumula-
tions of funds in this way had become sufficient to enable
them to afford a much better class of buildings.

We were soon at Dr. David Murray's office, having ridden
over quaint and handsome bridges and alongside of the castle
moat. This moat looked like a small river with a stone wall
rising in a graceful slant to a height of twenty feet or more,
and this wall enclosed a large region. The water for the moat
or ditch is brought fifteen miles or more and the entire work

is enormous in its solidity and extent. Entering a low building furnished with a table and a few chairs, we awaited the
arrival of Dr. David Murray, the Superintendent of the
Department of Education. On the table was a box containing an earthen vessel in which was a live coal for the smoker's
convenience, and soon a servant brought cups of tea on a
tray, bowing nearly to the floor when he entered the room.

The foreign University professors live in houses built in
our style, most of them in a large enclosure surrounded by
high walls with gateways at intervals, some permanently
closed and others always closed at night. There are a number of these enclosures in various parts of the city and they
are known as *yashiki*. In feudal times the lords, or daimyos
of the provinces were compelled to live in Yedo for a certain
number of months a year. The dignitaries came with their
retainers, artisans, and servants, in some instances to the
number of thousands. The yashiki to which we were going
was known as Kaga Yashiki, the Daimyo of the Province of
Kaga occupying it in feudal times. The other yashikis in
the city bear the name of the province of the daimyo to
whom they belonged. Reliable books on Japan will inform
the reader more specially about these enclosures. The great
wealth of some of the daimyos, the magnificence of the pro-
cessions when they started overland for Yedo, and the great
awe which these ceremonial columns inspired are among the
most impressive features of feudal times. The Daimyo of
Kaga came with ten thousand men; the Daimyo of Satsuma
with his retainers traveled over five hundred miles to reach
Yedo. The sums expended in this way were very great.

Kaga Yashiki is now a wilderness of trees, bushes, and tangled masses of shrubbery; hundreds of crows are cawing about; here and there are abandoned wells, some not covered, and treacherous pitfalls they are. The crows are as tame as our pigeons and act as scavengers. They sit on the fences bordering the railway and caw as the train goes thundering by and they wake you in the morning by cawing outside the window.

We visited the Imperial University with Professor Toyama. It was a strange sight to see the students, all in Japanese costume, studying Gray's Botany, at work in the chemical laboratory, performing experiments in physics, and using English textbooks. A preparatory school for the study of English is connected with the University and all students must understand English well before entering the University. I had an interview with the Director of Educational Affairs for the Empire, a fine-looking Japanese who could not utter or understand a word of English. Another very scholarly looking young man, who acted as interpreter, accompanied him. It bothered me somewhat to talk through an interpreter in this way, as the whole interview was very formal, though very pleasant. The refined conversation in Japanese was very attractive to listen to. Dr. Murray sat by, and after the conversation had ceased and we had parted, the Doctor said I had left an excellent impression. Fortunately my practice in lecturing without notes came in well at this interview, for I framed my language with the greatest care, complimenting the Director on the progress the country was making.

In the afternoon Professor Wilson, with whom we dined,

took me to the "Wrestlers," where numbers of wrestlers have their bouts. The surroundings were odd enough; little tea-houses, a few bronze gods, ten feet in height, and the usual swarm of Japanese. We bought our tickets, consisting of pieces of wood, seven inches long, two and one half wide, and one half inch in thickness, on which were printed a number of Chinese characters. The "circus" was made of poles standing upright, with rafters laid flat across, on which, for a ceiling,

Fig. 13

was straw matting and the walls were of the same material. A rude gallery, or rather two galleries, ran round the building and were equally primitive. In the centre were four upright posts between which was a raised portion and a ring of nearly twenty feet in diameter, with a canopy of red cloth above (fig. 13). At each post there sat an old Japanese, evidently some sort of a judge, while a stern-looking fellow, highly dressed, acted as umpire. To see the huge and corpulent wrestlers come into the ring straddling their legs, lifting them up and down as if they were trying them, slapping them vig-

orously, and then when ready stooping down for a few minutes facing each other, examining each others' muscles, for
they were entirely naked save for a loin-cloth, was a novel
and interesting sight. When they finally got ready they
rested their hands on the ground and then suddenly sprang
at each other, the feat being to push or throw one or the other
out of the ring. Sometimes the struggle was very short, at
other times active and with tremendous strength shown; and
sometimes one of them would be simply pushed back from
the ring and at other times they would get some fearful tumbles. One wrestler was thrown out of the ring landing on his
head and shoulders, which were scratched and bleeding when
he got up. We sat very near the ring so that I might look
back upon the audience. The ground was parted off by mortised beams making areas about six feet square which answered for boxes. Within the enclosure all the space was
yours, and some of the audience had writing materials and
were taking notes of the struggle; others had their little vessels with hot coals and a little tea-kettle and were making
tiny cups of tea at intervals. What interested me as much
as anything was watching the Japanese as they looked curiously at Professor Wilson's eight-year-old boy. This sweet
little fellow sat on the side of the enclosure where he could
see the performance. As the entire audience was kneeling on
the floor and Harry was up high, they could all see him. His
light curly hair and blue eyes were as novel a sight to them
as bright red eyes and blue hair would be to us, for foreigners
are not yet so common in Tokyo as to be familiar objects.
Now, this light-skinned and delicate-looking boy speaks Jap-

anese just as well as he does English. Judge, then, of the astonishment of the Japanese when the boy turned round and asked, for his father's sake, an explanation of some part of the performance and then gave it to us in English. The delighted faces of the Japanese to find that he could speak their language was charming to see, and so repeatedly during the performance I asked Harry to ask the Japanese a number of questions for the sake of seeing their looks of admiration. The wrestlers were very large and strong, some of them perfectly enormous, they were so fat; but there seemed to be more brute strength than agility manifested. Over and over again they would grapple, and the umpire, detecting something wrong, would stop them, and they would unlock and each go to a corner of the arena, at one of the posts, where an assistant would hand them a swallow of water which they would blow into a spray over the body and arms, then they would take a handful of dirt and rub it in the arm-pits, and

FIG. 14

come back to the centre of the ring, crouch down, and go through the same manœuvres six or eight times before they could get rightly started. Sometimes they would get in this attitude (fig. 14), and one would say, "O-shi" and the other, "O-sho," and this they would repeat many times. All the while the most vigorous efforts were being made by each to maintain his position. At length the umpire would say something and they would stop their struggles and step out of the ring, the bout being evidently a drawn game. The perfect quiet and order prevailing, though no policemen were present, the good humor and politeness shown, and the entire absence of any odor or close smell impressed me; and when the show was over and they all came swarming out, there was no crowding, pushing, or loud talking, no rushing to whiskey saloons, for there were none; but many stopped near the little booths surrounding the place and took a quiet cup of tea or a tiny cup of saké. Again I contrasted this behavior with that accompanying a similar performance at home.

When we drove away, my friend, having an engagement that prevented him from carrying me to the railroad station, called a jinrikisha and told the man in Japanese where I wanted to go and for half an hour I was traveling through the narrow streets of this vast city. I never met a single European, and, of course, did not know whether I was going in the right or wrong direction.

Immediately after leaving Tokyo on the train one notices in the waters of the Bay of Yedo five small, low islands of identical shape running in a line parallel with the shore. You are not surprised that these islands should be fortified, but are amazed as to what peculiar formation or denudation could result in producing such curiously symmetrical islands. You are told that they are artificial and were all built within the space of five months. When Commodore Perry went away he stated that he would be back in five months, and in this interval the Japanese not only built the five islands from the bottom up, but surmounted them with forts and even mounted cannon on some of them. The incredible industry and the swarm of workmen and vessels required remind one of the resources and exploits of the ancient Egyptians, only the Japanese had taken days to do what these ancient people had taken years to accomplish. The islands appeared to be four hundred or five hundred feet square and perhaps a thousand feet apart. In the park in Tokyo we had noticed boulders that were unquestionably glaciated, but were afterwards told that these stones had been transported probably hundreds of miles from the north on Japanese junks.

In our rambles we have come across a few cemeteries appearing very much like our own graveyards, but differing, of course, in the form of the stone monuments and in the absence of the long, narrow mound and in the agreeable absence of those pretentious and obtrusive products of stone-yard art. With all the other sensible and sanitary features characterizing the Japanese the custom of cremation is one. What proportion of bodies are cremated I do not know, but it is large.

At night you occasionally hear a curious clacking sound beaten in regular rhythmic raps. You find that these sounds are made by private watchmen who at intervals go about the grounds to inform the owners that some one is on guard.

At times, night and day, you hear a plaintive sort of shrill whistle. This sound is made by blind men and women who go about the streets to advertise their calling, which is that of masseurs. You call one in, and for half an hour or more the masseur will hammer, pinch, rub, and maul you in such a way that when the work is finished you feel like a new man, and for this delight you pay the sum of four cents! Thousands and thousands of the blind throughout the Empire earn their

living in this way. They go to a regular school and are taught
the proper methods of massage. These unfortunate people
have been rendered blind by smallpox, but since the common
sense of the nation saw the merits of vaccination and promptly
adopted it this loathsome disease has been banished forever
from the country. We could not help recalling the incredible
idiots in our country, who, too obtuse to understand the value
of numbers and statistics, resist this beneficent process. Such
people by the laws of survival of the fittest are ultimately
eliminated by smallpox and thus the race goes on in its advance. The sign, "I am blind," is never seen on street beggars; indeed no street beggars are seen. The various cries of the street venders of food and other
articles arrest your attention at once by their quaintness and you even follow the peddlers along the
street to hear their calls. The cry of the flower
vender sounds precisely like the terminal cluck of
a hen.

The devices for the display of objects in the shops
are often simple and interesting. Thus a fan shop
had a rack made of a long piece of bamboo with
openings cut between the joints and into these places FIG. 15
the fans were inserted. A similar holder is found in
the kitchen to hold wooden spoons, spatulas, skewers, etc.
(fig. 15).

The infinite variety of simple objects that one sees in a
single ride along the streets keeps one on the alert, amused and
delighted all the time. In the balcony of those houses which
may have a second story the balcony rail will show a hun-

dred varieties of lattice, carving, nature effects in wood, etc. In one balcony rail I saw a rough plank with irregular holes in it (fig. 16): one would say, a rude and ungainly object fit

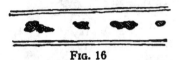

FIG. 16

only for fire wood, and yet the Japanese enjoy the natural results of nature's caprices: the fungus-stained wood, a plank cut from the outside of an irregular tree-trunk, the holes in the plank being made by the depressions.

I have had enough experience with a jinrikisha to learn that one must sit quite still in riding. The man, pulling, holds the shafts rather high and just balanced, so that any sudden movement forward, as in bowing, may bring the man on his knees and throw you over his head; or, in recognizing some friend who has just passed, you turn your head and body around, leaning back at the same time, and the chances are that the jinrikisha tips back and you are gently dumped into the street to the mortification of the man, who stands bowing and go-men-na-sai-ing, and to the amusement of the crowd.

The decorative impulses of the Japanese run to everything, and even a baby's head is not exempt from this impulse, as one notices the adroit way it is shaved, leaving tufts over the ears, a semi-lunar area in front, a circle on top of the head, and a little queue behind.

As the horses are never shod as with us, it is an odd sight to see horses and bulls wearing straw shoes. These have a heavy matted sole and are tied behind the hoof. Along the road one sees discarded shoes, not only of the four-legged beasts of burden, but of those of the two-legged kind.

Figure 17 shows one way of holding a child to the back, the mother having her hands crossed behind and holding in her hands the baby's toy.

FIG. 17

Somewhat astonished at learning that the death-rate of Tokyo was lower than that of Boston, I made some inquiries about health matters. I learned that dysentery and cholera infantum are never known here; some fevers due to malaria occur, but are not common; rheumatic troubles show themselves among foreigners after several years' residence. But those diseases which at home are attributed to bad drainage, imperfect closets, and the like seem to be unknown or rare, and this freedom from such complaints is probably due to the fact that all excrementitious matter is carried out of the city by men who utilize it for their farms and rice-fields. With us this sewage is allowed to flow into our coves and harbors, polluting the water and killing all aquatic life; and the stenches arising from the decomposition and filth are swept over the community to the misery of all. In Japan this material is scrupulously saved and goes to enrich the soil. It seems incredible that in a vast city like Tokyo this service should be performed by hundreds of men who have their regular routes. The buckets are suspended on carrying-sticks and the weight of these full buckets would tax a giant. This stuff is often transported miles into the country, where it is allowed to remain in open half oil-barrels for a time and then is distributed to the rice-fields by means of long-handled wooden

dippers. Besides this substance for the enrichment of the soil
a great many cargoes of fish manure are brought from Hakodate. Without manure they do not cultivate; the soil is not
rich in productive materials, as it is mostly of volcanic origin.
A Japanese saying is, "A new field gives but a small crop."

The absence of sunstroke is another interesting fact, for
the people go bareheaded under the hottest sun, and the men
have the tops of their heads shaved. At home it is believed
that intemperate living induces sunstroke; here the people
are temperate in their habits of eating and drinking.

The streets and smaller alleys are generally well watered.
The people abutting a street may be seen sprinkling it with

Fig. 18

large bamboo dippers. In Tokyo men
go along the streets having suspended
on carrying-poles deep buckets of water. A plug is lifted out of a hole in the
bottom of the bucket and a spreading
stream of water pours out, the man in
the meanwhile almost running to scatter
the water over as wide an area as possi-

ble (fig. 18). The buckets for lugging water are made on such
sound principles and so simply that Eastlake would have

highly approved of the taste and utility displayed.
Two of the staves are continued above the rim to
nearly twice the height of the bucket and a transverse piece from one to the other forms the handle
(fig. 19). The carrying-stick, made of hard wood,
is found throughout Japan, China, and Korea. A
man will be seen having two large baskets suspended from

Fig. 19

the carrying-pole, in one of which will be a large fish and in the other several heavy stones to balance it! One would think there was a waste of energy here. Deep buckets of water for drinking purposes are seen swinging from these carrying-poles, but floating in each bucket is a circular piece of wood of nearly the diameter of the bucket, and this simple device prevents the water from slopping over. Low, shallow tubs are seen with three of the staves extending below the tub a short distance forming legs which support the bucket from the ground, and from this receptacle live fish in salt water are peddled. The simplicity of construction and the strength and durability of objects, at least in the hands of the Japanese, are noticeable.

Among the earlier features in this country noticed by foreigners is the fact that in many operations we do just the reverse of the Japanese, and this feature has been commented on a thousand times; nevertheless, I cannot help recalling it. The Japanese plane and saw toward them instead of away from them as we do; they begin a book on what we should call the last page, and at the upper right-hand corner and read down; the last page of our books would be the first page of theirs; their boats have the mast near the stern and the sailor sculls from the side; in the sequence of courses at dinner candy and cake are offered first; they drink hot water instead of cold and back their horses into the stall.

A "tea-firing" building, one hundred by one hundred and fifty feet, is an interesting place with its long row of furnaces, or rather large kettles enclosed in brick with openings beneath for fire. These rows of kettles covered the spacious

floor, which was the ground (fig. 20). The kettles were made
of some composition that resembled tin or zinc and the fires

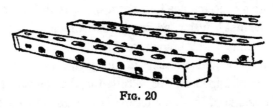

FIG. 20

were kept up by charcoal, the universal fuel of Japan. Each
man, woman, or girl tended two of these kettles, his duty
consisting in stirring the leaves with the hand to prevent
them from burning. One may imagine the aroma the tea loses
in firing, when it is stated that the atmosphere of Yokohama
is at times charged with the delicate fragrance of the herb.
The heat of the place was oppressive. The men were naked
except for the loin-cloth and many of the older women were
naked to the waist. Each person had a convenience for making cups of tea and many of them were smoking their tiny
pipes. Babies of all sizes were running round between the
rows of furnaces or sitting up on the brickwork. Some were
on the backs of their mothers. At almost every occupation
or trade the children are present, either carried on the backs
of their parents or of older children, or led by the hand. It
seems reasonable to believe that the continual presence of
children at every kind of activity may account for the dex-
terity the Japanese manifest in taking so readily to every
kind of handicraft. The tea for export has to be thoroughly
dried before packing in their sheet-lead boxes, which are her-
metically sealed by soldering. The slightest moisture would

lead to mould and deterioration. The tea for home consumption is only slightly fired and therefore retains most of the aroma. As a consequence lukewarm water is all that is necessary for the first infusion, while with us, "unless the water boiling be," etc., is a well-known maxim.

The number and novelty of delightful experiences one encounters in Japan makes a task for the journalist. The theatre was one of these novelties. It was an exhilarating experience to start off with a number of friends for the theatre. To be whirled along at a lively rate in single file through crowded streets, at every second having new sights, new sounds, and new odors, — the last not always pleasant, — is an experience never to be forgotten. We are soon at the theatre, a quaint-looking building decorated with long strips of cloth embellished with Chinese characters absolutely unintelligible to us, bright-colored lanterns, and a medley of grotesque signs. Within we come to a large rude sort of hall dimly illuminated, having a gallery on three of its sides. The place looked more like a huge barn. The floor was parted off by a framework leaving interspaces six feet square and a foot or more deep, and these bins were the boxes in which entire families could find room (fig. 21). The Japanese sit with their legs bent under them, and not like the Turk, who sits crosslegged. There is no chair, stool, or bench. It was quite as interesting, or at least equally novel, to watch the audience as it was to watch the acting. Here are entire families; mothers nursing babies, children inattentive to the play and sleeping, the ever-present fire vessel over which water is being heated for tea, old men smoking, and all so quiet, re-

.fined, and courteous. The two aisles are floors on a level with
the tops of the bins, and the people walk along these plat-

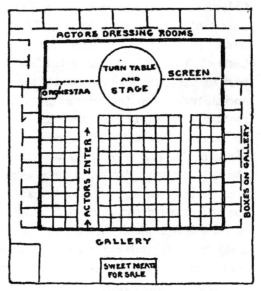

FIG. 21

forms, and then on the edge of the boxes, which may be five
inches wide, to their respective places.

The stage is low and the orchestra, at one side, is concealed
by a black, painted partition. In the centre of the stage is an
immense turntable, twenty-five feet in diameter, level with
the floor. When the scene changes there is no lowering of the
curtain, but the turntable slowly rotates carrying actors and
all, bringing into view another scene that the stage hands have
been busy about and carrying out of sight the scene already
used. It was interesting to watch the audience in their re-

ception of the play. They certainly showed more feeling and animation than I had seen displayed by a Chinese crowd in a Chinese theatre in San Francisco, and I may add parenthetically that the Chinese theatre at Shanghai differed in no respect from the San Francisco one save that a big, round Connecticut clock kept time on the San Francisco stage. We were told that the play represented some classical drama of ancient times. The language was difficult even for the Japanese who interpreted for us. He could catch a word only now and then. It was interesting to see the actors dressed in garments of the style of centuries gone by — the samurai with the long and short swords. A tipsy scene was acted with a great deal of drunken vigor; a stuffed kitten was dangled from the end of a long pole and stole a letter. Coming up the raised aisle from the entrance several actors stride along with a regular stage strut and swagger, the grandest of all having his face illuminated by a candle on the end of a long-handled pole held by a boy who moved along too and kept the candle constantly before the actor's face no matter how he turned (fig. 22). The boy was dressed in black and walked backward.

Fig. 22

He was supposed to be invisible, as indeed he was in imagination to the audience, but to us he was quite as conspicuous as the actors. There were five footlights, simply gas tubes standing up like sticks, three feet high, and unprotected by shade or screen, a very recent innovation; for before they had these flaring gas jets it was customary for each actor to have a boy with a candle to illuminate his face. The prompter, instead of being concealed, as with us, walked about deliberately on the stage, coming up behind each actor in turn (my table has just been shaken by an earthquake, June 25, 1877, — another shock, and still another), crouching down as if he were hiding, and prompting in a voice loud enough to be

FIG. 23

plainly heard. Figure 23 is a rough sketch of the stage. Above the stage for a drop affair there hung down a mass of stiff cord on which were closely strung bits of bright-colored paper. The orchestra was in action all the time — a lazy, absent-minded thrumming on the Japanese banjo with now and then a toot of a flute. The music was not so energetic or so loud as in the Chinese theatre. The menial subjection of women in past times was illustrated by the constant crouching attitudes assumed by those representing women, for we are told that men or boys always play the female characters. Between the acts a huge curtain was run across the stage and upon it were the most enormous figures in high colors with all the grotesqueness one sees on some of their fans. The

theatre in every detail was a novel sight, and only the faintest
idea of it can be given in this brief account.

Sunday was an interesting day to one brought up in the
old New England manner. Every trade and occupation was
in full activity; the boats in the harbor were just as busy as
on a week-day, and the old pile driver opposite the hotel was
hard at work; scavengers and waterers were in the street;
all the native shops were open, and so far as I could see there
was not the slightest observance of the day. I went to Tokyo
in the afternoon to visit the Imperial Museum in Uyeno
Park. The workmen in the park were busy on the grounds,
the shutters of the Museum were closed, but twenty naked
carpenters (the loin-cloth worn in every case) were at work
on tables and cases. The Museum was a perfect surprise to
me — a collection of birds finely mounted, a beautiful case
of native crustaceans, large alcoholic collections, and many
other groups of the animal kingdom represented; and it was
odd enough to notice that every label was in Japanese. The
advance in educational matters and the adoption of foreign
educational methods is bewildering.

In riding through the streets of Tokyo I observed many
new things. Nearly every house has a staging on the ridge-
pole with a few steps leading to it. Here one may go the better
to observe the progress of a conflagration, for the fires in this
city are often terrific in their swiftness and extent. The dwellings are usually light and apparently flimsy affairs, rarely
over one or two stories in height, but there are fireproof buildings behind or by the side of these dwellings which have walls
of clay or mud two feet thick or more. The door and the

shutters of the few windows are of the same material, very
thick, and made precisely like our safe doors at home with
three or four separate jogs. The houses are separate, though
standing close together. When endangered by the approach
of a conflagration the heavy window shutters and the door of
the fireproof building are closed and clay is then plastered
over the cracks and chinks. Before closing it up, a number of
candles are placed in a safe spot on the floor within and are
lighted, thus gradually consuming all the oxygen and rendering ignition less likely. Now, while they are supposed to
know nothing about the chemistry of combustion, they understand and put into practical use a principle which, so far as
I know, has never been practiced elsewhere. These buildings
are called *godowns*, an Indian word, the native word being
kura. The merchant and housekeeper hastily stow their
property in these godowns and neighbors avail themselves
of the protection thus afforded. After a great fire these black
buildings tower up from the ruins, not unlike our chimneys
under similar circumstances at home. The smoking ruins
of some of them recall the experience of some of the so-called
fireproof safes at home.

The visitor to Japan and other Oriental countries very
soon remarks on the almost universal use of bamboo for a
multitude of objects. Along the river great lumber yards of
bamboo are seen, the bamboo standing up in huge masses.
It would astonish an Occidental if he could see a list of the
objects made from bamboo. I have seen rude hoes of bamboo
with which small stones were being hoed out of a cart for road
repair; a serviceable, broom-like rake is made from a single

piece of bamboo, one end being split into eight pieces spread apart broom-like. It was used as a broom, a rake, and a pitch-fork.

Going through the strange-looking streets it is odd to hear the click of the American sewing machine. The prompt way in which the Japanese adopt new ideas is the surest indication of the fact that this ancient nation is free from that deadening conservatism that marks the Chinese.

In coming from the University I walked up to a group of four jinrikisha men and wondered if they would all rush for me as do our hackmen at home; but, no, one of them stooped down, picked up four straws of varying lengths, and then drew lots. No feeling was shown as the lucky one drew me away to the station. Time had to be made to catch the train and during the ride the wheel of my jinrikisha bumped into the hub of another one ahead. The men simply smiled their apologies for getting in the way, and kept on. I instantly contrasted this behavior and the customary swearing resulting from a similar accident at home. In my numerous rides I have noticed how carefully they turn out of the way for a cat, dog, or hen that may be in the road, and thus far I have never noticed the slightest evidence of impatience or ill treatment of animals, and the men never scold. This I record not as based upon my own very limited experience, though I have kept my eyes open, but from the testimony of those who have lived in the country for many years.

The chopsticks are the oddest devices to take the place of a knife, fork, and spoon. The food which really requires a knife to cut is served already cut in small pieces, the soup one

drinks from a bowl, and the chopsticks act as a fork in picking up bits of food and as a shovel in pushing rice from the
rice bowl as the rim is held to the mouth. One is surprised,
however, to see the chopstick idea come into use in many
other ways: a pair of iron chopsticks is used to pick up live
coals; the cook uses a pair to turn his fish or cake; the jeweler
uses a delicate pair of ivory chopsticks in putting together a
watch; and on the street one notices the rag-picker and
scavenger with a pair of chopsticks three feet long with which
he picks up rags, paper, etc., from the street and drops the
material into a basket carried on the back.

In going through the streets one notices the remarkable
absence of beggars. The absence of deformed persons is also
noticeable. One is amazed at the number of jinrikishas! In
Tokyo, I was told, there are sixty thousand! It seems beyond
belief and the statement may be incorrect.

A visit to the local market in whatever country one travels
is an interesting lesson in natural history. The world traveler
should make a note of the two important places to visit, the
local market, and, in Europe, the local art gallery. At the
market he gets a view of the local natural history, but, in
Europe especially, he sees not only the peasants in their native costume, but the home-made boxes, baskets, and the
like. A visit to the market in Yokohama was a series of interesting sights. A large area, roofed over with matting and
having alleys running through it, contained the greatest collection of living fish that I ever saw. The various forms of
tubs, trays, and baskets alone were interesting, filled with
living fish, of many species, brilliant in color or quaint in form;

the exhibition was unique. A peculiar flat basket with the bottom made wider than the rim is useful in holding fish, as the form prevents the slippery creatures from sliding out (fig. 24). The shallow tubs filled with various species of edible

Fig. 24

mollusks were fascinating; sprays of water showering upon them kept the color-markings bright and fresh. Specimens that the collector at home would regard as rare and valuable objects were displayed by the basketful. Here was a boy opening a beautiful little species of bivalve, preserving the soft parts and throwing the shells away by the bushel. Shallow tubs filled with the most remarkable looking prawns of large size, crabs of grotesque shapes and quaint forms, rare in our museums at home, were here in quantities. Immense oyster-like creatures were exposed on the half-shell, their

Fig. 25

hearts still beating, an evidence that they were alive and fresh. The pearl shell, *Haliotis*, known as *abalone* on the Californian coast and as *awabi* here, was offered for sale as an article of

Fig. 26

food (fig. 25). Shallow bamboo baskets, each containing three shells, were exposed for sale, the shells covered with beautiful seaweed and tubular worms, a perfect little forest of sea life. The most curious sight to me were the cuttlefish, some of large size, both squid and octopus (fig. 26), some alive and others boiled and ready to eat.

The various creatures were all kept alive by a simple device. A huge circular tank resting on a low stand was kept
filled with water by men who traveled back and forth from
the ocean to the market with heavy buckets of salt water
suspended from carrying-poles; and I may add, parenthetically, that I have met these salt-water carriers many miles
inland on their way to some inland market. From this tank
of water runs a long, bamboo tube, perforated at intervals,
from which fine streams of water spurt for a considerable distance. Shallow tubs filled with fish receive these streams,
and thus fresh sea water is not only supplied to the fish, but

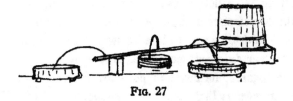

FIG. 27

aerated as well (fig. 27). One is amazed at the great number
of species of fish displayed as food. There are in Japan several
fish-raising establishments; salmon is artificially raised.[1]

The vegetable portion of the market was poorly supplied,
apparently very few kinds of vegetables being known before
the advent of the foreigner. A curious kind of radish, called
the *daikon*, is a staple article of food. It is a foot and a half
long, of the shape of a beet, and greenish white in color.

[1] Professor Baird, the first Director of the United States Fish Commission,
told me that in our seas we had as many edible species of fish as there are in
the Japanese seas, but we catch only those fish which can be caught in great
numbers, while the Japanese fishermen bring in all fishes caught, and these are
patiently sorted in the market.

It is eaten raw as a relish, and is also fermented and converted into something resembling sauerkraut, and, as a friend with me expressed it, was odoriferous enough to drive a dog out of a tanyard. You recognize the odor as it is being transported through the streets, and it is hardly less offensive to encounter than the offal-carriers. The tomatoes were very poor-looking and much deformed; the peaches small, unripe, hard, and green. One can hear a boy bite a peach from across the street, yet in this hard, green state the Japanese seem to prefer them. The pears, apparently of only one variety, were round and without sweetness or flavor; it was difficult to tell whether they were pears or apples, as they had the appearance and shape of large, symmetrical russet apples. The fruit seems to lose its sweetness, and sweet corn has to be renewed every few years, as it soon loses its sugar. The beans in pods are displayed on curious little mats of bamboo to which they are sewed (fig. 28). The hens' eggs were very small, and it was an odd sight to see large boxes filled with eggs and all of them much smaller than we ever see except those preserved as curiosities.

FIG. 28

It is delightful to be in a country where the people are honest. I never think of keeping my hand on my wallet or watch. On my table, with door unlocked, I leave my small change, and the Japanese boy or man coming in fifty times a day leaves untouched everything he should not touch. He took my ulster and spring overcoat to clean, and soon came back with some small change which he found in one of the

pockets; then he returned again bringing three San Francisco horse-car tickets. I am informed that some stealing
takes place when the people have been associated for some
time with the so-called civilized races, but in the interior dishonesty is seldom known and, indeed, is a rare occurrence in
treaty ports. The best evidence of the honesty of the Japanese is seen in the fact that the houses of the native population
of thirty million have no locks, keys, bolts, or buttons; indeed, no doors to lock. The sliding screen in the daytime is
the only door they have, and this is so fragile a structure that
a child ten years old could pull it down or break a hole
through it.

I had my first taste of saké — the Japanese national bev-
erage — at a tea-house. It is a fermented drink made from
rice and, I should judge, not stronger than our lager beer,
though instead of a half-litre mug, such as we use for beer,
the Japanese sip it from tiny shallow porcelain cups. (Fig.

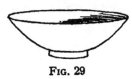

FIG. 29

29. Saké cup, natural size.) It is
always drunk hot, but I preferred it
cold and drank several cups of it
without feeling the slightest reaction.
It certainly did not seem even as
strong as claret. On the whole I found it pleasant and entirely unlike any wine or liquor I ever tasted, having a flavor
that suggested the odor of geranium leaves. Thus far I have
seen no staggering drunkards, though now and then at night
you pass a man singing, an indication that he has had too
much. The Japanese may be considered a temperate race.
That the Japanese are a gentle and tranquil people is indi-

cated by the fact that they are never seen to drum with their
fingers, nor do they whistle or rattle anything in their hands or
indulge in manifestations of nervousness as we do. I came from
Tokyo last night having in my hands an insect box, and as I
walked up the narrow street whistling some tune I drummed
on the box and the people looked out from their open houses
as if a full band were going by! Since the people are never
impatient they have no need to use expletives and an oath
is unknown, the hardest words they can say upon excessive
provocation mean fool and beast. Gentlemen never use even
these.

Dr. Eldridge, an eminent American physician, who has
practiced in Japan for a number of years and who has been
for two years connected with the Medical College in Tokyo,
has given me much information regarding his practice among
the Japanese and the experiences of other physicians some
of whom have been here sixteen years. The climate of Japan
is considered remarkably healthful. Smallpox, which has always been epidemic, is now coming under control, the Government taking vigorous measures to secure general vaccination and maintaining a vaccine farm for the purpose. In this
matter as in many others, the Japanese are far ahead of occidental nations. Scarlet fever is almost unknown, never epidemic; diphtheria also is rarely seen, never epidemic; severer
forms of bowel complaint, such as dysentery and chronic
diarrhœa are very rare; phthisis is not more common than in
the Middle States of our country; malarial diseases of severe
nature are uncommon, even the milder forms in most regions
not being common; acute articular rheumatism is rare, mus-

cular rheumatism very common; typhoid and typhus are rarely epidemic, the latter uncommon; relapsing fever is occasionally seen; skin diseases are common, especially the contagious forms. It is said that injuries and fractures of the bones heal very slowly and often imperfectly. Rice has but half the ash material of wheat, and the water does not supply sufficient inorganic matter necessary for the bones.

While many of the Japanese display beautiful white teeth, yet one sees bad teeth also. Some show a remarkable protrusion of the incisors, and this deformation has been ascribed to the custom of children nursing so late; children nurse until they are six or seven years old and this is supposed to pull their teeth forward. The Japanese are already studying foreign dentistry, and with their remarkable and delicate mechanical ability they should in time develop skillful dentists. More solid advance has been made in foreign medical practice in Japan than in any other department of Western science. Medical colleges and hospitals are already firmly established. A chemical laboratory was immediately started to analyze all imported drugs to see that they were pure, and so rapid is the adoption of the medical practice of Western nations that already the empirical Chinese practice is doomed. Next to religious belief peoples cling most tenaciously to their medical belief, no matter how crazy and idiotic it may be. The rapid displacement of the Chinese medical cult for the rational and scientific practice of Western methods is overwhelming evidence of the remarkable character of this people, seeking the best from every civilization and promptly adopting it. We are comparatively slow in learning from

other nations. We know there are better methods of municipal government in Germany and in England, better ways of
road-building in all Europe. Do we adopt these methods
promptly?

We are familiar at home with the Chinese circular brass
coin having a square hole in the centre. In Japan a similar
coin is seen and also
a larger oval one with
the square hole in the
centre. We have of-
ten wondered what
the hole was for. It

Fig. 30

seems that they string the coins as beads on a rough straw
cord or stack them on small vertical sticks standing erect on a
block of wood (fig. 30).

There is one subject, among many subjects, that foreign
writers are unanimously agreed upon, and that is that Japan
is the paradise for children. Not only are they kindly treated,
but they have more liberty, take less liberty with their liberties, and have a greater variety of delightful experiences
than the children of any other people. As infants forever
riding on their mother's back or somebody's else back; no
punishment, no chiding, no scolding, no nagging; such favors
and privileges are they allowed that one would certainly think
that they would be spoiled, and yet no nation possesses children that can approach the Japanese children in love of parents
and respect for the aged. Honor thy father and thy mother,
is an ingrained characteristic of the Japanese. As the children get out of babyhood they begin to work, apparently

good-naturedly. One sees little boys in the street scooping water with their hands from buckets and sprinkling the road, and among all classes one observes the natives either sprinkling the paths about the house or sweeping them with short-handled brooms. The cleanliness of the Japanese is always remarked upon by foreigners. A Japanese never enters his house except in his stockings, literally stepping off his wooden clogs or straw sandals as he enters the house. Children of the poorest classes play in front of the house, but instead of enjoying their fun on the ground a straw matting is spread for them. Every town and village has its bathhouse, and it is hot-water bathing always.

With rare exceptions, such as Bar Harbor, Newport, and places of that standing, one sees in hundreds of regions along sea walls in our country, outhouses, refuse, and other abominations, conditions that our Village Improvement Societies and Municipal Leagues are combating. Indeed, were it not for these unsightly conditions, in town and country alike, these societies would never have come into existence. As one approaches Tokyo by rail a cove is crossed bordered by a long sea wall lined by simple dwellings, yet everything is neat and refined. It seems incredible when I recall that in country village and city alike the houses of rich and poor are never rendered unsightly by garbage, ash piles, and rubbish; one never sees those large communal piles of ashes, clam shells, and the like that are often encountered in the outskirts of our quiet country villages. In refined Cambridge, a short cut between the houses of two scholars led through a deep depression of the land. This land was so disfigured by a certain type of rubbish that for years it was facetiously called the "tin canyon"! The Japanese in some mysterious way manage to bury, burn, or utilize their waste and rubbish so that it is never in evidence. At all events, the egg-shells, tea-grounds, and all the waste of the house is spirited away so that one never sees it. In our extravagant way of living in contrast to the simple life of the Japanese we have much waste to dispose of and it is truly waste. At home the well-to-do have cleanly surroundings, the poorer classes in country and city alike being responsible for much of this untidy condition.

The first general impression that one gets of the Japanese as one sees them in groups is that they all look alike and individual distinctions come only when you have been in the country some months. You are amazed, however, when the Japanese tell you that at the outset we, including French, English, Italians, and other Europeans, all look alike to them! Upon inquiry as to wherein we resemble one another they invariably reply, "You all have fierce, staring eyes, prominent noses, and white skin." It is only after some time that they, too, begin to recognize individual differences. In the same way their peculiar eyes, somewhat flattened bridge of the nose, and darker skin make them all look alike to us. To foreigners who have been in the country some months the Japanese show as many individual differences as ourselves. Besides appearing alike, they are all short of stature with short legs; black, thick hair; rather protruding lips, parted, showing white teeth; prominent cheek-bones; dark complexion; hands small, delicate, and refined; in manners, gentle, polite, and good-natured, with smiling faces. Among the lower classes it is amazing to see their excessive good nature. A jinrikisha man, for example, will smile and laugh in the heartiest way while demanding a few more pennies than you have paid him and which he has reasons for believing are not enough. You repel him harshly, but that makes no difference; he smiles and retires with a kindly grin.

A foreigner, after remaining a few months in Japan, slowly begins to realize that, whereas he thought he could teach the Japanese everything, he finds, to his amazement and chagrin, that those virtues or attributes which, under the name of humanity are the burden of our moral teaching at home, the Japanese seem to be born with. Simplicity of dress, neatness of home, cleanliness of surroundings, a love of nature and of all natural things, a simple and fascinating art, courtesy of manner, considerations for the feelings of others are characteristic, not only of the more favored classes, but the possession of the poorest among them. That others also feel this is shown by a remark made by an American who belongs to the highest rank of society at home. We were at a country inn for a few days. After a polite concession to some of our mistakes by one of the maids, he said, "The manners and refinement of these people are equal, if not superior, to those of our best society at home."

CHAPTER II

A TRIP TO NIKKO

A TRIP to Nikko, sixty-six miles by stage to Utsunomiya and nearly thirty miles farther by jinrikisha, gave me my first experience of the country. We started from Tokyo at four o'clock in the morning for a ride of three miles to where we took the stage. It was strange enough to ride through this great city, at this early hour as quiet as the heavens above. Here we met other friends who were going with us. An officer of the Educational Department was to accompany us as interpreter, and two Japanese attended us to do our cooking, packing, lugging, etc. Our stage was very much like the little wagons the expressmen get up for carrying parties to the beach — seats running on both sides, our knees bumping together. The road, however, was smooth and level, and the pair of Japanese horses kept along at a good rate, a change being made every eight or ten miles. We passed through a town about six o'clock in the morning, and in one street there were hundreds of people with baskets and trays of vegetables, fish, and fruit for sale; an open market, in fact. As we went through this crowd the driver blew a high-toned blast on a small trumpet and the betto who ran ahead gave a curious whoop; in fact, when any one appeared in the road ahead, either on foot or in jinrikisha, the driver and the betto would yell and howl as if we were going at the rate of an express train and everybody was deaf and blind. We could hardly understand this exhilarating racket until Dr. Murray explained to us that it was only within a few months that the stage-line had been established and the whole enterprise was a great novelty. After leaving the market town we met scores of people struggling along with heavy loads hung from their carrying-poles. Such loads! I have tried a number of times, without success, to lift them from the ground, and these people will travel miles with them. We met several girls walking to Tokyo, ten miles and more, to do their shopping! Even at half-past six in the morning children were going to school. Now and then a Japanese would pass with an American hat on his head, though with the usual dress of a Japanese. In several instances we met a Japanese with only a thin pair of cotton drawers clothing his legs, though, as many go bare legged, it did not seem so strange.

For miles we went through a region of rice-fields, and here I saw the water-wheel used as a tread-wheel for irrigating purposes. Figure 31 shows a man coming down the road with

Fig. 31

the wheel and box carried in the usual manner. In the same sketch is a man treading the wheel and raising water from the ditch in the rice-field. The box is first fitted into the embankment, the wheel drops into appropriate sockets, a long pole is driven into the mud alongside the wheel, and holding on to this the man keeps his equilibrium and turns the wheel with his feet. The road we traveled was smooth and straight and a much better road than I ever saw in New England outside the cities. The farmhouses were neat and tasteful and, with their heavy thatched roofs, picturesque. Now and then we would pass a Buddhist or Shinto temple. These were of all grades from simple little shelters to large and imposing structures with enormous thatched roofs. These buildings overshadow the low-studded houses of the people, as the cathedrals in Europe overtop the dwellings surrounding them. It is interesting to observe that in Japan the Shinto and Buddhist shrines and temples are always placed in the most picturesque spots, — at the head of a ravine, in a grove of trees, or on the top of a mountain. I was told that many Buddhist temples had been abandoned owing to the withdrawal of Government support. We passed a few large places of worship which were being utilized as school houses (fig. 32). While a school was in session in one of these abandoned temples we walked near the steps and listened and admired. Supported as the temple was on its great wooden columns it was like an open pavilion and one could look through it from front to back. From one side the pupils could see us, and some of them were smiling roguishly as we stood there staring at them; another class had its back turned. A large blackboard was standing on props, and besides a few Chinese characters there were our numerals depicted. The teacher was reading from a Japanese book and the pupils were repeating after him in a most singular and vociferous sing-song drone. At the foot of the broad stone steps and on the steps were long rows of wooden clogs and sandals just as the pupils

FIG. 32

had left them on entering the school. I could not help think-ing what a mischievous boy might accomplish in mixing them, but, happily, the children of Japan are brought up in gentle ways, though full of fun. The expression in our country that "boys will be boys" — an apology for hoodlumism, the greatest menace to our country — is never heard in Japan.

The entrance to these various shrines is marked by a curi-ous gateway or frame (for there is no gate) known as *tori-i*. The name is said to mean "bird-rest." If one finds this struc-ture on the side of the road he may know that it indicates a shrine of some kind, which may be deep in the woods. The device originally belonged to the Shinto faith and was made of the plainest logs, sometimes of immense size. When Buddhism was introduced from China the tori-i was adopted. The various figures and drawings of the tori-i made by foreigners are rarely correct. In Japanese books on architecture certain proportions of the structure are indicated by diagrams. For example, the angle made by the end of the upper cross-beam must have a certain relation to the base of the upright post and a dotted line is drawn to indicate this angle. The tori-i is often built of stone, the vertical as well as the horizontal elements above being monoliths. In the Province of Hizen there is a large tori-i made of porcelain.

In riding along the road one sees bunches of twigs tied to the trees. This is the kindling collected by the people, garnered, and tied up in this way to dry.

In one town which we passed through I saw for the first time two beggars, and shocking sights they were. One had lost all the toes of one foot, the other had a face that appeared as if it had begun to ferment and swell up, and such rags! They bowed with a quick sort of bob several times when I gave them some coppers. A small coin valued at a tenth of a cent is very convenient for such purposes. I bought at one shop some object for six and one half cents, giving a ten-cent scrip, receiving in change a handful of coppers of various sizes, which I pretended to count very carefully as a safeguard to the next Yankee that came along, but I learned afterwards that such trouble was needless.

By quarter of eight in the morning we had traveled fifteen miles, and our jinrikisha, with all the luggage, consisting of canned soup and food of various kinds and a dozen bottles of English ale, was still ahead of us, though the man had started at about the same time we did. While most of the people were bareheaded and some had a blue cloth tied about

FIG. 33

the head, straw hats of various kinds were also seen. In the rice-fields the workers wore a very wide shallow straw hat and in the distance presented the appearance of animated toadstools (fig. 33).

Blind girls walking slowly along, playing on a kind of banjo and singing, were a common sight, and at one place was a man performing after the manner of Punch and Judy. With a doll on his left hand he was bobbing its head and singing.

The bright, light-red color of the pomegranate flower, as you see it amidst the dark foliage surrounding the house, is very beautiful.

As one goes along the road various domestic economies are in full view. Much weaving is going on with a loom just like ours in essentials, and, in the spinning-wheel which is turned in the reverse of our way, is another illustration of the contrary way of doing things. The farmhouses bordering the road are so open that you notice the polished floors from the light that comes in from behind. One would no more step on these floors with his shoes on than he would step on top of a grand piano. With the open character of the house one cannot help realizing the fresh air available all the time. The swallows build in the houses just as they build in our barns at home (fig. 34). In some houses I counted a dozen paper and lacquer trays placed under the nests to protect the floors, in other instances a little shelf is affixed to the beam directly under the nest. One sees but few flies

FIG. 34

about, and this is probably due to the scarcity of horses, in the manure of which the house-fly breeds.

In washing floors you do not see a woman on her knees scrubbing; instead the woman stands at the work and reaching down pushes the cloth back and forth while walking (fig. 35). Such an attitude would break the backs of most of us, but theirs have been strengthened from childhood.

FIG. 35

It is curious to see fragments of window glass utilized in making a semi-musical device by hanging a number of fragments near enough for the wind to clang them together producing a pleasant tinkling sound (fig. 36).

Every village through which we passed had a main street lined with little shops, and whenever we stopped

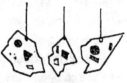

FIG. 36

a box containing a live coal buried in ashes was offered us to light our cigars, then a tray containing a few little cups of tea was passed to us, and sometimes a few sweet bits of candy or rice cake, insipid tasting, was offered. I am getting accustomed to the tea and find it refreshing. It is always very weak, very hot, and is drunk without milk or sugar. It is drunk by everybody, high and low, at intervals throughout the day.

So rare is the sight of a foreigner in these parts, or so intensely curious are the natives, that whenever we stop, the people, old and young, cluster about us to observe our behavior, and at times, when I made a motion to a little child, it would run away crying frantically. During the ride I often beckoned to the laughing children running after the stage to come to the steps and ride; they would instantly become sober and look inquiringly to some older person for an explanation. I finally came to the conclusion that they did not understand the gesture, and on inquiring of Mr. Arita, our Japanese attendant, I was told that the gesture should be made with the back of the hand uppermost and with the fingers bent together downward, several times, and quickly. When we passed the next group of children I made the proper gesture, and they instantly smiled and ran after the stage, and by pantomime I got a few to jump on to the steps. It is amazing how quickly a child gets about on her wooden clogs even with a baby on her back and most children are encumbered in this way. The following figure (fig. 37) illustrates the manner in which a soft band passes over the baby's back,

Fig. 37

under its arms, and under its legs at the knees, and is tied across the chest of the girl. The children are everywhere and are a constant source of interest. Many of them are not attractive, however, as in the country they suffer from catarrh.

Next to the universality of children in Japan the traveler notices the universal use of bamboo. Rafters of summer houses, balcony rails, baskets, flower vases, roof-gutters, even well-sweeps are made of it, and inside the house it forms certain structures and in the kitchen certain utensils. It is the universal substitute for our cuspidor, a short piece of bamboo being placed in a box with the fire bowl and used discreetly with head averted, and it is usually thrown away at the end of the day.

In riding through the country one soon notices the absence of flocks of hens. A single hen and cock roam together, though they are usually seen confined under an inverted wicker basket. There seem to be only two varieties of domestic fowl — a handsome, long-legged, big-spurred game cock with long, brilliant tail feathers, and a little bantam cock with enormous comb and legs so short that they can hardly be seen.

The peripatetic barber is seen with his curious brass-mounted box performing his task in the street. In some cases the barber appears to be a young boy, though usually men and even women are seen. The entire face is shaved; even women have their nose, cheeks, and all the surface of the face shaved. The prevalence of eye troubles, due in part to these traveling barbers, becomes very noticeable as one rides through the country; cataract, inflamed eyelids, and loss of one eye are seen as well as many blind people.

In the rooms in the taverns in which we rest are hung mottoes in Chinese characters, and it is interesting to watch our Japanese interpreter in his efforts to translate the meaning, and we are greatly puzzled that the language as written is so obscure to the people. In reading, however, if there is one character the meaning of which the interpreter does not know he is perplexed. There are very few connectives and evidently the context does not aid. Let us suppose the proverb, "Penny wise, pound foolish," written in four Chinese characters. Now, if the proverb was new and one character in the four was unknown to the reader, it would be impossible to interpret it. Thus, as "penny wise ... foolish," or "... wise, pound foolish," or with any other character unknown, it would be impossible to make any sense of it. Whenever our interpreter succeeded in reading these inscriptions, the meaning proved to be of a high moral character. They consisted of proverbs, good precepts from the classics, appeals to the beauty of nature, etc. These framed inscriptions were found in the poorest taverns, places where the men could drink saké; and as I heard the high sentiments embodied in these inscriptions and recognized the gentle art in the pictures I could not but recall the kinds of pictures and sentiments in similar places at home; that is, in the poorer saloons and the poorer taverns.

One of the many delights in riding through the country are the beautiful hedges along the road, the clean-swept walks before the doors, and in the houses everything so neat and the various objects in perfect taste; the dainty teacups, teapots, bronze vessels for holding the burning charcoal, beautiful grained panels, odd knots from trees, and woody fungus hollowed out to hold flowers. And all these beautiful things are in the houses of the common country farmers.

The artistic character of the people is indicated in many ways — in trifling matters even. If a child accidentally punches a hole through the paper screen, instead of mending it with a square piece of paper, the paper is cut in the form of a cherry blossom. Seeing this pretty way of mending holes in screens I recalled the broken windows in our country mended with an old hat or a stuffed bag.

The mill for grinding grain is turned by hand, and strong arms are required to turn it. A rod comes down from above where it is attached to the rafter, directly over the centre of the millstone, and the other end is attached to the side of the mill. The man grasping the rod rotates the stone (fig. 38). The rice is hulled by a sort of trip-hammer made of wood and weighted with stone.

Fig. 38

This is worked by a man stepping on the end of the beam, thus raising it and letting it drop. This device has endured in China for two thousand years, at least, as shown in pottery of the Han period. One may see this rice-pounding going on even in the city of Tokyo

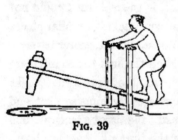

Fig. 39

(fig. 39). The man is naked and is concealed by a curtain consisting of strands of straw rope, a convenient device, for one may pass through this curtain without delay. It is a device that might be used for portières.

After the most delightful of rides on the coolest of days we reached Utsunomiya. It has been impossible to recall the infinite number of novel sights and experiences. For sixty-six miles rumbling along in rather a rattle-trap wagon, not a sight or a sound was encountered that was not peaceful and refined: the gentleness and courtesy of the country people, the economy, frugality, and simplicity of living! One experience I can never forget. A refined old lady sat next to me for some miles in the stage; I got into conversation with her hardly knowing a word of the language, but by pantomime and by drawing rude diagrams we managed very well. She had never conversed with a foreigner before or met one. The interesting questions she asked were precisely of the nature of those an intelligent and refined old lady would ask of a foreigner in our country.

I cannot describe the neatness of our rooms in the hotel. They open on a wide walk in the second story. Dr. Murray's Japanese boy soon cooked us an excellent dinner in our style, for none of us had as yet become accustomed to Japanese food. I ought to record the interesting experience I had with the children and other people of the inn when drawing, with a Japanese brush on Japanese paper, a number of objects such as toads, grasshoppers, dragonflies, snails, and the like. The little children would recognize the animal intended even when I had made no more than a stroke or two.

We were tired after the ride of sixty-six miles, and after the

above performance to bed we went. A night lamp was brought
in the shape of a large square lantern standing on two uprights, at least three feet from the floor. Only by the figure
(fig. 40) can one get an idea of
its structure. One side of the
lantern can be raised in its
frame to light a few pith wicks
that rest in a shallow saucer
of oil. One sleeps on the floor
in Japan, the soft mats form-
ing an excellent firm and level surface on
which to rest.[1] A huge green mosquito
netting in the form of a square box was
hung from the four corners of the room.
It was big enough for one to stand upright inside, and nearly filled the room.
The pillow was a little cushion stuffed
with buckwheat hulls, about the size of

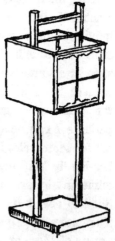

FIG. 40

a blackboard eraser. This was supported on an oblong wooden
box three inches in height. The pillow-case consisted of a
sheet of soft paper tied to the cushion. Feeling very lame
and stiff after the day's journey I called in the services of the
amma, or masseur. He was an old man deeply pock-marked
and blind. He kneeled down beside me and began on one
leg, pinching and rubbing with a sort of tremulous motion.
He moved my knee-cap back and forth a number of times
and kept up this vibratory kneading process on the back,

---

[1] Details in regard to the mats are figured and described in my book on
Japanese Homes. (Harper & Bros., 1886.)

arms, shoulder-blades, and neck, — and the ribs too, which I could not stand. It certainly rested me a great deal, and for this service, which lasted half an hour, his charge was four and a half cents.

In the morning we were up bright and early and now we had to make twenty-six miles by jinrikisha. It was odd to see the jinrikisha men gathered in front of the inn and half the village crowded about us examining with curious interest our clothing and our actions. It was hot and I had taken off my coat and waistcoat, and an unusually gaudy pair of suspenders which I wore won special interest. They were too vulgar in design and color to win admiration even from the countrymen. We had in all six jinrikisha men; great, brawny fellows, quite naked but for the loin-cloth, skin browned from constant exposure to the sun. They went at a fast walk or trot, until they came to a village, when they dashed through like mad. I could not help noticing that human nature is the same everywhere. Our old stage-coaches used to jog along the country road until they came to a village, when they would tear through at a gallop.

For twenty-five miles before reaching Utsunomiya and the entire distance to Hashi-ishi, close to Nikko, the road is closely bordered with magnificent cryptomeria, a species of pine. In some places the road is bordered by embankments over twelve feet high and on each side are dug deep channels to conduct the water. In certain places are wide dams so that the current is checked in its flow. The effect of the close fringe of stately trees, some of them five feet apart and never more than fifteen feet, continuous for twenty-seven miles, is wonderful. In many places the trees came together above. In a few places we saw deep holes in the tree-trunks made by cannon balls in the Revolution of 1868. Here and there were gaps in the line of trees, but in every case young trees had been planted and carefully propped (fig. 41). At times we noticed a tree with a large square chip taken out of the bark, and on the smooth cut two or three small circular stamp marks were impressed, and several feet above the cut a straw rope was tied about

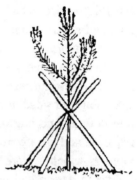

FIG. 41

the trunk (fig. 42). Trees marked in this way were to be cut down, and in every instance trees very close together were

FIG. 42

selected. To see this careful attention miles from a habitation indicates the most perfect care. For centuries it was the law of the Empire that when a tree was cut down another tree should be planted in its place, and the practice has been continued by the people. All the principal roads of the Empire are lined with a row and sometimes a double row of stately trees, chiefly coniferous. On the Oshu-Kaido we traveled for hours without meeting a single break in these lines of trees except at the villages. One rarely sees a house beyond the limits of the compact settlement; generally a little framework, or gateway without the gate, marks the entrance to the village, when the houses immediately begin, and you leave them abruptly as you pass out at the other end of the village street.

Along the sides of the road were telegraph poles, and as there was no room to place them on the embankment they had been planted in the middle of the deep gutter and the gutter had been neatly cut about the base of the post and into

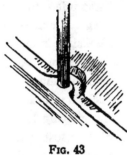

the embankment (fig. 43). It was curious to see the old New England well-sweep hung in precisely the same manner as at home, the beam and upright being made of bamboo. At noon we noticed everybody taking a siesta lying on the floor; children nursing from sleeping mothers, and everything to be seen, as the houses

Fig. 43

were open to the street, the farm-hands coming in from the fields bringing the ever-present appliances for making tea. The mountain views were beautiful and reminded one of the Housatonic Valley.

At work or at rest the Japanese sit on the inner side of the foot and leg; that is to say, the legs are bent beneath them, the heels apart, and the upper part of the foot resting on the mats. One often notices a callosity or thickening of the skin on the upper and outer side of the foot and understands the cause only when he sees the attitude of the foot in sitting. The blacksmith sits on the ground at his work, though the helper stands; the carpenter saws and planes on the floor, and it is an odd sight to see the carpenter's shop with no bench or vise.

We met at times pack-bulls carrying enormous loads on pack-saddles of clumsy forms. For miles we met only stallions, and in and around Tokyo stallions only are seen. After getting beyond Utsunomiya all the horses were mares without a single exception, and this curious way of setting apart large regions, where only male or female horses are seen, I am told is peculiar to Japan, though, doubtless, it will be found in China and other Eastern countries. It was interesting to see the villagers engaged in a game of chess, a game more complex than our chess. I tried to imagine such a sight in one of our New England back towns. In no instance did we pass a deserted house or people living in an unfinished one. We saw dwellings in construction, but where people were living the house was always complete, no staging clinging to the sides, or areas unshingled or unclapboarded. Most of the roofs were thatched, and each region or province had a different kind of ridge to the roof. A few houses were shingled, the shingles not much thicker than our playing-cards and hardly bigger; bamboo pegs, the size of shoe pegs, taking the place of our shingle nails. It is no wonder that a town burns down when a house gets afire, for the shingles are like thick shavings and instantly take fire from the sparks.[1]

The cleanliness of the Japanese is amazing; houses are clean and wooden floors polished, surroundings cleanly swept, and, yet, the country children of the poorer class usually have dirty faces. The wooden buckets in which the sewage is carried to the fields are white and clean as our milk pails. In Japan milk, butter, and cheese are unknown. In their cook-

[1] See *Japanese Homes* for details of the house.

ing, however, the cleanliness is not always apparent, and to enjoy one's dinner a knowledge of its preparation would not act as an appetizer. This statement applies only to the poorer classes, as it probably does the world over.

We saw on the banks of a stream a fisherman managing ten poles at once. He stood upon a knoll with his feet resting

upon the ends of the poles which radiated like the sticks of a fan, and thus he, like a huge spider in the middle of the web, could detect which pole was being disturbed (fig. 44).

FIG. 44

The Japanese pillow is an odd affair and at first sight seems very uncomfortable, and yet I have tried one for a two hours' sleep and enjoyed it. To use one all night gives one a cramp in the neck when unaccustomed to it. The pillow was evolved to meet the peculiar method of arranging the hair. The elaborate coiffure of the women and the rigid queue of the men, waxed and arranged to last for a number of days, required a head-rest where these conditions would not be disturbed. In hot weather the air circulates about the neck, and this is very agreeable. Figure 45 represents our pillows brought up for the night, and figure 46 is a sketch of

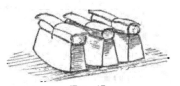

FIG. 45

Mr. Arita sound asleep. I have mentioned the mats covering the floor of a Japanese room. These are arranged in a certain order; thus, a six-mat room is shown in figure 47. In an inn a mat is allowed for each person, and the keeper always prefers Japanese guests to foreigners, for the foreigner not only wants the whole room, but

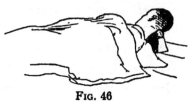

Fig. 46

a table and a chair besides. These, when procurable, have

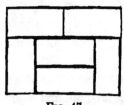

Fig. 47

wide strips of wood on the legs; otherwise they would go through the mats. The foreigner also takes with him a cook who demands much space in the kitchen; for it requires a long experience to accustom one's self to Japanese food, which seems tasteless and insipid; even their candies and sweetmeats are without flavor. How I have longed for a good drink of cool milk; even a plain slice of bread and butter. However, everything else is so delightful that I give no thought to the food.

We met the mail on its way to Tokyo; a man, naked and running at full speed, dragging a two-wheeled cart painted black, with the flag of Japan flying from a pole on the cart. The runners are changed often and make better time than a horse (fig. 48).

Fig. 48

At certain important corners of the road and in conspicuous

places prominent monuments are érected to the god of mercy to horses. Here is a sketch of one of them (fig. 49). It was

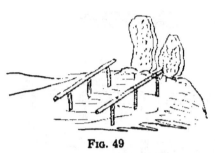

FIG. 49

impossible to draw the written script, so the sketch shows a meaningless scribble. It conveys the admonitions such as our Society for the Prevention of Cruelty to Animals at home would have: "Loosen your check-rein when going up hill," "Water your horses," etc.

We never ceased to admire the ingenious way in which the thatched roof is treated; so much taste displayed in such a material. It is said that a good thatched roof will last fifty years.[1] The remarkable feature about the thatched roof in Japan is the fact that each province will have its own style, so that one familiar with the various types might land in that country in a balloon and determine the province he was in by the appearance of the ridge-pole of the house. Samuel Colman, the artist, criticized our roofs on account of their monotonous appearance; a straight ridge instead of some graceful curve and ornamental ends, and this kind of a roof from California to Maine. Here the ridges are in many instances elaborate structures. Plants grow from the matted straw, and on some I have seen a superb crown of blue iris completely covering the ridge-pole. Figure 50 shows a roof

[1] In *Japanese Homes* the subject of the roof is treated to some extent with sketches.

with corners nicely finished, with ridge compactly held by bamboo slats. Projecting from the eaves are sprays of sweet flag arranged in groups of threes, which were placed there on the 5th of May — the boys' festival. I was impressed with the fact that in this country there is among its holidays one set apart for the boys,

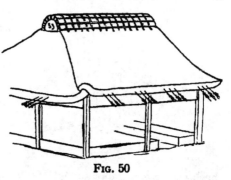

FIG. 50

and that it should be so universally observed; for every house, even the poorest, had these dried twigs hanging in threes from the eaves. The girls have a holiday on the 3d of March.

The Japanese hoe is a very clumsy-looking object (fig. 51). It is much lighter than it seems. The iron part is thin and the wooden part fits into it like a dovetail joint. In using it the man has to stoop a good deal, but the habits of these people in bowing low, in carrying children on the back when young, and in planting their rice all tend to develop a back of great strength. It is odd to see a little baby or child rise from the floor without the aid of its hands. Their legs are much shorter than ours in proportion to the arms, and it is commonly believed that sitting on their legs as they do accounts for this shortage, but that is absurd. The

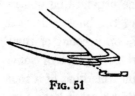

FIG. 51

flail is quite unlike ours. The handle is made of bamboo, the end shaved down and bent as in figure 52, to hold the thresh-

ing part. A number of men will be seen using the flail, which has the advantage of moving in one plane. It does not pursue a devious course like ours, which in the hands of a novice is liable to crack his head. The grain is

FIG. 52

neatly spread on mats by the house to dry, and the hens and chickens have the freest access to it. I have never seen one driven away. The farmers have long racks with which they lug grass or grain from the fields (fig. 53). They are longer than a man and are carried high on the back. When they rest the lower end touches the ground. The grain is lashed on in big bundles and the load would almost fill a small hayrack.

Along the road we occasionally found a round, bright-red strawberry which was entirely without taste. I have thus far seen three different kinds of wild strawberries. Flowers are grown in masses around the house. The hollyhocks are very beautiful; the yellow and red flowers from their brilliancy appear almost artificial; indeed, some I have seen in bouquets deceived me as to their nature. The pomegranate is the most beautiful of all. As

FIG. 53

we get into the interior we see wonderful hedges of the red azalea, precisely the same beautiful plant that we see in our conservatories at home.

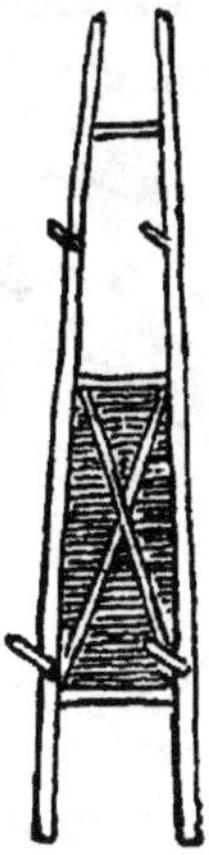

In the tea-houses where we stop for a little rest our eyes

are roaming everywhere: the rooms are clear of everything, the mats clean, the ceilings of cedar boards and all the woodwork unfilled, unoiled, unvarnished and unpainted. The whole side of the house is open to the sun and air, and yet snugly closed at night by wooden sliding screens and, in the daytime, if necessary, by light framework screens covered with white paper. The few ornaments in the room consist of flower vases and a *kakemono*, which, instead of a picture, may be the writing of some distinguished man

FIG. 54

or Buddhist priest, giving some precept or moral phrase from the classics. Figure 54 is an inscription simply framed, with red silk cushions to protect the frame.

FIG. 55

The care and taste displayed in the forms of their windows, when they have them, is shown in figure 55. The drawing shows a circular window, four feet in diameter, made in a plain gray wall; outside is purposely trained a pine, and a stone lantern is seen. If a view of some mountain peak can be brought into the circular outlook it is considered ideal. These openings may be double gourd-shaped or square, but always in good taste. We were in raptures over these features, always so quaint and beautiful—

FIG. 56

features that are never seen in our houses, but which might be adopted.

Figure 56 is a sketch of a woman who was having her hair made up by a female barber. The combs of wood were saturated with pomade and the barber's hands also, as she puts a daub of pomade on the back of her hand for convenience in using. Hair done up in this way holds its shape for several days.

The infinite industry of the people is shown everywhere. In speaking of the planting of their crops I have mentioned the thousands of acres of rice-fields where little bunches of rice-plants are transplanted by hand, but I was not prepared to see the barley, wheat, and buckwheat actually transplanted in rows, and thorough weeding also done by hand. I was told that there were two hundred and seventy varieties of rice; there are two principal kinds — the ordinary and a glutinous variety.

CHAPTER III

THE NIKKO TEMPLES AND A MOUNTAIN VILLAGE

THE village of Hashi-ishi (stone bridge), near which are the
world-famous temples of Nikko, is to be our resting-place for
several days. In coming from Tokyo we have ascended two

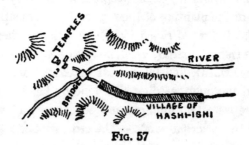

FIG. 57

thousand feet. The village is stretched along by the side of a
big roaring brook with wide channel and high banks (fig. 57).
The entire surroundings are just as wild in craggy ledge, mountain forest, tangled bushes as are wild places in the White
Mountain region. To appreciate the unique and surprising
character of the Nikko temples one must bear in mind all
this wildness and inaccessibility. The street of the village is
upgrade the entire distance. It has a slight curve, has a stone
pavement, and directly in the middle is a strong current of
water running in a stone gutter. There are also gutters on each
side of the street (fig. 58). At intervals the central gutter en-
larges into a square well at which women are seen washing

tubs and pails, or bathing their arms or legs. The water comes from a mountain brook and is as pure as crystal. The

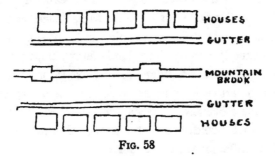

Fig. 58

drinking-water is taken from other wells. The roadway is interrupted by steps at intervals, and the whole appearance indicates that no wheeled vehicles ever use it. Nothing but pack-horses are seen, and even jinrikishas find it difficult to make their way over the steps.

We stopped at the best inn, a charming long reach of quaint buildings running away from the street, with beautiful balconies, cleanly swept courts, odd shrubbery, dwarfed pines, stone lanterns, curious fences, and everything fascinating. We selected the apartments at the extreme end of these buildings and have two rooms on the first floor and two rooms above. Our balcony is nearly as wide as the room and is covered by an overhanging roof. We move our table out and write at night by the aid of two kerosene oil lamps hanging from the rafters above. These lamps are the only evidences of European or American contact except ourselves. We have seen nobody but Japanese. Not a fragment of newspaper, poster, cigarette box, or anything foreign. Now, while I am writing here at ten o'clock at night, the insects are very welcome but annoying. I have my insect box beside me and cannot resist pinning some of the moths, they are all so beautiful. Many of them are familiar as belonging to the same genera as those we have at home, but different in color and pattern. Now and then a strikingly familiar form lands on my paper, but even in these cases there is a difference. I must record here a dish of wild raspberries we had for supper, twice as big as ours, polished like a blackberry, seeds very small, with a flavor of raspberry with a wild, woodsy taste, quite delicious and really an entirely different fruit from ours.

After getting settled we look about the village, and enjoy the magnificent mountain scenery; the roar of the river back of us reminds me of Carrigain Brook. The next morning we started for the temples of Nikko, the greatest temples now standing in the Empire. These temples are associated with the burial-place of the first Shogun and the third Shogun, the first dying two hundred and fifty years ago. We passed over a quaint bridge, close to which is another heavily covered with red lacquer. This bridge is supported near the ends by huge stone posts two feet in diameter and fifteen feet high, rising from the turbulent river. The cross-pieces are of stone and mortised into the upright posts. The bridge on each side of the river is closed by a high fence and no one is allowed to cross it. In past times only the shoguns were allowed to cross; even the daimyos in their pilgrimages were not permitted to cross this bridge.[1]

[1] An interesting fact connected with this bridge is that, when General Grant visited Nikko, in his trip around the world in 1879, the fence was taken down that he might cross, but his modesty led him to decline the honor.

I must confess the utter inability of doing the slightest justice to the temples and tombs, so wonderful are they, so elaborate, so vast and magnificent. In two hours I became completely exhausted. I have little photographs of them, but these do the scantiest justice to the minute ornamentation, the intricate wood carving, the bronzes, wrought-brass work, brilliant coloring, and the thousand details that cannot be recorded. No drawings have yet been made of these marvelous structures. One gateway is named in Japanese the "whole day gate," because one can examine for a whole day the details of its elaborate carving. After crossing the public bridge we ascend a broad avenue with a step every six or eight feet and a massive stone wall on each side, for the avenue is cut out from the side of the mountain, and all about the old forest trees loom up just as they do in the wildest parts of Maine. It is useless to try to give an idea of the magnificence of these wonderful structures, and what makes it all the more impressive is that the entire group of buildings is on the steep slope of the mountain-side in a wild forest of primeval pines, while the undergrowth of tangled vines and flowers, throwing out the sweetest perfumes, gives the richest framework for these elaborate works of man. This wild forest comes up closely in contact with the foundation of every wall and temple. It is as if the exact boundaries of the Nikko temples had been outlined in this deep forest and everything had been cleared away and the temples and walls then built. The first shrines were built over one thousand years ago, but the present buildings were erected nearly three hundred years ago and a forest could have grown around them in that time. In addition to all this beautiful natural scenery is often heard the deep, flutelike note of a bird celebrated by the poets of Japan; a note quite as charming and striking as that made by our hermit thrush.

Figure 59 is copied from a German map of the Nikko temples. I have lettered a few of the buildings with corre-sponding lettering, for the rude sketches I made give no idea of the size of these buildings. Letter O represents a structure with three large halls, the middle one forty by sixty feet, and the side halls, shown by dotted lines, forty by twenty-five feet. These dimensions are underestimates rather than over. The walls of every one of these buildings are covered with elaborately carved panels brilliantly colored. The wood carvings are deep, the branches and flowers are separate, and the wood is dug out so deeply that it makes a dark

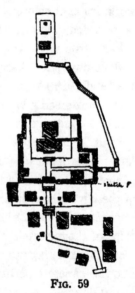

Fig. 59

background for the carvings. In the plan marked F there are fifteen panels on one side of the entrance and eight on the other.

These panels are six feet long, and each one has a different composition. One panel has storks, another swans, another one, represented in the sketch (fig. 60), shows a mythological bird, beautifully carved in high relief, full of life and action, the feathers and flowers brilliantly colored. Beneath the larger panels there are smaller ones just as elaborately carved, and

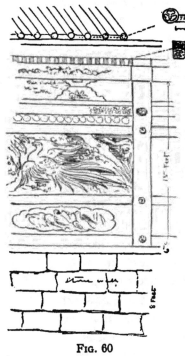

FIG. 60

all the brass plates, of which there are many, are delicately incised in intricate designs. One stands amazed, breathless, in the presence of this stupendous achievement.

Much of this work was begun nearly three hundred years ago and various buildings were added up to within two hundred and fifty years ago, and yet the perfect freshness shows the great care bestowed on these sacred relics. Within, such lacquerwork, such bronze, gilt, silver, and gold objects, such paneled ceilings, and every floor carpeted with cool straw matting, and outside massive stone pavements, stone walls, stone balustrades, stone figures and monuments! And all this incredible handiwork is planted on the steep slope of a wild, rugged mountain-side with not a rotten log or scraggy bush disturbed outside the walls, and even the stone foundations clothed with lichen and moss, with beautiful fronds of ferns springing from the rock crev-

ices. I gave up in despair any attempt to portray even
faintly this amazing revelation of Japanese art and workmanship. To approach the tomb which lies highest on the
slope, we pass through a massive gateway and enter upon
a broad flight of stone steps, green with age. The stairway
was ten feet wide, on one side a high stone wall, and on the
other side a rail wrought out of solid stone in lengths of
six feet, and four and a half feet high. There are two hundred of these steps, wide and spacious. It was wonderful to
walk slowly up and look over the massive stone railing
into a grand old forest of spruce and pines, and at the top
to find another richly carved temple rising in the midst of
this wild and sombre forest. After two hours of these marvelous sights we came back to our inn mentally exhausted and
somewhat physically so. At times the deep, sonorous clang
of the temple bell comes down from the forest above like the
note of some gigantic, deep-throated bird. The charm of the
temple bell in Japan comes from its being struck from the outside with a swinging wooden beam with its soft and battered
end, instead of with a heavy metal tongue dangling from the
inside as in our bells. The curious drum tap increasing in
rapidity is also a signal for prayers or some other priestly
function. These shaven-headed, mild-faced priests as they
go by attest to the potency of Buddhism for the swarming
millions of the East.

The following sketches (figs. 61 and 62) convey a rude idea
of the great stone staircase, green with age and damp from the
deep shade which covers everything. A perfect silence reigns,
as in all dense forests, broken only by the trill of the cicada,

or the deep, flute notes of the thrush (?). Figure 62 shows one of the stones of the balustrade, a single piece cut out of the

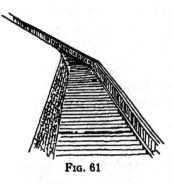

FIG. 61

solid rock and each segment united by brass ties. One thinks of the immense labor involved in all the work! The stones hauled from a distance, dragged up the steep mountain-side, hewn and fitted for a flight of two hundred steps, arrests our attention because all this work was done before the days of steam and rail. The interior of the temples is as impressive as the exterior. On each side of the shrine were massive vases each holding dwarf pine trees, four feet high, trained to a rod of bamboo, the whole affair—the trees with their irregular, crooked branches, rough bark, and hundreds of clusters of pine needles, the vase, bamboo, and all — composed of bronze,

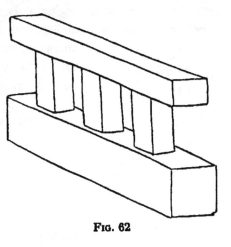

FIG. 62

and so truthfully rendered that one has to examine minutely to assure himself of its artificiality!

As we approached the temple we heard a peculiar chorus of voices which sounded like a chant, and we supposed a religious service was going on. It was simply a lot of workmen turning a windlass and hauling a big piece of timber to the foundations of another building under construction. We passed into the enclosure to see them work. It was an odd sight to see this crowd of naked, brown-skinned carpenters all howling a chorus for some time before making the slightest effort at pulling. At another place a double truck was being dragged and pried along by a crowd of workmen, and in the same way they would sing lustily, one man stand-

FIG. 63

ing out from the crowd singing a chanty, and when they all joined in the chorus a simultaneous effort would move the clumsy affair about six inches. Figure 63 shows the form of the truck, but no musical notation of ours would render the weird music.

FIG. 64

In coming along from the temple I made a sketch of two massive stone posts each wrought in one piece (fig. 64), representing a mythological beast that looked as if he had just jumped over the post and caught his tail.

It is a contrast to return to our restful rooms after all the bewildering work, the gorgeous coloring, and elaborate details we have been studying. Our rooms above and below are absolutely devoid of furniture, save the foreign table and chairs specially provided for us. We sleep on the floor. From the veranda downstairs we look out on a quaint little garden with evergreens, a few flowering shrubs, and clean paths. To

FIG. 65

the left is a veranda leading to the latrine (fig. 65), a good illustration of the artistic refinement of the Japanese in concealing what in a New England village usually forms an unsightly and conspicuous object. Observe the manner in which the Japanese carpenter, or better, cabinet-maker, has brought in the natural wood.[1] All the woodwork is just as the plane left it and much of it is in the natural condition. I found the little cupboards, closed by sliding screens, convenient to stow away my insect boxes and other things.

In the little shops lining the streets were many objects made for souvenirs of the place, and in every instance they were made from material collected in the immediate forest; a

[1] In *Japanese Homes* a redrawing is given of figure 65, with description. Figure 66 is also redrawn and described in the above-mentioned book; it represents one of the rooms in which we slept and is typical of the simple and refined character of the Japanese room.

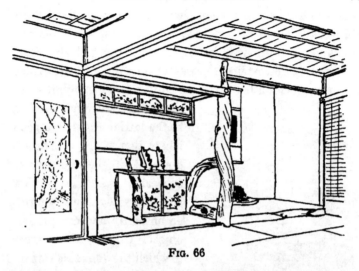

FIG. 66

woody fungus (*Polyporus*), scooped out and lacquered within, formed a cup; a twig of worm-eaten wood made a rustic candlestick; a bole from a tree hollowed out for a bowl; beautiful little wood trays with flower designs incised, and many other curious devices made from wood and bark (fig. 67).

In many parts of Japan, famous as places of resort, the souvenirs are invariably made from objects collected in the immediate vicinity. In our country one finds at Niagara

FIG. 67

Falls, Bar Harbor, and other places, objects sold as souvenirs that have been brought thousands of miles, and have, of course, no relation to the place. Indeed, I have seen at Bar Harbor souvenirs from Japan which the dealer will tell you are collected from the shore; or ammonites from the English lias are sold as fossils dug from the immediate rocks at Niagara Falls!

Figure 68 shows a bronze bell, three feet in height, and the

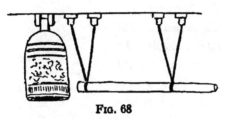

FIG. 68

round beam eight feet long, and the method of hanging by which it is struck. Figure 69 is a sketch of a Japanese insect collector examining my box of insects, and when I sketched him he was telling me their names in Japanese and I was continually thanking him, not

understanding a single word he said.

In collecting about Nikko I have noticed some remarkable examples of protective coloring, in one instance a small wood-frog which is found alongside the road, always resting on a large green leaf; the green of the leaf and the green frog absolutely

FIG. 69

the same shade. I have also noticed a green spider occupying a leaf in the same way. The spiders are abundant and interesting. One curious spider belonging to the geometric kind made a net horizontal instead of nearly vertical with the radiating threads nearer together than the usual forms and in the centre a mat, woven by many zigzag lines, perfectly white in color and very con-

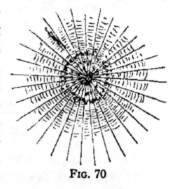

FIG. 70

spicuous, while the remaining web was almost invisible. The spider was long and slender and rested some distance from the centre and facing it; when the net was disturbed, it was violently shaken by the spider (fig. 70). Another web was unlike any kind I had seen before. It was a little nest of sheltering web nearly an inch in diameter, several ribbons running off in an irregular manner. The spider conceals himself beneath the canopy and rushes out when the radiating ribbons are disturbed (fig. 71).

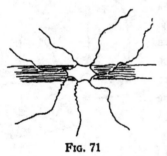

FIG. 71

On Monday morning, July 2, we started for Chiuzenji, some seven or eight miles distant, and all uphill. Nikko is two thousand feet and Chiuzenji is four thousand feet above sea-level. We had a *kago*, a simple palanquin carried by two men with a third to assist at intervals, and two sturdy fellows who carried on their backs all the bags, extra clothing, provisions, etc. A wooden frame, four and a half feet long, was strapped to the back and

upon this rack was hung our impedimenta. A thick piece
of matting was worn on the back against which rested the

rude knapsack or frame. Figure
72 is a sketch of one of the men
with insect net, shell scoop, col-
lecting-bottles, and other objects.
They must have weighed seventy or
eighty pounds. The two servants
brought up the rear of the procession, and as we filed up the street
the natives were out in full force
to see us go by. We passed up a
beautiful avenue leading to the temples and then turned up the valley
to the left. Here was a little cluster
of houses by the river, shaded by
deep forest and overshadowed by

FIG. 72

mountains, all volcanic, the denudation leaving them all with
rounded peaks. Figure 73 is a hasty outline of the mountain

peaks as we enter the
valley, so unlike the
mountains at home.
The road was good,
hard, and entirely free
from dust, as there
are no carriage wheels

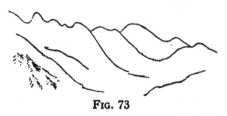

FIG. 73

to grind the pebbles into powder. After a walk of two miles
we turned aside from the road and descended into a little
hollow where were a shrine, a tea-house, a garden, and a

pond of crystal water fed by a mountain brook, which came tumbling down through the woods; the garden, pond, house, and all surrounded by the densest hedges of azalea in full bloom. As we saw it from the top of the hill it was one mass of red. The hedges were four feet high and six feet thick and blooming in a way that our poor hothouse azaleas never do. While we were sitting on the veranda sipping our tea and enjoying the garden, some travelers came along who were bound for Yumoto to bathe in the hot springs. It was a novel sight to see two of the girls go to the spring to bathe, dropping their garments to the waist. On discovering that we were looking at them, they shyly, but laughingly, drew their dresses up again, having learned that foreigners considered such behavior immodest. The whole affair was idyllic, and we realized more than ever that we were in a foreign land.

After leaving this charming place the road narrowed and we came to a dashing mountain brook, — the water clear and blue, the rocks piled up in masses, the ascent steep, and the views wonderful. The mountains were high and precipitous and the body of water much larger than one would expect in a place of this nature — really a mountain river rather than a mountain brook. A narrow pathway led in and around huge rocks and crossed the stream several times by little foot-bridges. After a mile or two of this tumultuous river we began to climb in earnest, either a steep incline or an interminable flight of stone steps, at intervals coming to a tiny tea-house which commanded some entrancing view. One place I particularly made a record of. It stood on a promontory, a bald point, not only embracing a magnificent view of the valley, but giving a view of three different mountain streams that converged below. Some of the travelers we had seen at the first resting-place overtook us, and we walked along together, the girls laughing and talking in Japanese, at times crying out, "O atsui, atsui," the only word I understood, which means "hot"; and it was a scorching day. One old fellow would ask me a question and I would respond, "You incomprehensible idiot, why do you not frame your speech," etc., etc., to which he would say "hai," which means "yes"; for the people we meet say "hai" to everything they do not understand. Two of our party took turns riding in the kago, and I tried it for about an eighth of a mile, but got out, as it did not seem like mountain-climbing to be carried by men in this way. It was an uncomfortable way of riding, though to the Japanese, with their way of sitting, it must be ideal; but the vehicle to us is a somewhat cramping affair and it requires practice to get used to it, as our long legs are in the way. I managed to get a sketch of it while resting for a moment. It is interesting to see two sturdy men walk vigorously along supporting the kago which hangs from a long,

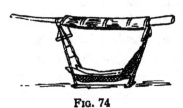

FIG. 74

round pole on their shoulders. Each carrier holds a long staff to support himself, the two keep in step, and the kago has a gentle, swaying motion. A third man follows behind to take the place of the first one who gets tired. Figure 74 represents the kago and figure 75 is a sketch from the inside while riding.

At óne place I turned over a bit of rotten wood and found
exquisite little land shells like
Pupilla, only reversed. (I recalled the figure of the species
in a French journal.) Associated with them was a little
shell apparently identical with
a common species in New England. Such beautiful but-
terflies were seen, of which I
secured a few. We were in-

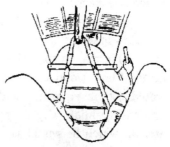

FIG. 75

terested in the number of stone figures along the road,
most, if not all of them, images of Buddha, and many of
them broken, some toppled over, and all lichen-covered
and bearing other evidences of age. Some were mounted on
stone pedestals, and one had had small stones piled on its

FIG. 76

legs and arms, each stone representing a
prayer (fig. 76). In coming up the mountain torrent it was delightful to stand on
the narrow bridges and be cooled by the
air which came from the dashing water
below. It seems odd to find no evidences
of glaciation; one boulder among the
thousands had the appearance of glaciation, but the edges are not rounded nor
eroded as are the New England boulders.

At a deserted shed used by travelers for a resting-place I
noticed for the first time that signatures had been written
on the boards and rafters, done with a brush in Japanese

script. I had before observed the absence of all disfigurement of public places by names, or rude pictures, or inscriptions, as is so common in our country. This deserted shed was so far in the wilds that this gentle abuse of making an autograph album of it did not seem an offense.

After a long, fatiguing, but glorious tramp we reached the shores of Lake Chiuzenji, a body of water, two miles across, bordered on one side by mountains fifteen hundred feet high or more, with abrupt slopes, and to the north the famous Nantai-san, eight thousand feet above the sea, rising abruptly from the lake. The lake bed was evidently a volcanic crater. There was no sand beach in sight, and the shore was strewn with fragments of volcanic rocks of all sizes and occasionally lava and pumice. Nantaisan is one of the famous mountains of Japan, called on the map Nantai, though it has several names, as with new mikados new names have been given it. After the Revolution of 1868 the Mikado gave it a new name and the old one, whatever it was, was dropped. This strikes us as peculiar, the changing of old names; thus Yedo was named Tokyo — Eastern Capital — after the Revolution. We have made similar changes, however, though in some instances these changes consisted in dropping Indian names for English names; thus, Shawmut became Boston and Naumkeag became Salem.

The dragonflies swarmed by millions. I never saw such numbers; they flew in your face, alighted on your hat and clothes, and were decidedly annoying. A great many ephemera and other insects which develop in the water, were also abundant. I spent the afternoon collecting along the shores of the lake. Not a trace of a living mollusk was found, though leeches were common on the rocks and a little crustacean also. Frogs of two species were common. I found to my amazement only the dead shells of *Corbicula*, a very common shell in the rice-ditches about Tokyo. I scratched around with my dipper in vain for a live specimen, and when I returned to the inn I learned that the Government had planted ten thousand live specimens in the lake, but that they had all died.

Fleas are the one fearful nuisance of the country. They are found wild even on tops of mountains. They invade the houses, and at night extra precautions have to be taken to avoid being eaten up by them. The bite, or sting, is very sharp, and one that stung me on the arm woke me up with a start and the tingling sensation remained for some time. My body is covered in some places by the red blotches of their bites. The universal use of straw mattings gives them great opportunities for shelter. The *futon*, a heavily wadded coverlet of cotton or silk floss, — rarely the latter except in the best houses, — takes the place of our bedclothes. You place one under you and as many more as you want above. Before we left Tokyo we had some nightgowns made in the form of large pillow-cases or bags, into which we got at night and drew up with a cord around the neck. It was a ludicrous sight at bedtime to see us stretched upon the floor with no signs of arms or legs; we looked like corpses. If we wanted to open a screen it was a comical sight as we waddled along and used the head in pushing aside the screen. This device succeeded in keeping out most of the fleas.

A list of the foods used by the lower classes would be interesting. Almost everything in the sea furnishes food for the masses; not only fish, but sea urchins, sea cucumbers, squids, and even some species of worms are eaten. Seaweed, a thin green leaf, is also eaten; it is dried and put up in tin boxes. It is apparently the common green seaweed, a species of ulva. Some of the preparations are appetizing in appearance, but to a foreign palate somewhat insipid. I have mustered courage enough to taste a few of the dishes, and have succeeded in swallowing but one of them, and that was a kind of soup, though I was nearly starved to death when I tried it. Water was boiled in a tin vessel with a sauce made from fermented bean, dark in color like Worcestershire sauce; into this were put thin slices of what looked like cucumber, and then followed large blocks of a substance which resembled new white cheese, fresh from the press; this was cut into triangular slices. This last substance was made from beans which had been boiled, strained to remove the skins, and then made into a paste-like block. This soup was certainly nourishing, and with a little practice one might come to like it. Another common article of food is made from seaweed and is known as *tokoroten*. It is in the shape of long, square pieces of a white substance and is always kept in water. At the side of the shallow tub containing it is a square wooden syringe having at the outlet a mesh of wire leaving twenty-four interspaces; the food, cut in strips the size of the syringe, is forced through by a piston, the wires cutting it into long, narrow strips. This is quite tasteless, reminding one of macaroni, and is eaten with a little sauce. Figure 77 is a sketch of the syringe and piston with end, natural size.

The village of Chiuzenji is deserted in winter, and even now, the first week in July, there are few houses occupied. Later, however, thousands of travelers will come to ascend Nantai, and then the houses are pressed for room. The country houses and inns use wood for cooking purposes, and the rafters of the kitchen are black with smoke, while the floors are polished.

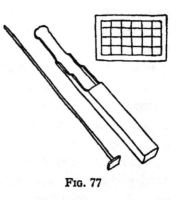

Fig. 77

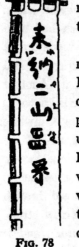

Fig. 78

As we get into the interior, clothing seems to be used only on state occasions; the children are entirely naked, the men mostly so, and the women partially so.

After a sound night's sleep we were up the next morning at five o'clock, as Dr. Murray and I were to ascend Nantai. We had to pay a dollar, ostensibly for a guide, but really for the priests of the temple. We had a man accompany us to carry heavy clothing, drinking-water, etc. Passing along the street for an eighth of a mile we ascended a flight of stone steps to the temple where long staffs were given us. In front of the temple were two long flags, one on each side of the gateway. The adjustment of a long, narrow flag to the pole was so ingenious that I made a careful drawing of it (fig. 78). (Since then I have seen many smaller ones in front of shops and other places made in the same way.) The flag is attached to a movable piece of bamboo which rests on the top of the bamboo flag-staff; loops on the side of the flag hold it in position, and as the wind blows the whole affair revolves on the pole. The flag

is made long and narrow to accommodate itself to the vertical style of writing Chinese characters, from above downward. I endeavored to copy the characters, or rather, give an idea of them. The flag was fifteen feet long and three feet wide, so I copied only the upper half of it. The characters give the name of the temple and mountain, etc. Figure 79 is a sketch of the foot of the flight of steps with the flags on the side and a tori-i just beyond. A quaint, high, and ponderous old gate is unlocked and opened, and passing through we found ourselves at the foot of a mountain path which leads directly to the summit of the mountain. Up to the spruces there are steps and beyond the path is worn over the roots and rocks. It was a direct

FIG. 79

climb of four thousand feet in altitude, and while there
was not a step of the slightest difficulty, — no stooping, or
crawling on knees, or digging toes or fingers in precipitous
sides, — it was the most fa-
tiguing and exhausting mountain climb I ever made. The
path was very steep and continuous; no level ridge or plateau to give one a rest. Figure
80 shows the angle of ascent
as we measured it. Figure 81

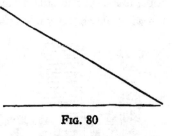

FIG. 80

shows the character of the steps, very rough and irregular
and tiresome to the last degree; something like walking
on railroad sleepers, only up-
hill all the way. Such curious plants, beautiful insects
again, and the sweet notes
of birds strange to us, and
all the rocks volcanic!

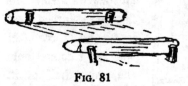

FIG. 81

And so we went up, up, the blue waters of Lake Chiuzenji
glistening through the trees and gradually other mountain
peaks coming into view. After what seemed an interminable
time we came to the line of spruces, and then the flowers were
more familiar. We saw the bunchberry flower, only smaller
than ours, and a berry that suggested the blueberry, not ripe,
however, and other flowers that belong to a northern flora,
only strangely mixed up with semi-tropical types. As we
neared the summit the views of the mountains were magnificent. Those near us were far below our level, which was

8175 feet above the sea. On the distant mountains we noticed lines of snow in the gorges. The contours of the peaks were markedly unlike those of the White Mountains. On our way up were resting-places where the natives who make annual pilgrimages stop for a cup of tea, and it was refreshing to encounter these places. It was a delight to see no trace of a

FIG. 82

foreigner; no bottles, boxes, or newspapers. At times we would pick up an oblong piece of thin board like a diminutive shingle, on which were inscribed Chinese characters which we were told represented prayers.

We were now within a hundred feet of the summit, one side of which was a precipitous slope of a thousand feet or more, the edge of an ancient crater. A little below the summit was a solidly built shrine

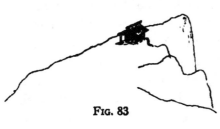

FIG. 83

sheathed with bronze and painted black (fig. 82). Its appearance from the highest point is shown in figure 83.

The doors were locked, but within, we were told, was a statue of Buddha. Upon a platform or veranda in front were a number of rusty coins, and all about the summit were spear-heads and broken sword-blades, so rusty and corroded that they must have been there for centuries. No one apparently had disturbed them, and I could not resist the temptation of securing two small rusty fragments. These were offerings to the shrine. On the highest point shown in figure 83 there is a deeply worn place in the rock where the swords were broken in past times. More remarkable still were a number of queues which had been offered as a sacrifice or to emphasize a vow. We were told that nearly, if not all, the high peaks in Japan were marked with shrines. A wonderful conception, such devotion to their religion, and to these places in August thousands throng to say their prayers as the sun rises, many of them traveling hundreds of miles and enduring hardships to do it. I could recall nothing at all parallel to this in our religious exercises except our Methodist camp meetings.

We spent an hour on the summit and the views were wonderful, Fujiyama looming up high on the horizon, a hundred and fifty miles away. The higher you rise the higher appears the horizon. Seeing Fujiyama from this altitude one gets a vivid realization of its immense size and the vast territory it covers. In the sketch (fig. 84), the slopes of the mountain are altogether too steep, and yet they appeared so when sketched. A curly mass of clouds concealed the base of Fuji, and a mountain the height of Mount Washington would have had its peak immersed in this layer of cloud.

Coming down we found more fatiguing than going up. I would rather descend Carrigain a dozen times than bump down the interminable flight of steps. The distance from the

FIG. 84

summit to the base is said to be seven miles, but it seemed twenty before we reached the bottom, and we were glad to rest and sleep for an hour, using the Japanese pillow for a head-rest, cool but still somewhat awkward. At five o'clock we started for Yumoto, eight miles distant, and I walked away feeling as fresh as a lark.

Our path led along the lake for nearly two miles — a path

with bushes meeting and brushing one on each side, and yet
a well-trodden path, as it is the only highway between
Chiuzenji and Yumoto. At times we met the natives, half
naked, or the odd-looking pack-horses with burdens on their
backs. Here comes a woman nursing her child in her arms as
she travels along, and soon we pass another, naked to the
waist, browned by the sun, leading a pack-horse, and actually
holding a baby under her arm like a bundle and the baby
nursing in this uncomfortable position. After the path left the
side of the lake it rose gradually to an elevated plateau. The
path heretofore had been through a dense forest with an
undergrowth of bushes such as we see at home. Now we came
out, with the rays of the declining sun hot and dry, and illumi-
nating with a peculiar light the flat area of some miles which
we were to cross. This area is doubtless the bed of an extinct
volcano, the bottom of a crater, in fact. A fly, not unlike the
black fly, began to annoy us, bringing the blood at every
sting. Butterflies were seen all the way, flocks of them in
great profusion, and many brilliantly colored beetles in the
path. Large patches of iris, blue and purple, great tracts of it,
were everywhere; but what amazed us most were the masses
of azalea through which we literally waded for miles. We
noticed the red haze of these
flowers from the top of Nantai. The plateau was sur-
rounded by high mountains,
Nantai looming above them
all and seeming to get nearer

Fig. 85

the farther we got away. Figure 85 shows how Nantai looks

from the plain. It was quite dark when we reached the woods again, and we were tired out, though not too exhausted to admire a beautiful waterfall which we had seen when two miles away.

At eight o'clock at night we entered the little hamlet of Yumoto, a number of houses closely crowded together and nestling in the very heart of high mountains. A peculiar, disagreeable odor of boiled egg filled the air, and this came from the hot sulphur springs which abound here. We quickly found an inn with rooms wide open to the air, and without unpacking a thing, fell on the mats and were soon fast asleep. It was dark when we reached the place, and we had seen nothing, and to wake up in the morning and look out on the magnificent prospect, the odd buildings, the people in their curious clothes, or no clothes at all, with the strange odors intermingled with the sulphur odor, the unusual sounds, was as if we had landed on a different planet. Impatient to see the place we walked through the little village with its two or three narrow streets, the entire extent not over a thousand feet. Before starting out, however, we had some difficulty in finding an opportunity to wash our faces, for, of course, there is no such convenience as a washstand, bowl, or pitcher of water in any Japanese house. Heretofore we have had brought to us a copper or brass pan, a bucket of water, and a long-handled bamboo dipper. At Hashi-ishi there was a tall sink for washing the face, as shown in figure 65. We finally found at one end of the veranda a wooden sink on the floor with pail of water and brass basin, in which we managed to wash our faces, though it was very awkward stooping down to it. At another place I saw a bucket on a shelf, or support; instead of a faucet there was an iron pin to pull out of a tube which stuck out like a faucet as in figure 86. The stream was so small that it took some time to get enough water for hands and face.

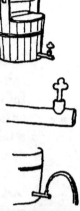

The baths are stretched along the side of the street; rude wooden sheds open in front, within which are the tanks, which are eight feet long and five feet wide, the water pouring out from a wooden pipe at the inner side of the tank, or simply running over the edge of the tank from the spring just behind. In one six or seven persons were bathing, in a crouching position, with the water up to their shoulders, at times dipping up water and pouring it over their heads. But the

Fig. 86

most striking sight was to see both sexes in the bath, young and old, and the whole affair open to the street along which many were passing, though a low screen partially intervened.

Here I must digress for a moment and express some plain truths about the subject of nakedness, which in Japan for centuries has not been looked upon as immodest, while we have been brought up to regard it as immodest. The exposure of the body in Japan is only when bathing and then everybody minds his own business. On the streets of the city or country I never saw a man looking at the ankles or legs of a girl; I have never seen a low-necked dress. I have, however, seen at Narragansett Pier, and at similar places, girls with the tightest of bathing costumes with legs and contour exposed, in full sun-

light, lounging about in the sand with men having still less on.
I lived for ten weeks beside a famous bathing beach in Japan
and never saw anything remotely approaching such a sight.
The men when naked always wear a loin-cloth. It is related
that when an English frigate entered a port in New Zealand
and the sailors went in bathing entirely naked, the chief of the
village sent earnest protests to the commanding officers com-
plaining of the immodesty of the men being without clothing,
for the natives always wear an apron or girdle around the
waist.

I spoke of overtaking travelers on our way to Chiuzenji;
in climbing up steep places I offered to help two pretty girls
over the difficult places. I was not in any sense flirting with
them, though such attention was regarded as such by the girls,
who were on their way to the hot baths, and they declined my
offers modestly with "Go men na sai" (Excuse me). At the
baths Dr. Murray wished to know the temperature of the
water as it poured from the pipe, and being somewhat lame
asked me to hold a thermometer under the spring. To do this
I had to stand on the edge of the tank with one leg far in on
the inner side, stretching out my arm to reach the stream. It
will be understood that I was somewhat abashed and did not
dare look at the people in the tank. Judge of my surprise on
hearing a pleasant "Ohayo" from two voices in the tank, and
looking found my two modest girls of the day before naked in
the water! The fact is they seem like little children, and I can
positively avow that we seem infinitely more immodest to the
Japanese than they do to us. The sight of our people in low-
necked dresses dancing together in the waltz, a dance they

do not have; kissing in public places, even a man greeting his wife with a kiss in public, and many other acts cause the Japanese to regard us as barbarians. If in going along the street one looked into the bathing-tank, the bathers would probably comment on it in much the same way that we should if a greenhorn were to look into a dining-room window while we were at the table. There are a few acts of theirs that seem very immodest to us; there are many of our acts which seem very immodest to them.

There are several baths along the road; some open to the sky; others with a shed-like covering as in figure 87. It was a strange sight, — the water pouring out from the ground in a voluminous stream, a boiling spring literally, for it was so hot one could not bear the hand in it for a second. In one

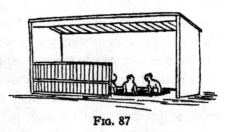

Fig. 87

spring we lowered an egg for ten minutes and it was thoroughly cooked. The springs all seemed to have the same sulphurous odor, and yet a dignitary of the village informed our interpreter that they varied in their therapeutic properties. One spring was supposed to be good for pain in the chest and leg, another was good for stomach disorders; another for weak eyes; and another for troubles in the head, and so on. Each spring was supposed to have different curative virtues!

It was an extraordinary experience going along the road, Dr. Murray with his notebook, and I entering these baths one after the other, standing on the corners of the tanks, and reaching out the thermometer to the streams which trickled from a spout, and numbers of men, women, and children following us curious to see what we were about. They did not mind the bathers nor did the bathers mind them, as indeed they should not. It was the height of modesty and simplicity; no prurient prudes in the crowd. Each bath contained from two to eight or more bathers, and some of them were sitting on the edge of the tank; young girls, middle-aged women, and old men wizened with age, all bathing in the same tank. I have been blunt and explicit in explaining this phase of Japanese life, for it is one of the extraordinary anomalies of this people. With ten times the graceful politeness that we have, with gentleness of manner and sweetness of disposition, yet they are wholly lacking in appreciation that nakedness is immodest, and, utterly lacking it, you are no more abashed by it than are the Japanese, and therefore conclude that what would be immodest for us is not for them. The only immodesty displayed is the behavior of foreigners in looking at nakedness, and this behavior the Japanese resent and turn away from. For example, on one occasion when we were returning home, having seven jinrikishas, six for our party and one for baggage, we clattered down through the village street. In front of one house and almost directly on the road was a woman bathing in one of the deep wooden tubs. Now, one might think that without a thread on she might have retired to the rear of the house, or at least have bathed her body in installments; not so, however, she contemplated us as we passed without once ceasing her operations. Not one of our jinrikisha men turned his head to look, nor would any other of the thirty millions of people have done so. I could not resist calling Dr. Murray's attention to her in a hurried way, and the woman, noticing my gesture, turned partly away from us, probably taking us for country bumpkins, or barbarians, — as, indeed, we were.

Having finished our temperature measurements at Yumoto, we hired the only boat in the place, a huge sort of gondola, and with two men for boatmen started to explore the fauna of the lake. When the boatmen came aboard, a girl accompanied them bearing the universal box of live coals and a tea-kettle. We wondered why she invited herself to come in this way, but she stayed, and so I utilized her by having her hold my glass jar while I picked shells out of my scoop, and in various ways we got her to work her passage. She held our hats while we looked over the sides of the boat for specimens. Judge of our surprise when we got back to shore to find that she was the owner of the boat and that we had to pay her for the use of it! As these people have a good deal of fun in their constitution, she must have enjoyed the way we had treated her. I found a specimen of *Lymnæa*, suggesting a Maine species, and a tiny *Pisidium*. Just after we started and had got into a new patch of lily-pads, a hunting-ground for shells, a wind began to blow in vigorous gusts, and despite the desperate efforts of our boatmen in poling and sculling, they had no control over the boat. To help them I took a pole, but soon realized that a bamboo pole was a novelty to me, and so, for fear of getting a ducking, the boat and all being so entirely unlike anything we have at home and behaving so absurdly,

I let matters take their course. We were driven across the lake into a cove, where we collected for a while hoping that the wind would go down. The men then undertook to pole the boat back again. I took the pole and tried again, but, impatient to shove her somewhere, managed to ram her on a hidden rock. Here we were for some little time, the boatmen finally jumping overboard upon the same rock, and after tre-

FIG. 88

mendous exertion fairly lifting the boat off. The wind, at the same time, drove us into the cove again, so we all jumped ashore and walked back to Yumoto. Figure 88 shows a hasty sketch I made of the village from the boat.

Arriving at the inn we hastily packed our belongings, and the Doctor hiring a pack-horse, we started to walk back to Hashi-ishi, a distance of seventeen miles. After the experiences of the day we were somewhat tired when we started uphill and down, over plains and through mountain brooks. And this was the way we celebrated our Fourth of July. I spent so much time collecting insects that I was left alone, and for hours enjoyed the supreme novelty of being in the interior of Japan, where no English was spoken, my vocabulary limited to "How do you do?" "Good-bye," "Wait a little," and a few isolated words. The day was intensely hot and I was reduced to my undershirt and drawers, all my clothes having gone ahead on the back of a coolie. The buttons giving way at the outset, a safety pin held me together, and so I went on singing, "Boom goes the cannon" and "Star-Spangled Banner," on account of the day; netting butterflies, picking up beetles, and altogether greatly enjoying the strangeness of the situation. I had a round-topped Japanese hat to protect my head from the hot sun, and my closest friend would not have recognized me (fig. 89). It is astonishing how these people can go bareheaded under a broiling sun, though now and then you see the broadest of broad-brimmed, matted hats. After crossing the flat area again, I came to the path in the dense woods, and suddenly met a savage, wolfish-looking dog, which

Fig. 89

barked viciously at me, but retreated, as the path was too narrow to pass. We kept on, the dog retreating and howling. I must confess that my scant clothing seemed exceedingly diaphanous, and I had no pistol. Soon three Japanese came in sight. The dog went by them and we rubbed as we passed. Then the dog, fearing to lose them, finally bounded into the woods and ran by me. I could not understand the dog's fear of the wood. I was glad to get rid of him, though not particularly alarmed, as, judging from the dogs I had already seen, they are harmless beasts.

I overtook my party at Chiuzenji resting and waiting for me, and having eaten our dinner we started again. In going back to Hashi-ishi the views were much grander than when going up. The descent enabled us to look down on wild and precipitous ravines and all the imposing character of the deep gorges was more impressive than when ascending, for in the effort we were too hot and fatigued to think of anything else. Our provisions were giving out; the crackers were all gone, though the claret and beer still held out, an indication of our extremely temperate habits. (One should get accustomed to Japanese food and saké, as I did in a year or two, and much trouble and expense would be saved in transportation and cooking, as well.) With rice, canned soup, and chicken we got up a Fourth-of-July dinner, drank the health of His Imperial Majesty the Mikado, and our President and the dear ones at home, sang patriotic songs, and drummed on the table, amazing and delighting the people of the hotel who peeped at us through the screens.

CHAPTER IV

TOKYO AGAIN

For two days it rained steadily and that gave us ample time to write our letters and journals. At five o'clock in the morning we started for Tokyo, our jinrikishas with the tops up like an old-fashioned chaise, and a sheet of oiled paper tied on in front to keep out the rain (fig. 90). We were literally locked up, and away we went with an exhilarating line of seven jinrikishas, half the men naked, the rest with a loose jacket on their backs as the only clothing. It was quite cold, yet they fairly steamed with the exercise. At times

Fig. 90

it stopped raining and we would have our tops down. These men ran almost continuously for thirty miles with no long rest. I noticed that when there was a strong incline the gutters were dammed at intervals of ten or fifteen feet, retarding the current of water and thus preventing the gullying of the channel. The trees in every case had been sawed off instead of chopped, thus saving wood. At times we passed huge fragments of rock with evidences that an attempt had been made to split them; but instead of drilling round holes they drill square ones. Such odd characters we saw on the road. We passed a pilgrim who had a little drum which he struck at intervals, and he made a noise between his lips, a sort of prolonged grunting strain which sounded like an expiring bagpipe. These sounds were his prayers which he was constantly uttering in his pilgrimage. These men, who travel hundreds of miles in their visits to various shrines, may be carpenters, merchants, or farmers. They often start off without a cent, depending upon charity for their food and lodging, though they may have money enough at home.

At one place where we stopped for lunch a man was reciting a poem or some such thing, and his voice had a most tense, artificial strain. He held two long blocks of wood and emphasized his remarks by striking them together at proper intervals. Nobody about the house paid any attention to him, so we each gave him a cent and kept him at it for some time longer. Upon the road we were traveling was a wall of giant pines or cryptomeria lining the road similar to the one already mentioned. Here as elsewhere the swallows build their nests in the houses and even in the best rooms, a shelf being put up to prevent the floor from being soiled.

Along the road at short intervals were guide-posts giving distances to the next places. After thirty-five miles the roads had become so bad and the wind had increased so in violence that our jinrikisha men got tired and wanted to go back, so they were paid off, and after a dinner, which cost them four cents, back they went. Some of the villages we passed through were poor-looking and the inhabitants evidently poverty-stricken. Strangers rarely ever came this way, and entire households turned out to see us pass, and whenever we stopped a large crowd would gather. While the people were the very

lowest, and their faces were coarse and the children were very
dirty, and the houses were poor, there was no trace of brutality
or maliciousness in their looks or any expression of haggard
despair such as one sees in the slums of our great cities. At
one village where we stopped for lunch the landlady squatted
down on her knees near us, and grinned and laughed at us
whenever we took a mouthful, and finally became so annoying
that Dr. Murray asked her sharply in Japanese what she
wanted, and she took the hint and went away. The poor
creature was ignorant and intensely curious, and every minute
detail of our complexion, our clothing, food, behavior, the
knife and fork, all were entirely new and strange to her, and
her manners were certainly bad.

Even in this dirty town it was interesting to contrast the
inn where we stopped with the many inns I had seen in New
England and in other
parts of our country.
Figure 91 is a rough
sketch of one side
of our room: rough,
worm-eaten wood for
a shelf, the natural
trunk of a tree for
the mid-post, a sim-
ple kakemono. The
details were solidly

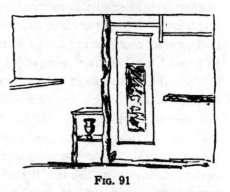

FIG. 91

constructed. This room looked out upon a beautiful garden
in which was a little wooden tank holding water. The wood
had come from the seashore. It was, indeed, a bit of wood

from a vessel, black in color and bored by teredo. In it were a rock, aquatic grass, a bronze crab, etc. (fig. 92). It was beautiful, and would have been eagerly sought for to grace our best rooms at home. A translation of some inscriptions on the walls of the room proved them to be precepts from the classics. When I recalled the things that decorate the walls of similar places at home, —prize fights, burlesque horse-race, or naked women, —we agreed that the Japanese were far superior in refinement. Now, all this exquisite taste was in one of the poorest villages and shows how universal the appreciation of artistic things is in this pagan country.

Fig. 92

At this place we had a row with our jinrikisha men. They saw we were in a tight place and were going to take advantage of us, as they often do in so-called civilized countries. We threatened them with our canes and they became docile; indeed, they had not been ill-natured, and matters became smooth again. It was a drizzling rain all the time and cold too, yet our naked fellows never seemed to mind it. It was curious to see how indifferent the natives were to the rain; children with little babies on their backs were out in the twilight and all wet to their skins. As it became dark the ride grew tiresome, the low-thatched houses looked dark and smoky, and a cloud of smoke would be rising from almost every thatched roof as if the house were afire. Whenever we stopped to drink tea there were always little points of interest in the poorest of houses. For example, the ingenious way they have of making screens of rope, bamboo, and even shells, strung as beads, which hang like a fringe before the door; an admirable idea, as it admits the air, conceals the interior, and one can walk through it without obstruction. I remember seeing in one of the villages the roof of a small house covered with large perfect shells of *Haliotis* and cuttlefish bone. These had been brought from the sea as articles of food and the shells had been placed on the house-top.

When we finally got to the end of our jinrikisha journey, we found ourselves in front of a large house all open beneath as in the case of all the inns. It was very dark and rainy, and it was a weird sight to see the jinrikisha men steaming from their long run, sitting in picturesque groups drinking tea, — mind you, not rum, — the warm light from the painted lanterns throwing shadows beyond them, and making their brown, glistening bodies almost red. They appeared like savages. There seemed to be no end of families in the house; there were at least a half-dozen, and many women. Figure 93 shows a group of children watching us from the outside. We were

FIG. 93

shown into a room where we dropped on the floor tired out.

FIG. 94

From the ceiling hanging from long poles were hundreds of cards of silk-worm eggs ready for exportation to France (fig. 94). These cards of paste-board were fourteen inches long and nine inches wide, and, we understood, they were worth five dollars a card. Good cards contained from twenty-four to twenty-six thousand eggs. The cards were hung back to back, each card having the owner's name on the back. A company in Yokohama controls the price of eggs. The company buys up all there are in the country, and one year, in order to keep the price up, actually destroyed all above a certain number. The man who evidently owned the place was an intelligent fellow and through an interpreter we got a lot of information about silk culture. He had a beautiful little boy, and though I have been here a month and have seen hundreds of children, this boy is the first one I have held in my arms and even on my shoulders, the family showing their appreciation by smiling.

The married women, with their polished, blackened teeth, are a shocking and startling sight to a foreigner. When the blackening is first applied they keep their lips apart for a while that the color may set. Thus holding the lips apart becomes a habit; at all events, they are rarely seen with the lips closed. The young man brought us fans and asked for our autographs on them, and on the fan he gave me I drew a lot of insects, shells, etc., which pleased him greatly. In return he gave me a bagful of confectionery. The sugar plums were good, but to a foreigner the candy is insipid, having no flavor whatever.

At this place, Nowata, we were to take a boat on the river Tonegawa. Nowata was the head of navigation. As the final *a* is pronounced like *r* it seems an appropriate name for the head of navigation, "no water." Ten o'clock at night came before we could get a boatman to scull us sixty miles to Tokyo. The night was totally dark and rainy, and it was difficult to induce the boatman to go, particularly as the last time he went down the river he had been robbed by river pirates. Dr. Murray and I represented to him that he and I were terrible fellows and would tear to pieces any number of pirates if they dared to approach the boat. This danger was probably greatly exaggerated, though at the time it added an exciting zest to our trip. So after bidding "sayonara" to our pleasant hosts, we started through the wet fields and bushes to the river-bank, illuminated all the way by a number of paper lanterns, in the hands of accommodating boys. The boat was a long, clumsy sort of craft, with a place in the middle having a little roof of matting more like a thatched roof in pieces. There was no light on the boat, as it would interfere with the boatman steering, so we had to grope around to find a place to lie down. I sat up for an hour enjoying the novelty of the situation, the boatman silently sculling with a long, steady swing, the others sound asleep, and such perfect quiet — no sound, in fact, except the shrill chirrups of many strange insects, most of them higher or shriller than those I am familiar with at home or else they marked time differently from ours. While smoking and half dreaming I caught myself, now and then, suspiciously watching some dark object near the shore. I was the only one who had a pistol, and it was at the bottom of a promiscuously packed bag. Where the cartridges were I did not know, and in the dark the luggage had been piled up helter-skelter, and finding even the empty pistol was out of the question. At all events, when I lay down to sleep I thought that if we were attacked the bamboo pole should be my weapon. Long before daylight the boatman, alarmed at

something, called Dr. Murray, who got up and watched for
a while and finally concluded it was a false alarm. (I record
this incident, as it was the last time I carried a pistol in Japan.)
The boatman had probably lied about the river pirates so as
to get higher pay. After a few years' residence in Japan one
realizes that a man is safer in the wilder regions of Japan at
any hour, night or day, than in the quiet streets of Salem, or
in any other city in our country.

We awoke at six o'clock in bright daylight, and after breakfast, cooked on the boat by the faithful Yasu, we lay back

upon our pile of luggage
and enjoyed the novel
sights of the river, boats
of all sizes and the curious-looking houses. The

FIG. 95

banks of the river were low and the current sluggish, and so

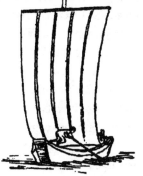

we went slowly along, yet not slowly
enough to get good sketches. The
boats on the river are very much the
same in style, but vary in size. None
is painted, and the absence of paint
on the houses, in towns and cities
alike, gives a remarkably dingy appearance to the streets, the houses reminding one of old sheds or barns in
our country. If paint is used at all it
is black and gives out a disagreeable

FIG. 96

odor like sour paste. The sketch (fig. 95) represents our boat.
Figure 96 shows another boat with sail up, but there being no

wind the man is poling it along. The boat sails are made of long, narrow strips of thin cloth laced together, leaving an interspace of three or four inches. The sails are very large and these interspaces relieve the pressure in high winds. The long bamboo pole is sheathed with iron, resembling a gigantic pen (fig. 97). The endurance of the boatmen is quite equal to the strength and endurance of the jinrikisha men. Our man, for example, began sculling at ten o'clock at night and kept it up with one or two intermissions until four o'clock the next afternoon, with no sleep and apparently no fatigue. At intervals we would pass crowds of coolies engaged in repairing the river-bank. In this work they were building walls of bamboo, driving piles, in some cases making a wall of huge bundles of twigs or bushes ten feet long which

Fig. 97

were laid with their cut ends toward the river. A most effective way consisted of long, tubular structures of bamboo, a foot in diameter and fifteen or twenty feet long, filled with large stones. These tubes were piled criss-cross at points of danger along the river-bank. The river has to be constantly watched, as it wears away the banks very rapidly.

We saw an ingenious device for netting fish. The net is arranged on two long bamboo poles, the ends of which are fastened to a simple framework attached to the boat; the framework being pushed forward the bamboo poles dip into the water, thus submerging the net. After a while the frame-

work is pulled back, raising the net from the water, and the
fish are tipped into the boat. Figure 98 shows the net out and

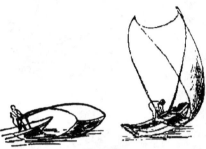

drawn in. The type of
houses along the river
is shown in figure 99.
Figure 100 shows an-
other boat.

After four weeks I
am beginning to recog-
nize the differences at
first glance between the
men and women; they

FIG. 98

both dress in long, blackish-blue garments. The men have no
beards, and in the country the women's hair is often so

tangled that little difference
is seen; but after a while
the distinctions begin to be
recognized.   The country
people — the peasants — are,
on the whole, rather plain-

FIG. 99

looking. The men are better-looking than the women, and

FIG. 100

now and then you see faces of intelligence.
I have seen a few girls that might be considered pretty.

Allusion has been made to the practice of
children carrying on their backs the babies.
Figure 101 represents a large boy fishing,

and hung to his back is his little baby brother or sister. I
have never yet seen a cradle, nor have I seen a baby left

alone to squall its eyes out; indeed, it is the rarest sound in Japan — a baby's cry.

From a foreigner's stand-point the nation seems to be devoid of what we call an ear for music. Their music seems to be of the rudest kind. Certainly there is an absence of harmony. They all sing in unison. They have no voice, and they make the most curious squeaks and grunts when singing with the

FIG. 101

samisen, or the biwa, which remotely resemble our banjo and guitar.[1] When the men sing at their work, however, their voices seem more natural and hearty, and this kind of singing they actually practice, as we learned the other day at Hashi-ishi. We passed a place where we thought a carousal was going on, and we learned it was a lot of workmen practicing their songs and choruses, which they sing at their work in hoisting, pile-driving, or moving great loads. It is an interesting sight to see twenty or thirty men bending to their work and ready to pull together when a certain part of the song is reached. It strikes us as a great waste of time to sing for a full minute or more before the slightest movement or effort is made.

[1] Later I learned from a student that our music was not music at all to them, He could n't understand why we cut it off by jerks; to him it was "Jig, jig, jig, jig, jig, jigger, jig, jig"!

The water-wheel device for irrigation purposes was on a large scale. There were three big wheels on the same shaft and six men treading them. Large tracts of rice-fields were being irrigated in this way. Whether these men were hired or whether the farmers take turns at this work, I did not learn.

One observes a marked absence of deformities or malformations among the people. This may be attributed, first, to the personal attention given to children, and, secondly, to the almost universal one-storied house with absence of flights of stairs down which children might fall. There are no doors to jam their fingers, no runaway horses, no biting dogs nor hooking cows; there are bulls but they are always in leash. There are no guns or pistols, no chairs to tumble out of, nor high windows to fall from; hence no broken backs. In other words, there are no conditions surrounding the children that would lead to accidents of a serious character. I have never seen a stone thrown, and no clan fights in cities among the boys as with us. One wonders why they do not scald to death in their hot baths.

Within ten miles of Tokyo a head wind sprung up, and so we landed and engaged jinrikishas, leaving the boy to bring along the luggage. We had another ride across a new tract of country. It was interesting because we were in the confines of one of the great cities of the world. The style of house was somewhat different; that is, there were new ways of treating certain portions, particularly the ridge-poles, which varied greatly from those of houses a hundred miles north.

The device for lugging dirt for filling or other purposes con-

sisted of a coarse mat with long loops. The dirt is hoed into
the mat and then, with carrying-
stick, two men lug it away, as in
figure 102.

FIG. 102

It is an interesting fact that
round the wide world children
are fond of making mud pies
and cakes. Along the road in
Japan little girls were moulding plastic mud into little round
forms, which in this case must have represented *mochi*, a cake
made of rice, as pies or bread are unknown in Japan.

One is continually surprised at the attitude of courtesy and
politeness invariably shown to the foreigner, even by the
poorest classes. I have repeatedly noticed that when they
address me they first untie and lay aside the cloth about the
head. When one jinrikisha overtakes and passes another on
the road, as ours did, as we were in a hurry to reach Tokyo,
the man would always apologize and say, as it was translated
to us, "By your permission, if you please."

We passed many beautiful hedges, in one or two instances
a double hedge, the inner one of trees densely growing and
squarely trimmed, and next a shrub hedge squarely trimmed
and reaching halfway up. It was quite effective, as it lined
the street for a considerable distance. The Japanese gardener
has a way of binding the branches to bamboo frames until the
twigs assume the position permanently. I saw a large gingko
tree that spread out like a fan in one direction at least forty
feet wide, while in the other direction it was not more than
three feet through, though it was so densely leaved that no

light came through it. These people lead the gardeners of
the world in the way they make the trees behave. The beds
of flowers we passed in going through the country were beautiful, particularly the hollyhocks, and the dazzling masses
of portulacas, and the blue hydrangeas with big clusters of
blossoms. The plum and cherry are cultivated, not for their
fruit, but for the flowers. So much has been written by travelers in regard to the famous cherry blossoms that further allusion is unnecessary; a number of varieties are known. The
peaches exposed for sale are small, green, and hard, as unripe
as a green olive, and they are eaten by the people in this unripe state. I opened several peaches and four out of five had
worms in them.

The odd ways of these people are everywhere visible and
arrest the attention. Over one entrance besides a few Chinese
characters was the impression in ink of two hands with fingers
wide apart.[1]

In a few instances we have noticed wise-looking elderly
men watching us as we passed them, and gravely shaking their
heads in retrospective contemplation, as if they were of the old
school and believed the country was going to the devil in permitting the long-excluded and detested foreigner to go freely
where he pleased. I could read all this in the expressive looks
they bestowed upon us. No such freedom, however, is permitted; the foreigner cannot go without a passport twenty
miles beyond the limits established for the four treaty ports
without being arrested and turned back. To go into the interior of the country the passport must not only specify the

---

[1] I learned years after that this sign was made to ward off smallpox.

actual route to be followed, but the number of days he is to travel. At every inn where we stopped our passports were taken by the innkeeper, or some officer, carefully copied, and returned to us with profound bows of apology for troubling us.

As we neared the city we passed large lumber yards. The boards, instead of being in promiscuous piles as with us, were tied together just as the tree was sawed up, so that in building the carpenter was sure to get the same color and grain of wood. Large lumber yards of bamboo are seen, the bamboo standing in masses and resting against some support. One also sees stone yards. Here one may pay fifty or a hundred dollars for some odd-shaped and weather-worn stone that may have been brought from Sado or Yezo. The Japanese furnish their gardens with stones, and these are brought from long distances. Any quaint form, or one with a natural depression to hold water for the birds, is specially desired. Stones that may be piled one upon another to represent a stone lantern, slabs of stone for diminutive garden bridges, stones for poetic inscriptions, and stones for other purposes are eagerly sought for by the Japanese.

Allusion has already been made to the staging on the ridge of the house from which the progress of a conflagration might be watched. I now observed a number of houses on the ridge of which was supported a huge tub filled with water and a long pole with brush at the end with which to extinguish any spark that might alight on the roof. In some instances the tub was covered with basket-work to hide its unsightly appearance.

Peddlers toting their stock in trade upon their backs were often met with. One peddler was carrying large boxes filled with little cages, in which were imprisoned green grasshoppers which kept up a constant trilling, singing much louder than a similar species at home. I bought one and stowed him away in a match box, and after eight days he was alive and vigorous. Children buy these insects from the peddler, feed them on sugar, and keep them as we keep canary birds. The tiny cages were made very tastefully and in a variety of forms; one had the shape of a fan, each compartment having an insect imprisoned.

It was delightful to get back to the hospitalities of Dr. Murray and to sit down again to a dinner of rare roast beef, real butter, and good bread. It is difficult to understand a country in which there is no milk, butter, cheese, bread, or coffee, and never has been. Butter is so distasteful to the Japanese that many cannot eat cake or other article of food in whose composition butter is used.

Since my engagement as Professor of Zoölogy at the Imperial University I have been busy making plans for a summer laboratory, arranging a course of study for a class of ninety students, and planning for the foundation of a museum of natural history.

Fig. 103

One sees often on the streets a man with a huge pack on his back; this pack covered by a blue cloth reminding one of a hand organ. The bundle is a large stack of books; in truth, a circulating library. The books are carried everywhere, and as there is no illiteracy in Japan these books go to every house, new books being left and old ones taken away (fig. 103).

The streets have no names, so far as I can learn, not even
the longest avenue in the city, except when foreigners have
in a few cases given names to the streets after some block or
bridge. The principal blocks or possibly all of them, have
names, but the streets never. A man lives in such a block and
one has to follow around the four sides, — that is he has to
traverse four different streets or lanes — to find the person
he is after. Dr. Murray started out with me to find a Japanese to whom I had a letter of introduction. Our jinrikisha men
inquired repeatedly for the block, and having found it they
went around three of the four sides reading the little wooden
or paper labels on each house before we found the place. In
this connection it is interesting to learn that in our country
the professional city directory makers get every name by
starting at one corner of a block and following around its four
sides, up every alleyway and indentation, and when the block
is completed crossing it off on the map they carry and starting
again from the corner of a new block. In that way the can-
vassers cover the entire city.[1]

In the houses little lights and offerings of food are placed on
a shelf containing a Buddhist shrine, the *kamidana*, or God-

[1] As an illustration of the often unreliable statements made by hasty travelers,
the erroneous statement above made in regard to the absence of street names in
Tokyo copied from my journal is a good example. As I could not speak a word of
Japanese, the misinformation must have been derived from my American associates,
who had resided in Tokyo for a considerable time. An interesting communication in
the first volume of the Asiatic Society of Japan, by Dr. W. E. Griffis, entitled "The
Streets and Street Names of Yedo," was read in 1872, published in 1874, three years
before the above record in my journal. I earnestly commend this article, in which
one will learn that there are hundreds of street names, many like our own, as, Front,
Pine, Willow, Cedar, and others of the most extraordinary character, such as
Abounding Gladness, Tomb Door, One Color, Mountain Breeze, Finger Valley,
and many others equally odd.

shelf, as it is called. These offerings of food are to the memory of departed friends.

At times one runs across the celebration of some festival in the streets. The other night the streets were filled with people buying and selling; a regular fair. I walked through the throngs for an hour observing the many curious things offered for sale, many of them the products of domestic manufacture and to be bought for a trifle — a half cent or the tenth of a cent. The streets were lighted by little candles and lanterns resembling fireflies and, at best, giving but a feeble illumination. The shelves on supports were tastefully arranged; in one case a little fence had been made by binding short twigs of some evergreen between two strips of bamboo. Hundreds of bouquets of flowers and innumerable little potted plants were seen, cunning little wooden trays, toys of all kinds, and the most ingenious paper lanterns. One was in the form of a cylinder of paper, within which was a central axis of wood supporting a windmill above, the heat of the candle

turning the axis; projecting from the sides of this were supported figures cut out of paper in the shape of a man on horseback, a jinrikisha, and figures of people. On the lantern a little bridge and landscape were painted, and as the figures moved round, the candle shadows were thrown on the cylinder of paper,

Fig. 104

and thus a moving picture was made of these objects crossing the bridge: a most entertaining toy for children, and its
price was one and a half cents. Figure 104 gives an idea
of its structure. Another white-paper lantern, round in
shape, had on its surface what appeared to be fresh drops of
water. I thought at first the appearance was produced by
glass beads or drops of transparent gum stuck on the inside.
The illusion was made, however, by little cylinders of silver
paper of three or four sizes pasted inside, and the light of
the candle produced a
shadow on the paper
with a bright spot pre-
cisely like a round
drop of water (fig. 105).
Nearly all the objects
for sale by these ped-
dlers had been made
for children. Games of
all kinds were on the
ground. One consisted

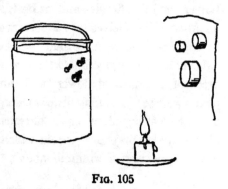

Fig. 105

of three figures standing on upright pieces of bamboo. The
boys bought ten little, button-like objects, stood four feet
away, and threw these at the figures; if one was struck, the
boy won an egg for a prize. Targets of various kinds were
shot at by boys blowing little darts through a bamboo tube
— a regular blow-gun.

As one rides through the streets he is constantly reminded
of the people's love for natural objects. For example, in front
of a drinking-booth, offering nothing stronger than ice water, or

soda water in bottles, one observes a huge, black, tangled root
of some tree six feet in diameter, resting at an inclination, and

FIG. 106

the beautiful porcelain cups
from which the customers drink
are placed here and there in the
roots (fig. 106). The root was
such as the farmers build root
fences with. It was kept wet to
make it the blacker, and with
the bright porcelain cups made a striking appearance. A
stand for plants was made by two planks of a ship perforated

by teredo, black in color with bamboo bands between (fig. 107). It made
a very effective and unique stand.

In wandering through the streets
of Tokyo I entered a public school,
first asking permission of the teacher,

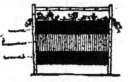

FIG. 107

who understood what I wanted. I was shown from one room
to another, and when I made my appearance in the different
rooms the teacher would stop the recitation, and at a word
of command the pupils all stood up and at another word all,
including the teacher, made a low bow almost touching the
desks. Then the recitation went on without interruption.

One notices in the Japanese face no strongly marked expression. This is the result of their training. As they never appear
to get mad or even excited, there is nothing to prompt the
deep wrinkles that one observes in the faces of foreigners.

A curious system of tattooing is seen among the lower classes;
at least one notices it in the naked jinrikisha men. The back,

arms, and legs are elaborately tattooed in grotesque designs in blue and red, some of the designs being quite artistic; a dragon, for example, extending down the back and legs and most delicately executed. What weird ancestry this survival must point to! In many cases one notices on the legs a row of scars which are made by burning a substance like punk, a painful operation, but supposed to be a curative for rheumatism.

Allusion has been made to the skill of the Japanese in dwarfing trees. I saw the other day a sturdy apple tree just two feet high; it was growing in an ordinary teapot and bore twenty apples. The apples were equally dwarfed, but sound-looking. What centrepieces for the table could be made if our horticulturists turned their attention to this ingenious art of the Japanese!

Thus far in my few weeks in this country I have come in contact, with few exceptions, with the laboring classes, — the farmers and work-people, — and yet what a record of sobriety, artistic taste, and cleanliness it has been! I hope before long to have access to the higher classes, for here the words "higher" and "lower" classes have their definite meaning. A book might be written on the lower working classes of Japan; their honesty, frugality, politeness, cleanliness, and every virtue that in our country might be called Christian.

A region in Tokyo known as *Asakusa* is one of the many novel sights to a foreigner! The great Buddhist temple towers far above the low dwellings of the neighborhood. The avenues leading to the temple are lined with booths on each side, mostly filled with toys or exhibitions of trained dogs or top-spinners. There may be tea-houses and cake-shops, but most of the activity and display are in the interest of children. Here is a place where one can buy a tray of seeds to feed the pigeons, which come down from the roof of the temple in great flocks and alight on the ground or upon the people who are feeding them.[1]

Within the dark recesses of the temple the coolly dressed priests were moving about and groups of people were praying. The only earnestness of expression I have thus far seen is when the Japanese are praying. The curious objects one sees in the temple often excite surprise and even contempt. An American missionary journal, reflecting on this subject, held up to derision an object which was seen on the walls of this religious edifice, namely a framed lithograph of the Pacific mail steamer, City of China. I could not believe it, and so on this first visit to the temple I specially searched for it, and found it among other souvenirs and emblems adorning the wall. It was, as described, a cheap, colored lithograph of the steamer, and from its rather soiled appearance I judged it had been there some years. On the glass at one side was an inscription in a few vertical lines. A few days afterwards I got a student to go to the temple with me and translate the inscription, and this is a free rendering: "This vessel rescued five shipwrecked Japanese sailors and brought them back to their native land. To commemorate this kind act on the part of the foreigner the priests of this temple have secured this picture and placed it among its relics." This was done at the

---

[1] Within twenty years we have vastly improved in this respect, and now one may see flocks of pigeons fed on Boston Common by men and boys, some of these birds actually alighting on the head, shoulders, or hands of the feeders.

time of bitter feeling against the foreigner and revealed a true Christian spirit on the part of the priests, and this picture is venerated by the Japanese.

There are many features in the temple that remind one of the Catholic cult; indeed, when Kaempfer, the Dutch doctor, who accompanied the Dutch Mission at Nagasaki, in the latter half of the seventeenth century, studied the Buddhist rites and ceremonies, with its monks and nuns, its holy water, incense, and rosaries, celibate priests, masses, chants, etc., he was forced to say, "Diablo simulanti Christum." In this temple on a stand is a wooden image, three feet high, polished and rubbed down to such an extent that the fingers and toes are almost obliterated and the merest traces of features remain. By the lower classes this figure is believed to have virtues of such a nature that if one has an ailment or pain he may be relieved or cured by simply rubbing the image on the part affected and then rubbing the same surface on one's self.

One can study the image and make an estimate of the prevalent diseases in Japan by the amount of wear! Thus the eyes are almost obliterated; the abdominal region is well worn, pointing to intestinal troubles; the well-worn knees and back of the image suggest muscular and articular rheumatism! (Fig. 108.) I stood for some time watching the poor people soberly approach and rub the figure and then rub themselves in the same place or apply the massage to the baby carried on the back. The faith cure and massage were all right, but when it involved the eyes, one would

Fig. 108

think that here the health officer should interfere, for certainly a contagious eye-trouble might be widely spread. As in other countries only the lower or ignorant classes share in these superstitions; the intellectual classes have long outgrown such senseless beliefs.

One may wander through the streets of Tokyo again and again and meet new sights to record. In one shop for the sale of sugar it was interesting to observe little boys, certainly not over eight or ten, doing all the work of weighing the sugar with steelyards, or rather bamboo yards, doing it up in bags and making change. A large crowd of customers were making their daily or weekly purchases, and in their work the boys were as active as ants. A meat-shop was a great novelty a few years ago, and even now only a few are seen in the larger cities. Refrigerators are not known, ice being very expensive. In the front of a shop was a large piece of beef, and a woman sat near it fanning it to keep the flies away.

FIG. 109

An illustration of the tolerance of the people and the good manners of the children is shown in the fact that no matter how grotesque or odd some of the people appear in dress, no one shouts at them, laughs at them, or disturbs them in any way. I saw a man wearing for a hat the carapace of the gigantic Japanese crab (fig. 109). This is an enormous crab found in the seas of Japan, whose body measures a foot or more in length and whose claws stretch on each side four or five feet. Many looked at the man as he passed and some smiled. It was certainly an odd thing to wear upon the head when most of the people go bareheaded.

I attended a festival known as "Opening of the River." Precisely what it means I did not learn. The celebration takes place on the Sumida River and the city pours its thousands on the river and into the tea-houses along the banks. Three of us started from Kaga Yashiki at eight o'clock in the evening, and of all the wild rides in jinrikishas this was the wildest one. We were late in starting, the streets were dark except what dim light came from the paper lanterns which everybody carried; the men were in a hurry, too, and they ran at top speed yelling, "Hai, hai, hai!" for people to get out of the way; and such narrow squeezes! We bumped into each other as the forward jinrikisha stopped, we slewed round corners, cut through narrow streets, and passed every jinrikisha we overtook. At the river the sight was entrancing, the wide river as far as the eye could reach being thickly covered with boats and pleasure barges of all descriptions. We had permission to pass through the grounds of a daimyo, and his servants brought chairs to the edge of the river for our accommodation. After sitting for a few minutes we concluded to see the sights nearer, and at that moment a boat came slowly along the bank, the man soliciting patronage. We got aboard and soon were sculled into the midst of the crowd. It would be difficult to imagine a stranger scene than the one presented to us; hundreds of boats of all sizes, — great, square-bottomed boats; fine barges, many with awnings and canopies, all illuminated with bright-colored lanterns fringing the edge of the awnings (fig. 110), and in every case a carpet or rug spread in

the middle of the boat, and upon it knelt the family with
friends surrounding an array of big and little dishes and saké
bottles, while geisha girls were thrumming the samisen and

FIG. 110

singing in their curious, falsetto voices. The broad river was
completely covered with these lantern-illuminated boats;
scenes of gentle revelry in some, children in all of them,
and good nature and good manners everywhere. Across the
river near the bridge brilliant fireworks were being discharged,
and we managed to reach the place after an hour's work in
pushing through this labyrinth of boats; bumping, backing,
and, at times, turning in the opposite direction. While most
of the boats were drifting on the water, others were in our
predicament in trying to land or in seeking other points, and
yet not a harsh word or rebuke was heard. Abounding good
nature everywhere. It was a startling sight when we got near
the place to see that the fireworks were being discharged from
a large boat by a dozen naked men, firing off Roman candles
and set pieces of a complex nature. It was a sight never to be
forgotten: the men's bodies glistening in the light with the
showers of sparks dropping like rain upon them, and, looking back, the swarms of boats, undulating up and down,
illuminated by the brilliancy of the display; the new moon

gradually setting, the stars shining with unusual brightness, the river dark, though reflecting the ten thousand lantern lights of all sizes and colors, and broken into rivulets by the oscillations of the boats. In our efforts to return to the river-bank where we had embarked, we met many boats going in the opposite direction, the boatmen with their long poles avoiding one or assisting another, and not a cross word in all this confusion, only "Arigato," "Arigato," "Arigato," (Thanks, thanks, thanks), or, "Go men na sai" (Excuse me). Such a lesson in refinement and gentleness, from boatmen too! Little by little the realization of why the Japanese have always called us barbarians is dawning upon us.

After we landed we had another exhilarating ride home. It was Sunday night and nearly every shop was open even at eleven o'clock. I sat up until midnight discussing with Dr. Murray the attributes of the Japanese. Among other things we discussed fires, and Dr. Murray said he had never been at one and promised to go with me when the next one occurred. Off we went to bed, he upstairs and I in a room on the ground floor literally filled with mosquitoes. I managed to get under the netting without letting one in, but their humming kept me awake, and shortly after we got to bed the fire alarm sounded. The fire alarm bells are on high posts with a ladder leading up to them (fig. 111). A man climbs up and strikes with a stick the number of the district. The sound produced is harsh and unmusical, a ridiculously feeble sound apparently not reaching five hundred feet. However, these bells are scattered closely all over the city and are within hearing of everybody. I was out of bed instantly and quickly dressed, when the Doctor

appeared and said that the fire was not far away. We rushed
out of the yashiki and both of us jumped into one jinrikisha,
and within half a mile came to a blazing fire which
illuminated the trees and the faces of a throng of
Japanese. It was a row of houses at the gateway
of another yashiki, which was enclosed by high
walls. Of the many extraordinary sights I have
thus far seen in Japan, a Japanese fire company
in action at a fire goes beyond them all. The engine itself is not over two and a half feet long; a
stout wooden box with no wheels, and so light
that two men pick it up and carry it on
their shoulders for miles, using the long
beam, by which they pump it up and down,
as a carrying-stick. The sketch (fig. 112)
shows the engine at rest at the fire station
hanging on two pegs from the side of a
shed-like building. Below this hangs a ladder made of stout bamboo the rungs of
which, consisting of strips of wood, are firmly tied, making
a light, strong, and serviceable ladder. One man can easily

FIG. 111

run with this if he can
steer it through the nar-
row streets. There is no
hose. A wooden pipe,
six feet in length, is
joined to an upright

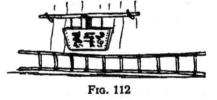

FIG. 112

wooden pipe which rises from the centre of the engine and
is jointed at the base in such a way that it may be made to

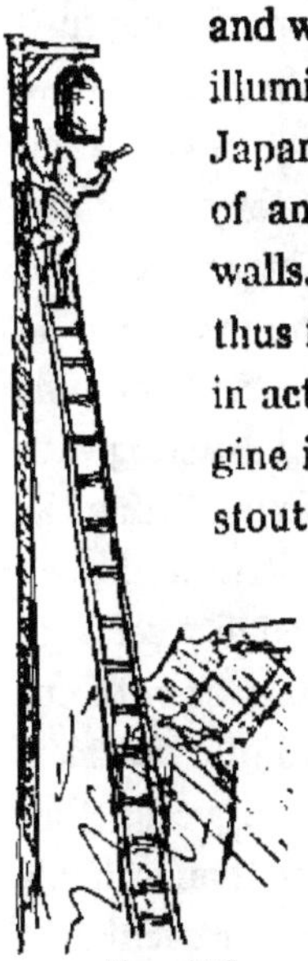

move up and down, or from side to side. It seemed the most ridiculous and puerile device ever conceived for the purpose of extinguishing fires. The buildings were blazing furiously when we arrived and the heavy roofing tiles were crashing to the ground as they were being shoveled off the roof. This we could not understand, as they were the only incombustible things in the house structure. Two or three fire engines were on the ground, and the men, two on each end of the brake, — no room for more, — and the pipe man standing on the box guiding the stream and assisting with one foot, were all pumping up and down frantically, lifting the engine from the ground at every pump. The stream thrown was about the size of a lead pencil and consisted of a series of independent squirts, as there was no air chamber as with our hand engines. The pumps were square instead of cylindrical and everything so dry, having hung in the sun for weeks, that more water spurted up in the air from the cracks than was discharged through the pipe, and the pipe man was immediately deluged with water. The joint of the pipe seemed to be dislocated in some of the engines, and only one out of three or four could play an effective stream (fig. 113). The fire companies are private and each company has a standard-bearer, the standards being geometrical structures of various shapes made of thick pasteboard, painted white, with the number of the engine in black, this being mounted on a long pole. These standard-bearers take a position as near the fire as possible, on the roof even of a burning building, and the companies whose standard-bearers are in evidence get a certain amount of money from the owners of the buildings saved.

In the sketch, I have endeavored to give an idea of the leaky engine, of two men who are bringing water, and a standard-bearer upon the yashiki wall, but you must imagine a number of these engines, nearly all leaking, men fetching

Fig. 113

water, others with ladders, fire poles, and sticks, beating, punching, tearing down buildings, and all yelling, and most of them carrying a lighted paper lantern! There being no such thing as a hose the engines have to be brought up close to the flames, and as the firemen are naked or nearly so, it would seem as if they must be blistered.[1] So far as courage and

[1] We learned later that the firemen do have a uniform of thickly wadded material, helmet and all, and that in checking a conflagration the men are engaged in tearing down the houses in its path and the engines play on the firemen engaged in this work and not on the flames, and these little squirt devices can be quickly taken

activity are concerned and the ability of standing heat and
smoke, they were as brave as our firemen, but aside from that
it seemed that a lot of little American boys would do better,
and as I stood among them I laughed again and again at their
absurd behavior. It is no wonder that acres of the city burn
over every year or two, and great destruction of property and
even of lives occur from the flimsy and inflammable character
of the wooden buildings; and this destruction will go on until
the Japanese modify their building laws so as to prohibit the
use of thin wooden shingles, and until they organize a decent
fire department with effective engines.

When we returned from the fire at one o'clock a few shops
had been opened in the hopes of catching a little trade. In
speaking of shops one observes that in the evening until ten
o'clock or later most of the shops are open. In the night time
the shops seem to empty themselves into the streets; at all
events, the streets near the buildings on each side—for there
are no sidewalks—are lined with straw matting upon which
are piled various wares, wooden, metal, and pottery, lacquer,
fans, toys, candy, etc., and all illuminated with a variety of
lights, from a rude dip with paper wick to a kerosene lamp.
Trade and barter seem to be the exclusive occupation of the
larger part of the population, and most of the shops have
rooms in the rear, which are the dwelling-places.

The other afternoon a distinguished old Japanese by the
name of Ito called on Dr. Murray, and I had the honor of being

---

up and rushed to the fire; the lanterns, furthermore, help them in the dark, narrow
streets, and so the absurdities of the affair are not so great. A fine collection of the
fireman's outfit may be seen at the Peabody Museum in Salem, Massachusetts.

presented to him. He is an eminent botanist and was president of a Japanese Botanical Society in 1824. He had come to
bring to Mrs. Murray the first lotus in bloom. He was in full
Japanese dress, though he had abandoned the queue (fig. 114).

Fig. 114

I regarded him with the greatest interest, and thought how
Dr. Gray and Dr. Goodale
would have enjoyed meeting
this mild and gentle old man
who knew all about the plants
of his country. Through an interpreter I had a very slow but
pleasant conversation with him.
On his departure I gave him
copies of some of my memoirs,
of which he could understand
only the drawings, and a few
days after he sent me his work on the flora of Japan in three
volumes.

Mention has already been made of the castle moats from
which spring in a curving incline the massive stone walls
which surround the castle. This wall encloses a vast space in
the city proper. The moat is like a great canal, and in riding
about the city one crosses it by bridges many times. In places
the moat is filled with the lotus plant which, if I mistake not,
is very closely allied to our pond-lily. The leaves are a foot
and a half in diameter and stand above the surface of the
water. The flowers are very large and of a delicate pink color.
These flowers are all in bloom now, and they are so thick with

their huge leaves that where they grow, they actually conceal the water beneath.

The absence of sidewalks in so great a city as Tokyo seems odd enough. The street beds are hard and smooth and it is strange to see the crowds of people traveling along in the middle of the street. So recently have they become acquainted with the jinrikisha that it is difficult for the older people to understand that they must clear the track. The jinrikisha men go tearing through the street and come within a hair's breadth of running over people, who do not seem to understand the necessity of getting out of the way. It is only within a short time that they have had an omnibus, which is simply an open covered wagon with a man always running ahead, to warn people of its approach. There is no reflex action manifested, and people move slowly aside in a dazed sort of way, when under like circumstances we instantly jump aside. These people are very slow in such matters and wonder at our quick motions. They never seem to be impulsive, and one has to exercise the greatest amount of patience in contact with them.

CHAPTER V

I HAD come to Japan with my dredges and microscopes to study a group of animals, the Brachiopods, of which there are many species in the Japanese seas. I had been to the Bay of Fundy, the Gulf of St. Lawrence, and Beaufort, North Carolina, for the same purpose, only one species being found in each of these places. In Japan, however, thirty or forty species are known. I established a station at Enoshima, a fishing village and place of resort, seventeen miles south of Yokohama. I had been there only a few days when a young Japanese came to me and invited me to give a lecture before the students of the Imperial University at Tokyo. On stating that I could not speak a word of Japanese, he replied that all the students of the University had to understand and speak English before entering. Noticing that I did not recognize him, he recalled the fact that I had lectured in a public course at the University of Michigan, that I had spent the night at Dr. Palmer's, and did I not remember a Japanese student who lived with them? I recalled the fact and this was the man, now Professor of Political Economy. He wanted me to give the same lecture with blackboard illustrations. It was a novel experience for me with a large hall full of students with flowing clothing, the skirted, or rather split-skirted *hakama*, a cross between a pair of trousers and a petticoat. It seemed as if I were lecturing before a class of girls. This lecture led to my being invited to take the professorship of zoölogy in the Imperial University for two years. As my public lectures at home for the coming winter had been arranged, I had to get a leave of absence for five months, which was granted. This was probably to their advantage in the end, for during my absence I collected books and pamphlets for the University Library to the extent of twenty-five hundred volumes and made the beginning of a good scientific collection. I was to establish a seaside laboratory at Enoshima and collect objects for a museum which was to be built.

A contract had to be made in the two languages, and I sat in the office while two scribes were busy preparing the papers. I got a surreptitious sketch of them at their work (fig. 115). Day after day went by while getting together glass jars, alcohol, etc., for the labora-tory. The foreigner gets im-patient with the moderate way in which everything is done, but the people are so sweet and gentle that it is im-

FIG. 115

possible to swear or to show the slightest impatience. A professor of botany, Professor Yatabe, who was teaching Gray's Manual, a graduate of Cornell, accompanied me to Enoshima to select a site for the laboratory building and to arrange for its erection. The day, July 17, was intensely hot, so that we waited until four o'clock before starting.

We each had a jinrikisha with two men, and they kept up a
good run without stopping, except at a few hills, when we got
out and walked. When we got to the last village they ran
like fury, not showing the slighest evidence of fatigue. The
enjoyment of the ride with the breeze made by their speed
was mitigated by my commiseration for the men running on
such a hot day. One wonders why they did not drop dead
with sunstroke and fatigue.

In going south, even the short distance to Enoshima, a slight
difference is seen in the houses of the villages. In one village
every house had growing from the ridge of the roof a dense
mass of iris. The ride was very picturesque, charming views of
Fuji appearing every now and then. It is certainly a wonderful mountain, standing up so loftily above everything else.
At times we would pass through a ponderous gateway capped
with flowers. The tea-houses, or inns, will often have for a
sign a weather-worn, irregular piece of wood upon which the
name of the place will be painted in characters. The sweet
single pink that we raise in our gardens at home is here seen
growing wild along the road. The highly perfumed lily, *Lilium
Japonicum*, is not an uncommon object and the atmosphere is
scented with its sweet, nutmeg odor.

Enoshima is an abrupt and precipitous island connected
with the mainland by a long, narrow sand bar which is covered at high tide. The island bursts suddenly into view, for
just before leaving the mainland we ascend a long sand hill
and at the crest the island stands out of the ocean with the
sand beaches fringed with breakers as they come rolling in
from the Pacific. In crossing this long strip of sand I saw for

the first time the shores of the ocean. I had not allowed myself to look at the shore before, as there were so many things
to be seen on land. The semi-tropical shells I had cherished in
my cabinet as a boy or had been familiar with in museums
were here to be picked up in quantities: *Cypræa, Conus,* a big
Dolium, and other southern forms. The delight in store for
me in seeing these creatures alive may be imagined. The village of Enoshima is massed together in one steep, narrow
street, so steep, indeed, that at intervals there are stone steps
in flights of six or eight, at short distances apart. The street is
not over ten feet wide and the wooden tea-houses are two and
even three stories in height, so that the street is comparatively
dark. The vertical signs of wood and the vertical strips of
cloth of various sizes and colors shade the street still more and
the sun never reaches the surface, which is always wet. The
entire street is lined with shops on both sides, and many of
them are stocked with souvenirs made from the shells, sea
urchins and other objects collected on the shore.

· I had come away without a particle of lunch, determined to
subsist on Japanese food. Having found a tea-house and being
shown to a room, we clapped our hands, the customary way of
calling a servant; the house is so open that the hand-clapping
is easily heard in the kitchen. The servant answers, "Hai,"
in a long drawl. The room was literally devoid of everything
in the way of furniture or other objects, save ourselves and
our traveling-bags. First tea was brought, then a flavorless
candy and cake, not unlike sponge cake, these articles coming
first instead of last as with us. We sat on the floor. I was
nearly starved and ready to eat anything. The pretty way in

which the girls knelt and bowed as they passed the things was gentleness itself. After a while up came the supper on lacquer trays, and a large number of dishes, porcelain, pottery, and lacquer, and the chopsticks which were united like a split match and had to be separated for use, this form indicating

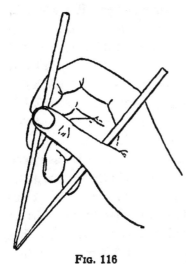

that they were being used for the first time and that they would be broken and thrown away after use. The chopsticks are held in one hand as in figure 116. The one held between the thumb and two fingers is moved back and forth as the pen is moved in writing. The other chopstick is held firmly by the third finger and crotch between the thumb and forefinger. I have already learned to use them slightly. These

FIG. 116

two simple devices take the place of every feeding utensil on the table. Meat, when served, comes to the table properly cut up. The soup is served in deep, covered bowls, small compared to our bowls, and the fluid part of the soup is drunk, while the solid pieces are picked up with the chopsticks. The rice is in similar bowls and is pushed into the mouth as you rest the bowl on the lower lip. The rice is so glutinous, however, that you can pick up lumps of it with the chopsticks. The cover of the rice bucket is often used as a tray in passing the rice bowl.

The cook uses metal chopsticks in turning food on the grid-iron or in the pan; iron or brass chopsticks are used in the *hibachi*, and these are united at one end by a ring; the jeweler uses delicate chopsticks in putting a watch together; the rag-picker on the street has two rods of bamboo, three and a half feet long with which he picks up paper and puts it in a basket, which he carries on his back. I watched an old woman making shell flowers, and where we should have used forceps she used a delicate pair of chopsticks in picking up the tiny shells. If our armies could be taught the use of the chopsticks, knife, fork, and spoon could be eliminated from the soldier's kit. Every prisoner should be taught the use of the chopsticks; every public institution should be furnished with them.

But to return to our first Japanese dinner. As it was spread out on the trays I was as much interested in the various plates and other dishes as I was in the food they contained. It was awkward to sit on the floor and to lift up many of the dishes in eating, and the chopsticks required constant attention, but the interest and novelty of the whole affair coupled with a fierce appetite led to a very agreeable experience. The fried fish and rice were quite delicious; the various pickles were not so agreeable and the little black plums were atrocious. On a large platter was a mat made of glass rods held together by silk thread, the rods as large as a lead pencil, and the mat a foot long and could be rolled up. It was an excellent device for draining

FIG. 117

food like boiled fish. Figure 117 shows its appearance in the dish. This device was used for a famous preparation of the

Japanese; namely, cold raw fish, cut in thin slices from the fish while fresh and alive. The idea of eating raw fish is particularly repulsive to our taste, though we eat raw oysters; nevertheless, foreigners soon get accustomed to it. The sauce made of fermented bean, barley, and some other grain seems to have been specially created for this kind of food. I ate a good deal of it and must confess that my first experience was fairly good, but my Japanese friend consumed

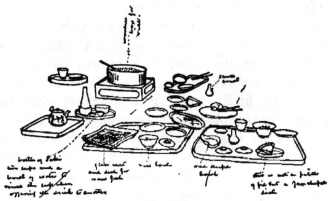

FIG. 118

with great gusto all that was left in the dish. It was hard work eating on the floor and my elbows soon got tired and my legs tired and awfully cramped. Though I managed to satisfy myself, a good slice of bread and butter, or either one without the other, would have helped things amazingly. Figure 118 shows the appearance of the floor after we had finished supper. After supper we went out to look up a place for the laboratory, and found a little structure unfurnished which we rented at thirty cents a day, and either to-night or to-morrow

we begin the work of collecting material for the future
Museum of Natural History of the University.

The breakfast was not so good: a weak fish soup, the fish
rather coarse and the other "fixin's" impossible, so I had to
order a stock of canned soups, deviled ham, crackers, etc., as
well as a kerosene oil lamp, knives, forks, and spoons. It will
save a lot of trouble if I ever can get used to this strange food.
I missed especially the morning coffee, as the Japanese drink
only tea, and so coffee had to be bought.

I want to record all facts concerning household adornment
and so note a tea-house we passed on the road, light, airy, and
cool. A curious effect was produced by hanging from the ceiling oblong strips of gold and silver paper held to the ceiling by
threads. Every breath of air made them turn and twinkle and
the effect was very pleasing. These strips were three inches
long and an inch wide and the entire ceiling was covered with
them about a foot apart. Another way of decorating the ceiling—which, by the way, is rarely decorated—is with colored
pictures of large fans. A room, sixteen by sixteen, had twenty
of these pictures, some of them expensive and very brilliant.

The ingenious way in which the Japanese conventionalize natural objects
is remarkable. I saw on a piazza rail
a board or plank in which had been
cut out the figures of cranes in different attitudes, and on an awning was

Fig. 119

a picture of Fuji and clouds, highly conventionalized (fig.
119).

When we washed our faces we found by the side of the brass

wash-basin a few Japanese toothbrushes made of wood; a slender strip of wood, one end sharp and the other end split

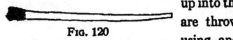

FIG. 120

up into the finest brush. These are thrown away after once using, and as the brush breaks down when used you are sure that it has never been used before (fig. 120).

The Japanese candlestick, of which there are many forms, was very interesting. It was made of brass and stood on the floor nearly three feet high (fig. 121).

FIG. 121

The next morning we arose early and went up the long street to another tea-house where the air was sweeter and the place so attractive that I engaged a room permanently; and such a view of Fuji as I had across the water! After settling this matter we climbed to the top of the island, going up steps cut in the solid rock. The island was heavily wooded and the summit crowned with a temple and shrines, and it was a great resort for pilgrims. Beyond the shrines the island terminated in precipitous cliffs facing the ocean. We descended a flight of stone steps to the narrow shore below, where we saw two Japanese divers for shells remain under water for a minute and ten seconds. When they came up we threw in a few cents and down they went again. Some little boys dived for pennies, and they looked funny enough kicking about below, in water clear as crystal. The shells clinging to the rocks were all so different from ours. The little crabs that live in holes on the beach run with amazing rapidity, and when I first saw them scampering over the pebbles I thought they were large flakes of soot, or furze. They go along somewhat like spiders and dart into a hole with a snap.

I dozed most of the way back to Yokohama, being very tired and the sun very hot, but enjoyed the foreign atmosphere of everything. In some respects boys are the same the world over. We passed a clay bank where some little boys were incising their names, probably, in Chinese characters. I have often seen at home boys carving their initials on similar surfaces.

The brooms the Japanese use in sweeping the mats or paths around the house are not unlike ours, only the handle is shorter and the bottom is cut at an angle to fit the floor so that the broom is not held vertically as with us.

I have observed in the train and other places that when a Japanese is reading his lips move and he often reads aloud.

Among the foreigners living in Yokohama Japanese fill every position of servants, cooks, coachmen, and clerks, and a Chinaman is rarely seen; yet in a few of the great banks one sees Chinese handling the money and keeping accounts; and in knowing every detail of international banking business, rates of exchange, etc., the Chinese excel all other peoples. For example, the trade is with Shanghai and Hongkong as well as with San Francisco, London, and Bombay, with many different kinds of money, weights, and measures. If rice is measured by the picul, which is over one hundred of our pounds, and

elsewhere it is sold by another measurement and with a different kind of currency, the Chinese compradors will instantly on
the abacus calculate the difference in Japanese money. The
price of rice is varying all the time as that of wheat is with us.
These men may be asked the price of rice in India or China, or
questions regarding the rate of exchange on London or New
York, and they can instantly answer and answer correctly.
They also excel everybody in the rapidity with which they
count money, — that is, silver dollars, — and in their power
to detect light-weight dollars or counterfeits. It is simply
marvelous to see the rapidity with which they will take a
roll of silver dollars lengthwise in the hand, first glancing
along the edges to see if they are the right thickness (the
Mexican dollar, the only one they use, is rudely made), then
allow them to slip like a cataract into the other hand, glancing
at the face of each one and hearing them chink against one
another, and then pouring them back in the same way to
glance at their opposite sides. While watching a comprador
I tapped with my finger as rapidly as I could to keep time with
the sound of the chinks and found that I tapped at the rate of
about three hundred and twenty a minute. This may be too
high an estimate, but the rapidity with which they were
dropped from one hand to the other was simply incredible.
In this process the man feels the weight, glances at the coin,
and hears the chink at the rate, certainly, of over two hundred
a minute. I watched the man with amazement as now and
then he would take out a light-weight coin. It is a monstrous
aspersion on the Japanese to say that these Chinese experts
are employed because the Japanese are dishonest. The truth

is that the Japanese have never been expert at figures, and no Englishman or American could even faintly approach these expert Chinese in reckoning with such rapidity all questions regarding exchange, weights, values, etc.

I examined another museum in Tokyo, an industrial art museum, and there saw many models of their coal mines, bridges, dams, and models to show how they protect their river embankments from erosion. There was also the framework of the roof of a Japanese house with several large stones on top of it to show its strength. The bridge models were of large size, five or six feet in length, and were very ingeniously and beautifully made. There was a model of a foot-bridge running across a river and suspended from the trees by ropes. In figure 122 is a rough sketch of a bridge pier showing the method of building a form of cantilever. A crib is first built, and unhewn trunks of trees, with their big ends inside, are held in place by fill-

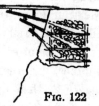

FIG. 122

ing the crib with stones; a succession of supports are constructed and finally a wall of stone is built around it.

In this museum were collections sent from the South Kensington Museum, — English porcelain and pottery. The cases were gracefully made and the glass was French plate. The halls were finished in cedar. Another low building contained a great number of objects which were obtained from the Vienna Exposition in exchange probably for their own exhibit: toothbrushes, pocket-books, soap, penholders, knives, and all the familiar things one sees in shops in our country. After having examined so many Japanese objects it seemed like a bit of home to see this room full of familiar material.

I was introduced to Mr. Farr, the manager of the Post-Office, and he said there would be no trouble about having my letters forwarded to Enoshima. He told me that last year they had sold $6000 worth of postage stamps to foreign collectors. Every bag that goes to America contains from fifty to seventy-five dollars worth of stamps for collectors abroad, — a clear profit.

The cloud effects in this country are wonderful; the air is so charged with moisture that long, shadow-like rays are thrown across the heavens, and such forms and colors! Some of the masses of clouds at sunset look transparent, and through them one can see dense masses of clouds beyond. In the morning the sky is clear, in the afternoon toward the north and west masses of clouds appear, and at sunset a glorious display of color is seen.

I have before mentioned the fact that the streets of those cities I have thus far seen are not named. In Yokohama the ground was laid out in rows of squares. I was told that the streets do not follow the original divisions, but as the land was

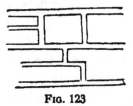

subleased in smaller portions the streets were made to run to them as in the accompanying diagram (figure 123). To find any place you have to know the number of the original lot. There is no sequence of numbers; as, for example, the Grand Hotel is 88, while 89 is three quarters of a mile away. The lots were orig-

FIG. 123

inally numbered from the water-front to the canal in sequence, beginning again at the water-front.

A curious decorative feature, known as *ishidoro*, or stone lantern, is seen in the gardens. Figure 124 shows two of the forms of which there are many kinds, usually covered with lichen, and all interesting not only in Japanese gardens, but would be in American gardens as well. A little lamp, or candle, is placed in the upper portion which is hollowed out for the purpose.

FIG. 124

It does not illuminate the region, but is simply a guide through the paths at night, just as lighthouses on the coast guide the mariner.

Back to Enoshima again (July 21), starting at four o'clock in the afternoon with the sun blazing down like a furnace. The rays actually burn as they strike the flesh, and how these naked-headed fellows stand it is a mystery to me. They all perspire profusely and the blue towel they tie about their heads is often wrung out. The evenings are deliciously cool and even on hot days a shady place seems cool. In riding over the same road again I notice more than ever the conveniences of the little shelters where one gets a cup of tea and a rice cake and leaves half a cent in payment on the tray. These places range all the way from the rudest shanty to a picturesque structure with an awning of straw matting extending over the entire road. Figure 125 gives the appearance of a rustic tea-place. We pass frequently on the road peas-

ants leading cows or bulls in strings of three. The latter seem much smaller and shorter-legged than our bulls, but evidently no more gentle than our creatures, as they have a hole through the septum of the nostrils in which is a ring with rope attached by which they are led. These bulls are being brought from

FIG. 125

Kyoto, a distance of three hundred miles to Yokohama, where they are to be slaughtered for the meat-eating foreigners. They were led along in a most quiet manner, no goading, no yelling, no barking dog to worry them. In every case they had on their feet thick straw pads, and often one sees a straw mat suspended above. I make a note of this; for in Cambridge, Massachusetts, large droves of cattle were driven by the college to Brighton, and the way they were harried by boys and men is one of the memories of a Harvard student.

FIG. 126

The farmers along the road often wear a square piece of matting across the shoulders, simply hung on the back to shield them from

the sun or rain. The pack-horses one meets often have prodigious loads of bamboo or lumber and are always led (fig.
126). With the number of pack-horses and cattle that one
sees on the road one is surprised at the absence of manure.

There seems to be a class of men — at least
they all are old men — whose duty it is to
sweep up this material, not for the road's
cleanliness, but for its value as dressing for
the land. Figure 127 represents one of these

FIG. 127

farmers performing the double duty of sweeping the road and
looking after the baby upon his back.

As the rice plants grow taller the
farmers look still more
odd with their enor-
mous straw hats and

FIG. 128

bodies just showing above the rice (fig. 128);
but to think of any human being working all
day long in a broiling sun with body bent
nearly double! Women as well as men share
in this work.

The sprinkling of the road in front of the
houses is done with a long wooden pump, as
shown in figure 129. It is three and a half feet
long and plays a fair stream. It is also used as
a fire protection.

In going through one village I passed a
number of brightly dressed children in a cheer-
ful flock around a woman similarly dressed,

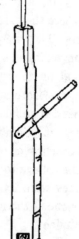

FIG. 129

carrying in her arms a newly born infant. I learned that

they had visited a neighboring shrine or church for some
sort of ceremony like our christening, and that it is customary
to carry the girls for this ceremony when they are thirty-three
days old and the boys when they are twenty-one days old. I
smiled at them when we rode by and waved my hand and some
of them responded, and we kept it up until the jinrikisha
turned a corner of the road

While in most parts of the world the fan is used for cooling
the face or for shading the eyes, in Japan one notices not only
a great variety of fans, but that they are utilized for many
purposes: an oil-paper fan is dipped in water and thus, in
fanning, the air is cooled; a fan takes the place of the bellows
in kindling the fire; a Japanese fans his soup if it is too hot and
the dancing girls make great use of the fan in their graceful
posturing. Fans are educational as well, information of various kinds being printed on one side, such as the best inns
and tea-houses to stop at, or the productions of the province,
while a map of the region is printed on the other side.

At one of our stopping-places I saw a man intently studying
a common fan. I begged the privilege of looking at it, and he
seemed quite pleased at my interest. On one side of the fan
was a map of Japan and on the other side a series of vertical
divisions headed by circles, some black, others half black, looking like half moons. It was a list of stopping-places between
Tokyo and Owari; the circles indicated the accommodations of
the inns, the empty circles indicating the eating-places alone,
the half filled circles the resting-places, and the black balls
showing where they "can eat and sleep you." Moral precepts,
poems, the praises of a tea-house are often written on fans. In

feudal times high officers directed the manœuvres of an army by waving a large fan, either white with red disk, red with gold disk, or gold with red disk. Sumptuous books have been published on the Japanese fan.

The abdominal, and I might say the abominable, protuberance often seen in little children and infants is astounding; it seems as if it would pain them; indeed, they looked as if they had been stuffed for the oven. It comes from gorging themselves with rice, which actually distends the walls of the stomach.

I have noticed with much interest the wall-paper designs. Those that I have seen are in the houses of the common classes and on the whole are quite as poor as the cheap wall-paper at home. They are better, however, in one respect, and that is that they are never bright-colored; usually the figure is white and shining on a slightly tinted ground. The designs are entirely different from ours and the wall-papers, instead of being in rolls, are made in oblong sheets a foot and a half in length. A number of different papers will be found in a single room. The one I occupy has five different kinds of paper, one kind on the ceiling, another kind around the upper part of the wall and the two sides of the room, and the other kinds on sliding screens. It was in no way attractive. It was an attempt on the part of some one to make a room after a supposed foreign style, and it was a miserable failure. In one design are irregular areas filled in with diaper and a formal design of a flower, and outside these areas are swallows, butterflies, and moths. In figure 130 is shown a drawing of a water plant known as *Paulownia;* it is represented in the crest of the

Tokugawa family; also a crude collection of pinks, convolvu-

lus, grapevine, and grasses enclosed in cloud outlines, and the interspaces, kennels with rabbits within. Another represents the rapids of a river with boats floating down filled with fagots and no man aboard to attend; it probably had some meaning. I was told that these designs were copied from brocade. What interested me was that they were most inconspicuous. One had to examine the paper closely to detect the design. Across the street I saw a screen covered with paper in which had been incorporated the outer sheaths of bamboo shoots, though they looked like strips from the inner bark of a pine, rich brown in color and quite effective (fig. 131). Green, threadlike seaweed is mixed with the pulp in making paper, with a very pretty effect.

FIG. 130

Enoshima being a favorite place of resort the shops are full of souvenirs and toys for children and always made

FIG. 131

from material got on the ground. A simple top was made
with the shells of two sea urchins (fig. 132);
a trumpet or whistle was made of a reed with
the shell of *Eburna* as a resonator (fig. 133)..
The top spun a long time and the trumpet
gave out a long, loud sound. They were
strongly and neatly made,
and yet in purchasing one
the smallest coin I had was

FIG. 132

a Japanese cent and rather than make
change I took three in all. The shell-work
in little boxes, and birds made of shells
perched in hanging rings and many other
graceful devices in shellwork, recalled to
my mind the shocking shellwork one used
to see at home: pyramids, monuments,
heart-shaped articles, and dropsical-look-
ing boxes thick with putty and utterly devoid of taste.

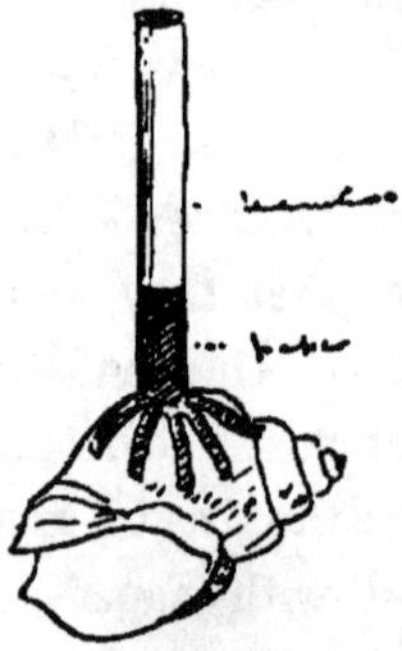

FIG. 133

I can look across my room to another angle of the house,
where in a room by themselves are four Japanese students
who in the morning are studying hard, clothed in their loose
Japanese kimonos and in the afternoon, when the sun is
blazing, they are naked and playing chess or *go*, both highly
difficult games. They are a laughing and pleasant group.
From their conversation in the forenoon I learn that they are
studying German, for I hear one say, "I shall go to London
to-morrow to meet my father," and another gives the German
rendering of it; and so from their room comes a rattle of
Japanese, German, and English, and now and then a sentence

in French and a good-natured laugh at some blunder. Their English is so good that I can understand every word they say.

Last night two of them came into my room at my request to explain to me the Japanese game of go. The game was originally brought from China, but now the Japanese excel the Chinese in the playing of it. Among expert players a single

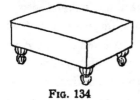

FIG. 134

game lasts for days, and sometimes an hour is consumed in making one play. The board is a low table eight inches high; a thick block of wood supported by four stout legs (fig. 134). It is squared off like our checkerboard, but the squares are smaller and are not colored light and dark as ours are, and there are many more of them, there being 361 squares, 19 by 19. The checkers are flat disks, like buttons, made out of a black stone and white shell, and they are placed not on the squares, but at the intersection of the lines. The player begins by putting down

a disk on any portion of the board and the object is to enclose the opponent's men by a continuous line of disks. When either side succeeds in doing this the disks enclosed are captured (fig. 135) and the squares are counted at the end of the game. The

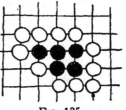

FIG. 135

battle rages at different places on the board. The famous players are classified: a first-rank player can give a second-rank player the privilege of playing two men on the first turn instead of one man, and I suppose a third-class player has the

privilege of playing three men. It is curious to watch two
experts play with only a few disks on the board. The player
will study the conditions for a long time and then place a disk
a dozen squares from the other checks or away up on the right-
hand corner, or in some other place, the reason for which only
an expert can see and the response is equally inscrutable. In
playing they always take the disk between the first and second
fingers, the second finger on top of the first finger. It is a most
profound game and few foreigners have mastered it. Mr. Kor-
schelt presented a paper on the game, with eighty-four illustrations, in the Proceedings of the German Asiatic Society.

The students kindly played a game for me. It was hastily
played for want of time on my part. One side got seventy-one
squares and the other eighty-four. There are other points in
the game which I did not understand.

There is also another, very simple, game which is played on
the same board and which would interest our people, and that
consisted of an attempt to place five disks in a continuous
row! It is a simple game, though players vary greatly in their
skill. I played a few games with them and they beat me every
time with a few men, and when they tried it
with each other they used over a hundred
disks. If you can get a situation in which
there are two lines of four, you win, as only
one of these lines can be stopped by the other
player. Figure 136 shows the position. A

FIG. 136

and B illustrate the two lines, only one of which can be
stopped by the other side. Various points may be started
on the board as in the game of go.

In many Japanese rooms there is a post running up in the centre of the wall, possibly to support the roof. On this is often hung a long piece of thin board, five feet long and nearly the width of the upright, and upon this vertical, narrow surface the Japanese artist manages to paint a picture or part of a picture that might be seen through a slightly opened door.[1]

Getting back to Enoshima I found my room reserved for me. The luggage had arrived safely and the building we had engaged for a laboratory was nearly completed. A hammock that Dr. Murray had lent me I hung from a post in my room to a post on the piazza. Though I was assured there were no mosquitoes they came in swarms, and I covered my face with a towel and then a thin coat; but it was too hot to endure this covering, and every time I moved or got up to fix things my pillow, consisting of three waistcoats and trousers folded in a shirt, would drop out and I had to rearrange it. Finally I gave up in despair, and my Japanese boy brought me a mosquito netting almost filling the entire room, and I slept on the floor. It was past midnight and I had just got to sleep when into my room came an anxious-looking fellow holding a lantern on the end of a stick in one hand and a letter and newspaper in the other. He jabbered away in his own tongue, which, interpreted, probably meant, "Is this packet for you which I have just brought from Fujisawa as special courier?" I was altogether too mad at being awakened to realize how happy I should have been if it had been home letters for me, and reading the name "Dunlap" I told the man to go to the

[1] The one figured in *Japanese Homes* was simply charming with its brown trunk of pine, the green leaves and the groundwork of cedar upon which it was painted. On the reverse side another subject was painted.

devil, which from the tone he evidently understood, for he instantly withdrew and I had another tussle trying to get to sleep.

The Japanese never seem to realize at night that some of the family or guests may be sleeping. They may be no worse in this respect than our own people. The houses of the Japanese are far more open than ours and the slightest sound easily penetrates the next room, and if loud the entire house is entertained by the song or conversation of a convivial crowd. The closing of the *shoji*, the slamming of the storm blinds as they are pushed in place, one after another, at night, are annoying to the last degree, for they are never handled quietly. From this universal racket I had supposed that the Japanese were indifferent to these disturbances when trying to sleep. On inquiry, however, I found that the Japanese were quite as sensitive as we, but possibly too polite to complain.

Since I have been here I have slept on the floor with my clothes forced into a shirt for a pillow. The Japanese pillow is all very well for a nap, but I dare not risk it for the night, as it makes one's neck lame unless one is accustomed to it.

I must again allude to the nuisance of the fleas — large-sized ones whose bites last a long time. I have fifty marks on my body, and with the hot weather the itching is intolerable.

While eating my dinner to-day a sharp earthquake shook the house, made the water in my glass oscillate, and rattled things generally. It felt precisely as if a corpulent man forty feet high had lurched against the side of the house with a bump. The different kinds of oscillations felt must be due to the different natures of the rocks. The displacement that produces the vibration would be different in degree with soft rock from what it would be if the rock were refractory.

Mr. Toyama and his friend came to-day, and while they ate dinner I was invited in and had a chance to taste boiled cuttle-fish, which was very tough, like hard gristle, with a flavor like mild lobster. I also endeavored to eat raw *Haliotis*. It was served in thin slices, and yet so tough I could not bite into it, could not even get the taste of it; it was like rubber. I am sure of one fact, and that is that our food is more nutritious, more rational, and easier to digest than the Japanese food; but in this statement I do not include many of our fat-soaked things, heavy hot biscuits and the like. The Japanese take eagerly to our food, and it thoroughly agrees with them; we do not take naturally to their food.

The friend of Mr. Toyama, a scholarly man, does not speak a word of English, but reads and translates with remarkable accuracy. He has translated many English works into Japanese and these are sold in great numbers. It certainly would astonish an American to read a list of the works already translated: Spencer on "Education," which has a tremendous sale; Mill on "Liberty"; Buckle's "History of Civilization"; a portion of Thomas Paine's "Age of Reason"; Burke's "Old Whig and the New" (ten thousand copies already sold), and many others of like character. Books of this nature, which are abhorred by certain sects at home, are here read with the keenest interest.

Figure 137 is a map of the Bay of Yedo to indicate the position of Enoshima.

Last evening I learned three games that are played on the

chess board. One student endeavored to explain Japanese chess to me, but it was too complex to understand. I learned this much, however; the chess board (fig. 138) has eighty-one squares and is not unlike the go-board in shape. These squares are not colored, but are marked by deep lines indicating the boundary of the squares. The chessmen are made of boxwood and are uncolored; that is, they are the natural color of the wood.

Fig. 137

They all have the same shape, though they are different in size; the royal pieces being the largest and the soldiers, or pawns, the smallest.

Fig. 138

The shape of each piece is like the key-stone of an arch, thinner at the lower end, and its name is written in black lacquer on the piece (fig. 139). There are twenty pieces, the court pieces occupying the first line, the pawns the third line, and two pieces resting on the intermediate or second line. The king is in the centre of the first line of squares; on each side of him are the golden generals; and next

Fig. 139

to these are the silver generals. The golden generals move forward diagonally, also directly forward and right and left, but backward only in a straight line; the silver generals have the function of our bishops, but may also move forward in a straight line. The flying wagon general moves like our rook, and one oblique, or diagonal general moves like our bishop. In each corner of the board is a piece that moves forward only, but if it gets over to the third row of the opponent it may change itself into a golden general. Two other pieces called horsemen move precisely like our knights, except that they cannot move backward. When they get into the third row of the opponent they too may become golden generals if they choose. The pieces are played with their smaller end forward, and in this way only can the pieces of the two sides be distinguished. To see two players at the game under the dim light of a vegetable wax candle, when it is difficult to define the pieces colored as they are like the board upon which they are played, is quite remarkable. The pieces are captured in the same way as in our game except that the pawns move straight ahead to capture. The most curious feature of the whole game, and that which makes our game seem simple, is that pieces captured may be replaced at any time or in any place by the capturer, so in a tight place these prisoners may be played one after another against the opponent and the one attacked may play his prisoners in the same way. It is a most elaborate game and requires a good mind to understand it. It is an extraordinary sight to see naked-legged jinrikisha men playing the game while waiting for a fare.

This morning with Toyama and two other Japanese I engaged a boat and sailed round from our cove to the other shore of the island facing the ocean. Here, near high-water mark, was a cave which we wished to examine. It was delightful to sail out with the dignified swell of the ocean lifting our boat up and down in grand style. The appearance of the front of the island, with its vertical cliffs crowned with a fringe of pines, was very picturesque (fig. 140). Running about on the rocks near the shore-line were a dozen naked little boys as brown as Indians, impatient to dive into the sea for the pennies we threw in. The cave seemed to be an immense fissure in the rock, which had been rounded out by the waves in former times when the land must have been submerged; now the waves reach only to the entrance. The rocks were

Fig. 140

light in color, so the dark entrance of the cave stood out strongly by contrast. About one hundred and fifty feet within was a Shinto shrine covered with gilt, which reflected the few light rays which came from the entrance, making a striking effect in the dark cave. The shrine was nearly ten feet high and as wide, carved in the most elaborate way. It was an odd place to find a shrine, this dark, damp cave, and yet in Japan, wherever you find a striking feature in the landscape, such as this place, the top of a mountain, the verge of a precipice or deep ravine, there you will find these religious and devoted people erect their churches or shrines. There was room on one side of this shrine to pass and penetrate farther into the dark recesses, and here we were provided with lights, and we plodded ahead a few hundred feet until we had to stoop to get along. It was absolutely dark except for what little light our candles afforded. At the extreme end of the cave was a board partition mouldy and rotten with age. A wooden grating was in the partition, and looking through it we saw a polished circular metal mirror about twelve inches in diameter, and this represented a Shinto shrine. Going back toward the entrance we came to an arm of the cave, and following that up we came to another grating through which we saw another Shinto shrine and mirror. The passage was hardly wide enough for two to walk abreast, and along the walls were symbolic figures — coiled dragons wrought in the stone and other emblems of mythology. I could not help reflecting on the devotion and piety of the early devotees who have left their marvelous rock carvings and prodigious temples in Java, India, and China. I scanned the walls closely for evidence of twilight insects, but it was not dark enough to find typical cave animals. To my delight I found two little spiders, two very small sowbugs, and, better than all, two cave crickets with exceedingly long antennæ, much smaller than ours, mouse-colored, and having a good set of compound eyes. I enjoyed my first look into a pool of sea water in Japan. I picked from the rocks at low tide a number of large chitons and greatly enjoyed the living mollusks as they crawled about, having only known them by their shells.

In the afternoon I started for Yokohama, stopping on the

way at the little village of Fujisawa, the nearest post-office to
Enoshima, hoping that my mail had been forwarded, as the
steamer from San Francisco had arrived. We got to the post-
office just as the mail was being distributed. Figure 141 gives
an idea of the postmaster as he appeared with a miscellaneous

heap of letters and newspapers
on the floor before him. It was
such a novelty to get my letters in a little Japanese village, and the innocent way in
which he gave me a bundle of
letters tied up, upon which
was attached a strip of paper

Fig. 141

with my name written in Japanese! I simply said, *Morse
san* and out they came; he did not look up, so absorbed
was he in the distribution of the rest. As a testimony to the
inherent honesty of the Japanese the postmaster at Yokohama told me that in the first year the Japanese entered
the International Postal Union the Department cleared sixty
thousand dollars above expenses and not a cent nor a letter
was lost or stolen. For the next six miles I lay back and enjoyed my letters. It fairly made my eyes ache trying to read
them all as we went bumping over the road at a lively rate.
I could not help realizing the novelty of riding alone through
the country, not speaking a sentence of the language and
everybody so kind and smiling, when but ten years before I
might have been assailed. Being in my shirt sleeves I attracted the usual attention, the people gathering about
whenever we stopped for tea and feeling and examining the

curious straps over my shoulders. The Japanese women are much interested in our woolen fabrics, their cloth being cotton, linen, and silk, and the weave simple. They will feel of your coat sleeve and critically examine its texture and with curious ejaculations express their wonder as to how it is made, and finally give up the puzzle in despair. On account of the heat I got out of the jinrikisha and walked up all the hills. At one hill I overtook six men struggling with a long beam on two wheels. My two jinrikisha men left their vehicle to assist in pushing up the load, and to their utter astonishment I took a hand in the pushing. When they reached the summit of the hill they gave me a volley of *arigatos* and profound bows. It was now past eight o'clock, the moon was full and bright, and I had the experience again of riding along and peering into the open houses as we passed.

I have before alluded to the festival in which they keep lights burning on the *kamidana* (god shelf) in memory of departed relatives. All the houses on both sides of the road were provided with a light and sometimes a row of lights on the shelf in front of a few objects of Shinto or Buddhistic significance. The rooms are low and above the kamidana the woodwork is black with smoke. Figure 142 is a sketch

FIG. 142

of one of these household shrines. They vary greatly in the number of objects displayed, in proportion, probably, to their piety and purse. There were little trays filled with rice for food offerings to the departed. In Shinto shrines these vessels are unglazed and for certain occasions made by hand without the potter's wheel. A few flowers and thin strips of board with the names of the departed inscribed thereon are also seen.

The flag is a long, narrow strip of cloth hung vertically by loops to the flagpole. The inscription, as in all the writing of Chinese characters, is written vertically.[1] The method of raising the flag is shown in figure 143.

In meeting people at the tea-houses along the road it is impossible to make them comprehend that you do not understand a word they say; they keep on talking to you, and generally in a louder tone, imagining you are deaf, or they have an expression on their faces as if they considered you an idiot or mentally weak. In vain you say, "Wakarimasen," the Japanese for "I do not understand"; finally, I would say to them earnestly, "What is your opinion of the Kansas and Nebraska Compromise?" at which they would look at

Fig. 143

[1] It should be constantly borne in mind that the characters used by the Japanese are strictly Chinese. So far as I know the Japanese never invented a character any more than we have ever invented a letter; the Japanese did, however, invent an alphabet by using Chinese characters in reference to their sound and finally abbreviated them to a single stroke or two; this the Chinese never did. Even with the example of a phonetic system — the Sanscrit — on their western borders, not one of the hundred millions had the ingenuity to devise an alphabet of their own. Dr. S. Wells Williams, the great sinologist, says their language has shut them from their fellow men more than any other cause, and Colonel Garrick Mallory, an authority on picture writing and hieroglyphics, says the practice of pictography does not belong to civilisation. The question arises in regard to the Chinese: Is the nation inert and backward on account of their method of writing or are the people fossilised and cannot adopt another method? A Japanese scholar informed me that the Japanese language was much impeded in its development by the introduction of Chinese characters.

me inquiringly and then grunt or laugh heartily, appreciating the point.

Having procured a number of things I needed at Enoshima I got off at noon, with the heat overpowering, for a ride of eighteen miles. The perspiration stood in large drops on my face and hands and the jinrikisha men fairly reeked; the rapid evaporation, however, enabled one to endure it. We passed many pilgrims on the road, this being the time (last days of July) when groups of artisans start on their pilgrimages to the temples. It is really a tramp in the country — an outing, — but they combine with this vacation a devotional spirit by visiting various shrines where they say their prayers and contribute their pennies. They go together in groups of a dozen or more and straggle along the roads in twos and threes. They

Fig. 144

are usually clothed in cotton cloth of the same pattern, a loose sort of gown, and thus appear to be in uniform, some of them having tied about the waist a bell which tinkles at every step. In hot weather the skirt is looped up showing their naked legs. Figure 144 is a group of two. They are always in a good-natured mood and always return a smile for a smile.

We overtook a crowd on the road accompanying the transportation of an immense bronze casting, probably a temple lantern. The design was in open work. It was suspended from a huge pole, at the front end of which was a cross-stick with a man at each end and probably a giant in strength supporting the rear end (fig. 145). The men were clothed in white with Chinese characters on the back running from the right shoulder to the left hip, and on the casting was a little banner also inscribed. When the men let the load down for a rest they all joined in the queerest sort of chant.

Fig. 145

Such are some of the many novelties one meets or overtakes on the road.

From my room is a wonderful view of Fuji across the water. A cove coming within fifty feet of the house, the fishermen in their quaint boats are always in sight, and at night, when they come in with their "catch," they sing in a responsive way, one saying, "Hiari!" and the other, "Ftari!" — or at least that is the way it sounds; and they keep this cry up with every stroke of the oars, the men of each side sculling alternately, for the boats are never rowed, but sculled from the sides.

As I crossed the sandbar on my return from Yokohama I noticed a long, heavy swell coming in from the Pacific, an indication that a big storm was brewing outside. The wind has been increasing in violence, and now it is blowing with the greatest fury, and as I sit writing the noise is a perfect roar from the wind and waves together. This forenoon before it became thick it was a magnificent sight to see the long swells sweep grandly in and the wind blowing offshore taking a mass of foam from the crests of the waves and blowing it back and far up in the air. The bay is at least five miles across and the swells extended the entire length; they seemed at least three

hundred feet apart and were of great height, and these wonderful masses of white spray torn from the incoming, semi-
circular swells, white as steam, was a sight far exceeding in
grandeur anything I ever saw, while the thundering crashes on
the beach must have been heard miles inland. The storm is a
typhoon. How severe it will be no one can tell, but it is blowing harder than I ever knew it to blow before and is increasing
in violence. The foot of the street is entirely blocked with
fishermen's boats pulled up there out of reach of the waves;
the houses are all closed with the wooden shutters, and the air
is hot and stifling. As my room is not particularly exposed to
the storm, my rain shutters have not been closed, and so while
stormbound I will continue the record.

CHAPTER VI

LIFE IN A FISHING VILLAGE

OUR little laboratory was finished this morning and now we are ready for work if our dredge rope and a few other things will only get here. I put a padlock and hasp on the sliding door, and while I was at work an admiring crowd of men, women, and girls and naked children with dirty faces stood by and watched me. They are all extremely curious people and minutely scrutinize everything that is new; even now while I am writing three women of the house have apologetically entered my room and are watching me write, as extraordinary a sight to them as their method of writing is to us. They write with a brush held vertically, and the lines run from the top to the bottom of the page, beginning on the right of the page and progressing to the left. We write with the penholder held sloping, with a metallic point as sharp as a pin, with a watery ink, as compared with their rich, black India ink, which they have to rub from a stick of ink every time they write. These women made surprising comments about everything on my table; bottles, jars, microscope, a meerschaum pipe, which must seem elephantine in comparison with their tiny metal-bowled pipe.

After I got the padlock on the door we moved in our two cans of alcohol, a lot of glass jars I had bought in Yokohama, dredges, and other laboratory material. The building sets on the extreme corner of a sea wall of stone with a narrow lane running along in front. Figure 146 is a rude map of the island, high and abrupt on all sides except toward the main land where

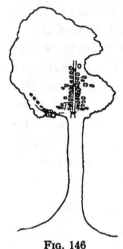

you pass under a tori-i to cross the narrow sandbar. Since writing the above the storm has increased to a howling hurricane, and having some fears about our laboratory I put on my rain coat and struggled down the narrow street, climbing over boats at the foot. The natives occupying the adjoining buildings had all moved their belongings to higher places on the island. From the window of our building the scene was terrific; huge waves were rushing over the neck of sand which was entirely under water. Such a roar and such a sight! There were three elements of peril: the building might be blown away; it might be dashed away by the waves; the stone wall might be undermined. The man we had engaged as a watchman could not be induced to sleep in the building, and so with his assistance and other help we packed in a lot of

FIG. 146

pails the jars that we had unpacked and arranged in the morning, and with our alcohol, dredges, and everything portable,

FIG. 147

we picked our way back to the main street and conveyed them to the inn where I was stopping (fig. 147). After I went to bed the driving rain came into my room, though the storm blinds were up, and my table and other things were moved to the opposite end of the room. I slept on the floor, which shook as if there were an earthquake, and it seemed as if the hurricane would burst in upon me before morning. When I awoke the storm had cleared off, though the sea was roaring. A visit to our laboratory showed that it had been well built to stand such a battering. Portions of the stone wall had been washed away on both sides of us, but our corner fortunately stood. The lower part of the street had been entirely swept away to a depth of four feet. The waves were still washing over the sand neck connecting the island with the mainland, and people were wading across both ways, some carrying others on their

FIG. 148

backs (fig. 148). A band of pilgrims on the other side were hesitating about crossing; with their broad straw hats in their hands and pilgrim staffs and their little blue banners flying they looked like a band of savages with their hats and staffs looking like shields and weapons. A courier has just come in to inform me that a lot of things have come for the station, but they cannot be got across on account of the waves. We shall finally get them as the waves go down.

Last evening I moved my table into the middle of the room and invited Professor Toyama and his friend, Mr. Ikkoto, and

my assistant Mr. Matsumura, to come in to enjoy my kero-
sene-oil lamp, a luxury the Japanese appreciate after having
studied with the dim illumination of a vegetable wax candle. Mr. Ikkoto brought in the work he is engaged in, that
of translating "What the Ancients Thought of the World"
from the "Popular Science Monthly." Mr. Matsumura is
studying my little "Textbook of Zoölogy"; Professor Toyama
an analytical table of the animal kingdom, and he was hard
at work upon it.

Nothing illustrates more clearly the simple and open character of the common people than the sketch (fig. 149) which I

Fig. 149

got in my ride from
Yokohama yesterday.
The jinrikisha men,
having passed the city
limits, where they are
compelled by law to wear some sort of a blouse, stopped to
take off their blouses, as it was intolerably hot. They are
not allowed to go naked in Tokyo, Yokohama, or in any of
the larger cities in deference to foreigners; of course it is
understood that they invariably wear a loin-cloth.

While waiting I wandered into a house to sketch the kamidana with its light burning at night, when I observed the
woman of the house sound asleep and the child she had
been nursing sound asleep also. I could not resist making
a sketch as an illustration of the fact that the houses are
literally open to any one who has the impertinence to in-
trude. I should not have entered without apologies had
she been awake.

Sunday, July 29. There is absolutely no way of distinguishing Sunday from any other day except perhaps in the larger cities where the few English shops are closed and the Government offices are closed too (a concession to foreigners), though you may always get in to transact business so far as my brief experience shows.

Pilgrims, travel-stained and weary, are crowding the narrow street going to the top of the island to visit the shrine; the various innkeepers, from landlord down to the last girl, line up in front of the houses, and while bowing low, emit curious, whining supplications soliciting custom. The houses are filled with these travelers from all parts of the Empire; the ting, ting of the samisen and the curious falsetto notes of the geisha make the nights anything but restful. In this narrow, crowded street I pass back and forth to the laboratory. I am the only foreigner in the village, and naturally am an object of great interest to most of them, as they come from the interior, and doubtless many of them never, or rarely ever, have seen a foreigner. Yet I am treated courteously and kindly by every one; not a shout or impertinent stare greets me; and the contrast between this behavior and the experience a Japanese, or Chinese, in his native costume would receive going down the village streets, or even the city streets, of our country, was humiliating to consider. The crowds are off for a good time and many are hilarious, yet I have seen but one intoxicated person, and he lay quietly asleep by the side of the street and people passed him looking regretfully at his condition; not a boy taunted him. Such instances kept me mentally comparing the two civilizations.

Mr. Knox, the writer, Mr. House, editor of the "Tokyo Times," Dr. Eldridge, of Yokohama, and Mr. Wertheimber spent the day and night at my inn, and when they departed this morning I went to the foot of the street to see them off. The sand neck having been washed away by the typhoon, they had to cross to the mainland by boat, and such a shouting and poling and hauling, with some hauling at the bow with a rope to get the loaded boat started, such a hubbub it was and so unlike anything I ever saw before! The landlord and servants were there profoundly bowing to their guests and bidding them good-bye and thanking them for their patronage.

The effects of the storm along the water-front in Yokohama showed the terrific character of the waves. The heavy coping stones of the sea wall were thrown over into the street, which was filled with pebbles and large stones. The remains of a large Japanese junk had been strewn in front of the hotel, and a large steam dredging machine, which had been at work for two months in the channel, had been carried a thousand feet, keeled over on one side, and all the buckets torn away.

The laboratory has two windows, one looking along the shore, the other along the sandbar to the mainland. Figure 150 is a sketch alongshore from the laboratory; the first building, which is in process of construction, is a fireproof structure known as kura, or godown. Mats are fastened to a framework to prevent the plaster from drying too rapidly. The sandbar having been entirely washed away, the people cross in boats or on the backs of stout fellows who wade across.

Coming from Yokohama yesterday I passed at different places on the eighteen-mile ride four beggars, and these are

seen at this time because the road is thronged with pilgrims
and will be thronged for several weeks. An odd way they have
of begging; the moment you appear in sight they kneel on the
ground with their heads touching the ground and remain in this
position without a sign of life. I had to ask my jinrikisha man
by pantomime if the man was at his devotions or was begging.
A rare sight is a beggar in Japan, and the absence of tramps,
vagabonds, and hoodlums adds greatly to the charms of the
country.

Fig. 150

Figure 151 is a sketch of our laboratory, and, so far as I know, the first zoölogical station on the Pacific.

Two weeks ago I should hardly have thought worthy of mention the effort to secure a hut for a station of this sort, as

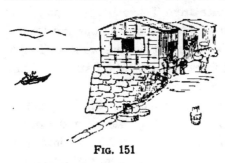

Fig. 151

at home I could run down to Eastport, for instance, hire a loft of a building on the wharf, get a carpenter and tell him what I wanted, buy preserving cans, and in half a day be ready for work. When I told Dr. Murray my plan of getting a small building and fitting it up especially for my work, he laughed significantly and said I should find a great many obstacles in the way, and I must say he was right. It was some time before I found a proper building and induced the proprietor to fit it up for me. He would do it next week; no, I must have it immediately or not at all; and then to explain everything through an interpreter; to try to hammer into the thick head of a country carpenter the idea of a long table against the wall, for they have no tables; to get four stools made, for they have no such thing, as they sit on the floor; to have shelves put up and to describe long windows closed with sliding shutters, and to get each sliding window and door locked, for they have no locks in their houses. The only thing I could do was to get a padlock and hasp in Yokohama and put it on myself; and to get the alcohol, jars, and copper cans, was indeed a task.

So impatient was I for jars that I went to Yokohama and hunted up a Japanese junkshop and tried to buy some salt jars, but while I could buy other jars, they would not sell these, as they had had an offer for them from Tokyo. Three days after, down came four men from Tokyo bearing upon their backs heavy packs addressed to me, and on opening them I found some very good jars made at the glassworks in Tokyo, and beside these about forty of the identical salt jars I had endeavored to buy in Yokohama!

When Dr. Eldridge saw the building, with its complete equipment of jars, copper cans, kegs, sieves, and cases of alcohol, etc., he was amazed, and as Dr. Murray is coming down next week I am impatient to show him that by keeping up a sufficient amount of steam, exhortation, and emphatic words a station can be equipped. My Japanese assistants, while willing to do anything, give no value to time. This is Oriental, I suppose, but nevertheless exasperating. This morning I was awakened at three o'clock by a courier with the announcement that the dredge rope had come. I was too sleepy to sign a receipt for it, but not too sleepy to make a generalization, based upon a number of experiences, that the Japanese never mind being disturbed at night nor do they ever seem to mind disturbing others.

I noticed some children at play, and they had modeled out of clay a temple the outside of which they had ornamented with the little circular tin disks which cap bottled beer and the like, which some foreigner had left and which the children eagerly collect and utilize in various ways. Little toy ishidoro and tori-i were placed about the temple, and a few sprigs of

leaves finished the surroundings. In several instances I have
watched children building things out of mud, sand, or clay,
and I have found their efforts following the same lines as our
children at home.

In looking over the roofs of houses the entire absence of
chimneys is at once remarked; there are no turrets nor cupolas
nor any projecting features. In the cities one sees the little

Fig. 152

staging on the ridge from which the progress of a conflagration
may be watched. The fireproof building will have massive
terminal tiles on the ridge, more or less ornamented. Figure 152
shows the roofs of the houses I overlook from my room, some
of the roofs being thatched, others covered with the thin
shingles already mentioned. The one with heavy ornamental
ridge is a fireproof structure. These buildings are crowded
together, and one may understand how immediately everything would go up in flame when a fire had once started.

Among the curious sounds that assail the ear inside and outside the house, none is more curious than a student reading Chinese classics. These classics are always read aloud, at least by students. It is a curious, weird sound with strange inflections, and at intervals a sudden jumping-up of an octave and a long sipping-in of the breath. Its very strangeness compels you to listen to it and it is impossible to imitate it.

The darkness of the rooms at night is oppressive. The tiny saucers of oil with pith wicks, having a flame of diminutive proportions enclosed in a paper lantern, enable one to find the lantern, at least, and snuggling about this the family gather to read or to play games. The candles are equally poor. What a boon the advent of kerosene oil is to the Japanese is shown by the rapid increase in its importation, and of lamps too.

This morning, July 30, I had my first dredging. Our boat was altogether too small and overcrowded; however, we went round outside and tried to dredge in the heavy swell that unceasingly rolls in from the ocean. A few hauls were made in fifteen fathoms of water, but the two men we had hired would not scull hard enough to pull the dredge along. It was hard work, and I had to overhaul alone the material brought up, as Toyama and his friend were seasick and lay helpless in the bottom of the boat. To-morrow we are to get a much larger boat, more men, and go out into deeper water. Returning to our cove I ventured a try there, hoping to get the objects that first induced me to come to Japan; namely Brachiopods. I had intended digging in this cove at low tide in search of the worm. Conceive my astonishment and delight when the first haul brought up twenty small *Lingula*, apparently the same species that I had studied on the coast of North Carolina. A number of hauls brought me up two hundred specimens which I have alive for study.[1]

A curious feature of conversation among these people is the constant ejaculation of "Ha" or "Hei." For example, one is talking to another and at every slight pause the other says, "Hei," and the first one says, "Ha." It is an indication that he is listening and understands and is a sign of respect. Also, in talking to each other they make a noise with the mouth as if they had burned the tongue with hot tea and were cooling it by drawing in air, or a sound similar to that made by a hungry boy when he sees something very good to eat. This sound is one of self-depreciation or respect.

This morning I had a larger boat with a sail and a crew of four men, and we dredged from eight o'clock in the morning until four o'clock in the afternoon. The entire expense was seventy-five cents, and the men worked like troopers every minute. Toyama, being seasick on the water, did not go. His friend had gone back to Tokyo, and so my assistant, Matsumura, concluded to try it, but we had not been out an hour before he began to lose all interest in dredging, and in a little while longer resigned himself to the miseries of seasickness and lay down in the bottom of the boat, and never moved until the boat touched the beach on its return. He was too sick to act as interpreter even, so I had to direct everything by pantomime. The sun was intensely hot and I got badly burned again. I do not remember the sun ever acting that way at

[1] The results of this work are embodied in a memoir entitled *Observations on Living Brachiopoda*. Memoirs, Boston Society of Natural History, vol. v, no. 8.

home, — burning through a shirt, — yet that is the way it behaves here. We went much farther to-day and threw the dredge into thirty-five fathoms of water and drew it many times. I got the most exquisite shells, most of them small, but some of them very beautiful. When noon came the men dropped their oars and prepared for lunch. They lifted a board from the bottom of the boat and each felt round for a fish he had caught the day before. I watched one as he prepared his lunch. The tail of the fish was cut off and flung overboard, the entrails removed, and with a big, rusty knife with wooden handle the fish was chopped into small pieces, head, eyes, bones, and all, and this hash was put into a wooden bowl. The man then opened a basket and took out a large portion of cold, rusty-looking boiled rice, and with two pickled plums chopped all together and added it to the fish. From a box was added a substance that had a very sour odor, something made of beans and allowed to ferment, a little water was added, and it was all stirred up together, and such an unsavory-looking mess I never saw before. The gusto, however, with which the man ate it to the last grain, showed that it was palatable to him, at least. Raw fish is a very common article of food, certain species being especially esteemed.

Everybody uses the flint and steel in lighting his pipe and every kitchen has its tinder-box. The matches I have seen in this country are the Swedish safety match.

We passed a number of boats; in some the men were fishing, in others pulling in their nets, and all were naked, and, with their dark, sunburned bodies and black hair, looked like savages. Such a novel sight it was to me sitting in the stern

of the boat and watching my four boatmen laughing good-
naturedly and sculling vigorously, swinging back and forth in

Fig. 153

unison and singing a weird kind of chant. Figure 153 gives a
suggestion of the appearance of the boat and the crew at
work.

My cook burned a hole in my undershirt, and with many
amiable grins explained the accident
by showing me an earthen vessel filled
with charcoal over which an open
wicker basket is placed bottom-side
up, and upon this the articles of cloth-

Fig. 154

ing to be dried are placed, as shown in figure 154; naturally the sparks snap out of the charcoal and the hole follows.
As I wear nothing but the thinnest undergarments, these are

FIG. 155

undergoing the process of washing and drying all the time.
   The accompanying sketches give an idea of three corners of
my room at the inn. Figure 155 represents the corner where I
eat; notice the table,—it is the carpenter's conception of a for-

eigner's table. The chair has been modeled from a tourist's
folding chair, only made rigid. The table is a foot higher than
ordinary tables, and the chair is too low, so that my head comes

FIG. 156

conveniently level with my plate. While eating, however, I
look out over a beautiful cove, a spacious bay, and magnificent
Fuji in the distance. Every day the aspect is different, and
now while making this sketch the view is indescribable. The

sun is within an hour of setting, all the low mountain ranges are a cold, light blue, thin bands of clouds between the ranges are brilliantly illuminated by the sun which brings out every point with wonderful distinctness, and the imperial mountain towers above all! To return to the room; the table is so high I have to rest my elbow on it to be comfortable. Corner shelves have been rigged up for me and on one I have my pith hat and a straw hat. The table has been set for breakfast and contains all the food for many meals beside. It is like camping out. The next sketch (fig. 156) shows my writing and work table with the lamp perched up on a salt jar; on the shelf above is one of my microscopes, a jar of alcohol, and box with pipe, tobacco, etc. On the floor is a tin case with my spare dredge which answers as a footstool, and on the table a jar to the left contains insect powder, and a jar of alcohol to the right is a receptacle for beetles and other insects that fly in during the night, and an occasional flea. The sketch (fig. 157) shows a corner where disorder has reigned since I have been here and will remain so until I pack up for good. There is too much to do in this world to fuss about trifles. The sketch shows my big valise in a perfect mess, the Japanese pillow upon which I sleep, a matting covering my mosquito netting, my binocular in a box, and a Japanese straw hat on the chair. This hat costing twenty-five cents is infinitely more comfortable than the pith hat costing eight dollars, and I wear it all the time, even at night when writing, as it forms an excellent shade for the eyes. On the shelf above, a box contains a number of the wonderful glass sponges (*Hyalonema*) several specimens of which are projecting over the edge of the box.

Were it not for my assistants I could never get through the work of assorting the material dredged. The sea bottom is very rich in marine life, and while I am studying the precious

Fig. 157

Lingula my men are at work separating the different groups: shells, sea urchins, starfish, and the like. Figure 158 shows the men at work. The one on the right is Professor Toyama, who pays his own bills, but assists in collecting; the middle one is

Mr. Matsumura, whose expenses are paid by the University; and the one on the left is the man I hire to sleep in the building at night, lug fresh salt water and do chores in the daytime.

FIG. 158

The general intelligence of everybody in Japan is well illustrated by this man. He assorts the material in the proper bottles after having had explained to him the crustacea, mollusks, echinoderms, etc. Later, when I went out in the suburbs to collect land shells, my jinrikisha men always insisted upon collecting for me, and when I showed them the tiny land shells I was after they would collect as many as I could. I tried to

imagine a hackman at home volunteering his services in such
a quest! I tried this man on some shell sand and pointed to
the almost microscopic shells I wanted, and he picked out the
little shells so skillfully, using delicate chopsticks for the
purpose, that I kept him at work most of the time.

In a newspaper just received the ravages of the typhoon are
reported; many vessels have been wrecked along the coast and
many lives lost. I have been unable to resist the attempt to
sketch the main street, and indeed the only street in Enoshima
(fig. 159). There are bad mistakes in perspective and the
street is made altogether too wide, but with these faults of
commission there are many of omission; I have not put in
half enough flags, nor men, nor women, nor children, nor cats
and dogs and hens. And speaking of hens I can walk up and
lay my hand on any one of them, and though it clucks as a
sort of remonstrance it makes no attempt to escape.

Since the storm it has been impossible to cross to the mainland except at extreme low tide, and a number of boatmen
have been doing a great business ferrying across loads of pilgrims who come in groups, often to spend the night only. It
is great fun to follow a band of pilgrims up the street. Nearly
every house along the street seems to be a place of entertainment, and it resembles running the gantlet of New York
hackmen; for everybody in the inns gathers in front to solicit
the patronage of the strangers, and such a curious hubbub they
keep up! The racket made at the first house being heard by
the second, and at the second by the third, and so on, — a
perfect whine of a score of voices.

Within the last few days my cook, owing to repeated objur-

gations, has braced up, and now I am living like a fighting
cock. This morning I had dropped eggs on toast and a broiled
fish, like the English sole; for dinner I had the most delicious

Fig. 159

fish in Japan, the *tai*, new sweet potatoes, and salted ginger-
root, tender and delicious, besides a tiny kind of melon and
preserved plums.

The other morning I flung a piece of stone at a dog under
the window; he watched the stone as it went by him, but

showed no fear. I hurled another, which went between his legs; still he wondered at it without showing the slightest concern. Later, I met another dog in the street, and deliberately stooped, picked up a stone, and threw it at him; he did not run away or growl at me, simply watched the stone as it went by him. Since boyhood I have observed that the mere movement of picking up a stone will cause a dog to slink or even to run away. Such experiences here prove that cats and dogs are not stoned at sight, and to the credit of our people I must say we have improved vastly in these respects since I was a boy. However, in the poorer regions of our cities the hoodlum class behave precisely as all boys did fifty years ago.

Nothing indicates the politeness of the Japanese people more forcibly than the fact that good manners are universal from the highest to the lowest classes. The kindness to dependents does not seem to spoil them; all know their places and keep them with respect. Confucius said: "Of all people, girls and servants are the most difficult to behave to. If you are familiar with them they lose their humility; if you maintain a reserve toward them they are discontented." My experience has been too short to be of any value, yet I cannot help reflecting on the fact that thus far I have seen only courtesy and good manners. I have been living alone for some weeks in a little fishing village associating with the poorer class of fishermen and petty shopkeepers, and the manners of all have been universally polite among themselves and to me. In meeting one another on the street or greeting one another in the house, they bow low again and again, and in this act they may stand nearly side by side and in the direction of their bows would miss each other by two or three feet. To see distinguished old friends meet is remarkable. Minutes are consumed in bowing, and after they begin to talk some complimentary expression or other sets them at it again. I have been positively ashamed of my vulgar curiosity in lingering and looking back at them. It seems a terrible waste of time to an active American, and Professor Toyama said the students at the University were economizing the time in such observances and their parents considered that manners were impaired by student life.

Upon my return from Tokyo the other evening I reached Enoshima at nearly midnight. It was an intensely dark night, and again I had the opportunity to see the gloomy character of the houses of the lower classes. When the storm blinds are put on, the house at night must be like a dungeon. The cheer of the open fireplace with its crackling fire is unknown in Japan. A few hot coals answer for heating and tea-making purposes, and in the kitchen the wood burned for cooking blackens the rafters above with the smoke. As you ride through the village you find little children out at nine or ten o'clock at night sitting on benches in front of the houses. You hear their prattle, but cannot see them. The sliding frames covered with paper which form the outside of the house in the daytime admit an agreeable light to the room and when closed keep out the wind. If a sufficient number of candles are burning within, the shadows thrown upon these paper screens by the inmates are often ludicrous. Hokusai illustrates the absurdity of some of these shadow pictures in his "Mangwa."

Here I was with a hundred dollars in my pocket, traveling
at night, through dark bamboo thickets and some poverty-
stricken villages, having a single jinrikisha man, now and then
meeting a traveler, sometimes a crowd of travelers, and I was
never spoken to. I had no pistol, no cane even, and yet so
assured was I of the gentle character of the people that I did
not feel the slightest apprehension. At one very dark place
we crossed a narrow bridge highly arched and covered with
turf, with no rail on either side, and hardly wide enough for a
jinrikisha (fig. 160). In the middle of the bridge we passed

FIG. 160

three men somewhat jolly
with saké. At that moment I
thought that here if anywhere
was a chance for trouble, for
these fellows had to stand on
the very edge of the bridge to
allow us to pass. They knew I was an "outside barbarian" by
my big sun hat and a cigar, and one push would have sent
jinrikisha and all into the water, twenty feet below; but not a
word from them. I finally fell asleep from sheer fatigue. Luck-
ily the road was smooth or I might have been dumped into
the gutter; awake, one unconsciously balances himself as the
jinrikisha sways back and forth on a rough road. When I
awoke we were at the beach, the waves roaring over it, and it
was dark as only the country can be in any part of the world.
Little glimmers of light from the cluster of houses across the
water, and a few bright fires on the shore where fishermen
were mending their nets or repairing their boats, with groups
of naked fishermen about them, were the only indications of

life. My jinrikisha man conjured up from the darkness two big baskets in which the bundles I had brought down were loaded, and tying the baskets to the ends of a long carrying-pole he started off through the boiling surf. Another man also appeared out of the blackness and offered to carry me across on his back; so I adjusted myself in the usual way, but this would not do. He dropped me and going behind thrust his head between my legs and lifted me as if I were a small boy and carried me on his shoulders. I could keep my position only by hanging on to his moist head, and as the waves rushed past making him unsteady, I, still half awake, felt as if I should be tumbled into the water at any moment.

If one should go over the road a hundred times he would see something novel or interesting. I noticed in a shop a big bucket of water over the edge of which hung a glass syphon, as seen in figure 161. A tiny spray from the end kept constantly cool and wet a tray of diminutive watermelons. In the little booths the melons are cut in two and a thin sheet of Japanese paper protects the cut ends. In the markets the water-

FIG. 161

melons have tied around the stems a little red ribbon, and I saw a man bringing a large load of them to market and each melon had its little red ribbon. The melons are round and small in size, not much larger than our cucumber, and resemble the Japanese squash so closely that the ribbon is used to distinguish them. The color of the flesh is dark red, a sort of congested red, and tastes like our melon, but is not crisp.

Many of the English in eating them devour the seeds as well. The pears are very agreeable when stewed, but there is not the slightest suggestion of a pear taste. They resemble a russet apple in color and are round like an apple. The plums are also very good when cooked. The tomatoes are the only fruit that tastes precisely like our corresponding fruit. The white potatoes are very small, and the sweet potatoes are much like ours, but the fibre is coarser and they are milder in taste. At the hotel in Yokohama a peculiar fruit, imported  from Singapore, was on the table. It is called *mangosteen* (fig. 162). The rind was blackish in color and very thick (the dotted line in the sketch shows the thickness of the rind). The color of the rind inside was the deepest purple, and the fruit within was of the purest white, resembling the white of an egg when beaten. It broke in divisions like an orange and had

Fig. 162

large seeds. Its taste was very agreeable and unlike anything I had ever before tasted, but suggested a slight flavor of apple with the mildest acidity; certainly a most delicious fruit and there is no reason why it could not be cultivated in Florida or southern California.

The other day going to Tokyo there were in the same car with me two little children dressed for company. They were not over five or six years old, yet their hair was done up in the most elaborate style; their eyebrows cleanly shaved; their faces and necks white with powder; on the outer corner of each eye was painted a little line of reddish paint, and the head was shaved in certain patches. One little girl stood at the car door looking out, and I made a rapid sketch of her (fig. 163). Notice the clear places shaved on top of her head, the little queue hanging behind. I had no time to do more than draw the simple outlines of her dress, but it was made of silk crape with large, irregular designs in bright colors. The sash around the waist, gray in color with no figure, was very heavy and bulky and tied in a big knot behind, the only device that kept her clothes on, for there is no button, loop, hook and eye, string, or pin — a most rational idea.

Fig. 163

On the outer border of the long pocket sleeve was a yellow silk cord running like a basting thread and terminating at the corner of the sleeve in a yellow tassel.

In riding through the country there has gradually dawned on me the entire absence of all marks, scratches, or other signs of the defacement of fences or buildings. No buildings in this country have so much as a mark upon them, and yet the workmen carry with them an equivalent of a pen or pencil, the *yatate*, with all the facilities of writing their names and inscribing choice sayings and proverbs if they chose to do so. I could not help contrasting this feature with the behavior of our own people in this respect. The defacement of our school-houses and other structures in our country districts proves this tendency.

On the road I saw long poles of bamboo with their leaves on and on the leaves had been tied a lot of bright-colored bits of paper: a decoration for some festival or an advertisement of some kind.

An Oriental custom is seen in the public story-teller who goes about to entertain crowds, in the street or privately, by

. FIG. 164

telling stories. In Japan story-tellers travel about, and under canvas gather an audience quickly. Though not understanding a word of Japanese I enjoyed the man and the interested and amused auditors. I listened for half an hour to a story-teller who came to the inn (fig. 164). It was curious to watch the workings of his face and interesting to hear the· sudden changes in his voice to represent the different characters. The students who formed his audience would laugh heartily when one character was represented by a slow and officious voice, and the story-teller shared in the enjoyment. He kneeled before a low table, a chessboard borrowed for the occasion, and had three objects as stage properties; a fan which he used now with the left hand and then with his right; an object which looked like a folding fan closed, but was in fact a thin piece of wood covered with paper, and with this he would strike the table in front of him with sharp clicks, more or less vigorously to accent the story; and the third object, a small block of wood which he would take up frequently and with it strike the table with a sharp snap.

The man who takes care of the laboratory is doing finely. He picks out little shells from dredged sand, cleans the larger ones, and seems to take the liveliest interest in the work. His entire time is given to us for all sorts of work at the princely wage of $1.25 per week.

To-day, August 14, the children are all gayly dressed in bright-colored clothes, and evidently a festival of some kind is being celebrated. When I reached the laboratory the janitor was engaged in cleanly shaving his children's heads. The youngest had been through the misery and was sound asleep on the back of his older sister. While I was endeavoring to sketch the group the baby awoke and began to cry, whereupon the little girl got down and walked back and forth jiggling the baby on her back with a sort of hitching motion and then got back on the stool again (fig. 165). I was told that the festival was in honor of their ancestors. In the forenoon the children either bring from their own homes or beg from others a small quantity of rice, and formerly they got together around

Fig. 165

a big kettle on the beach and cooked it; now it is cooked in the house and the children congregate in numbers with their lacquered cups to get their portion. Figure 166 shows a woman with a child on her back, the child holding a lacquered rice bowl in her hand waiting her turn for rice. The rice has a reddish tinge given to it for the occasion, comparable to our pink lemonade at circuses, I suppose. The color is derived from a kind of bean that is cooked with the rice. I mingled with them and tried to get some sketches, but the children were altogether too uneasy for me, and most of the girls were frightened because I tried to take up a little midget who was the least unattractive, for on the whole they were a plain set. I could hardly realize that they had the same reason to be afraid as our children would have if a Japanese

attempted to pick up one of them. The little boys seemed to enjoy my presence, and I laughed and cut up with them at a great rate.

FIG. 166

FIG. 167

To-day our man was mending the child's clothes, as his wife, who is a servant at the inn, has no time for such work (fig. 167).

The people are very adroit in tying knots. They make a cheap rope out of straw and the stoutest of twine out of paper. All their stagings for buildings are tied together instead of nailed, as the nail is apt to weaken the wood; the rope is wound about the point of contact many times and makes the firmest of fastening.

A sketch of an inn on the road from Yokohama (fig. 168) has a small English sign stating that foreign beer is kept here.

Fig. 168

The fringe around the wooden, shed-like roof in front is made of blue cloth, three feet wide, and slit up halfway at intervals of a foot to allow the wind to pass through.

CHAPTER VII

COLLECTING AT ENOSHIMA

YESTERDAY was a successful day at the laboratory. A fisherman brought in a bucketful of living cones and other large shells, bright-colored starfishes, and some rare mollusks I had never seen alive before, for which he asked twenty cents. We started up the river that empties into the sea near the neck of land where we cross, hoping to find some fresh-water shells, and succeeded in finding a few living *Corbicula*. Near the mouth we found a number of fine *Psammobia*, a large bivalve, and farther up we captured some lively and pugnacious crabs. A number of women and children were wading near the shore picking up *Corbicula*, which is an article of food. I bought two small baskets of them for two cents a basket. It would have taken us half a day to collect as many. Every living thing in the water seems to be eaten by the lower classes; all kinds of shellfish, every shrimp and crab as well as sharks, skates, and indeed all kinds of fish, seaweed, sea urchins, and sea worms. I ate some boiled *Trochus*, and they were not bad. The river was picturesque with the odd groups of boats, people, etc.: pilgrims coming down the river, old women picking up *Corbicula*, a man trailing a net for bait. Just as we were ready to return a boat came along with a party of pilgrims bound for Enoshima, and for two cents the boatman offered to take the four of us along. As the river was low, the tide being out, we had the privilege of literally working our passage,

as we jumped out of the boat many times and aided the others
in pushing (fig. 169).

The absence of flies of the common kinds in the country is
a noteworthy feature and to get one at any moment would be

FIG. 169

difficult. I remember at Grand Manan, at the entrance of the
Bay of Fundy, the intolerable nuisance of the flies in the fishing village, due to the fish cleanings being scattered about.
Enoshima is a fishing village, but the fishermen in cleaning
their fish carefully remove all the offal, and do this every day.
Then, too, everything they catch they eat, and so little is left
to decompose; furthermore, there are no horses, cows, sheep,
pigs, goats, or any other animals except man and fowl. Very
few hens are seen, and these are put away under baskets at
night. It is an interesting sight to see the roosters and hens
come up to the house at night and cluck around the basket
under which they are to go until some one comes and puts
them in one by one.

The street cries of the peddlers, already alluded to, are most
peculiar, and, of course, incomprehensible, as most of these
cries are in all parts of the world. I heard a cry so different
from those with which I had become familiar that I rushed

out and saw a man blowing bubbles from the end of a long bamboo .tube, but the bubbles were more beautiful and iridescent than those made from soap, of which the Japanese know nothing. The infusion was carried in two deep, slender buckets and the fluid was being sold to the children (fig. 170). Toyama inquired of the man as to the composition of the fluid, and was told that it was made from the leaves of a number of plants among which was tobacco. It was an odd sight, this naked man stalking

FIG. 170

through the streets blowing bubbles and at intervals uttering the most extraordinary cries.

My cook has his kitchen downstairs, consisting of a sink and two stone braziers. These braziers are made either of some kind of cement or cut out of a volcanic stone which is very soft; there is no oven, of course; they are simply receptacles for burning charcoal. On them the cook boils and broils, and in roasting a chicken he extemporized an oven by placing a square of sheet iron on top of the fire to support the chicken; then he put on a copper vessel, upside down, on which he started a coal fire, and stood patiently by, fanning the coals, and kept it up until the chicken was nicely roasted. Figure 171 is a rough sketch of the cook. The chicken cost a few cents and a good fish resembling a mackerel costs one cent. I mention these prices as an indication of the cheapness of everything.

A ride to Fujisawa with two jinrikisha men enabled me to

get a jarful of a handsome species of large fresh-water snail (*Melania*), as the men worked like beavers in picking them up from the river-bed.

I sent my mail by special courier to Fujisawa; distance, three miles; price, ten cents. The landlord came in to say the man was a running courier and that it would cost two cents

Fig. 171

more. I saw the man with sturdy legs start off at a good running gait, wading through the water and disappearing on the other side at full speed. Toyama wrote a special note which the courier carried asking the postmaster to send my foreign mail by special messenger, and an answer was brought back by the courier in an incredibly short time. He must have run at full clip over and back.

Yesterday we all went out on a reef exposed at very low tide taking with us a man who lifted the larger stones from the pools and turned them upside down so that we could examine the under surfaces. Such a harvest we made and such pleasure to find, hidden away in the crevices, large cones, a beautiful little *Cypræa* alive and fresh, and a number of *Stomatella*, the shell of which is exquisite; also *Haliotis*, abundant, and a number of genera, the soft parts of which were new to me; and besides all these treasures the quaintest crabs, starfish, *Comatulas*, strange worms and naked mollusks, chitons of large size, and a number of other species by the hundred. To-day we have been down again and with hammers have broken open the rocks and found a number of boring mollusks, such as *Pholas*, *Saxicava*, and *Lithodomus*. I have been exceedingly busy drawing many of them alive. Our building is gradually getting crowded and many of the jars and kegs are full. The wealth of material is amazing. I got tired bending over the microscope, and so for a rest made a sketch of our shanty. The window, or opening looking out on the beach, is my place of work, and sometimes it is difficult to study owing to the various and novel attractions outside. From the sketch (fig. 172) an idea may be got of the inside of the laboratory — frames covered with cloth on which the starfishes and sea urchins are dried, and all the clutter that such work entails.

Fig. 172

At the inn, as before mentioned, a number of students occupy a room next to mine, and a very pleasant lot they are. Most of them are medical students, and at the University the medical students are taught by Germans, so that these young men have to acquire the German language before they can enter. Some of them speak a few words of English. I go into their room frequently to watch them play their games, which, it must be confessed, are all much more profound than any of ours. Their chess is infinitely more difficult; in comparison ours is kindergarten. The game of go we have never acquired, and that of "five in a row" is as difficult as our checkers. I taught them checkers, and several games, such as chalking on the floor, etc. An interesting game is played with the hand.

Kneeling opposite each other the right hand of each player is flung out at the same instant. The hands must be in one of three positions: the palm open, representing paper; the index and middle finger open, suggesting a pair of scissors; the hand clenched, representing a stone. Now the paper can cover or conceal the stone; the stone can smash the scissors; and the scissors can cut the paper. Counting "one, two, three," the players fling their arms at the same time, and on the third stroke the hand must come in one of the three positions mentioned above. If your opponent comes out scissors and you come out paper, he has beaten you once, for scissors can cut the paper; if, however, you had come out stone, the stone can smash the scissors, and you have won. Either one winning three times in succession has won the game. You will notice little children when called upon to do an errand resort to this game, doing it once only, to see who shall go; drawing lots, in fact.

Another game is played with the two hands. The hands resting on the knees represent the judge; the arms held in the attitude of shooting a gun represent the hunter; and the hands held to the ears in the attitude of hearing represent the fox. Now these have the same relation to one another as in the single-handed game. The fox can outwit the judge, the judge can sentence the hunter, and the hunter can shoot the fox. The Japanese play it with great rapidity. They count three or make three motions of the hand, or clap their hands twice and at the third clap assume one of the three positions; and the motions are really made with the hands. Turning the hands up and out represents the fox; the two hands held as if supporting a gun indicate the hunter; and the hands with fingers pointing downward, the judge. It is impossible for us, watching ever so closely, to see which one has got three superior points in sequence. It is played very gracefully with curious sounds in rhythm emitted by the players, probably such expressions as "Look out!" "I've got you!" etc.; and with the spectators uttering similar expressions, and the chorus of laughter which follows as one or the other wins, make it very exciting. It may be added that if both players present the same form, they simply continue without interruption.

As I inquire of Toyama and Matsumura the "whys and wherefores" about everything, I am amazed often to find that they are ignorant of many things. I have noticed this feature with others, and have also observed a surprised look on their faces at some of the questions, and they smiled as if the question or subject was amusing. I have been intimately associated with Toyama and Matsumura for over three weeks, and yet they have never asked me a question as to how we did such and such things at home, or about the various objects on my table, in which, nevertheless, they take an interest, and with all this they are very curious to see everything. The students and literary class, while studying Chinese classics or modern literature, would probably consider it of no interest or importance to learn the death-rate of a town or of what diseases the people died.

I got Toyama to write down for me a list of girls' and boys' names with their meanings, names corresponding to our Christian names: —

Girls' names		*Boys' names*	
Matsu	pine	Taro	first boy
Take	bamboo	Jiro	second boy
Hana	flower	Saburo	third boy
Yuri	lily	Shiro	fourth boy
Haru	spring	Magotaro	grandchild first boy
Fuyu	winter	Hikojiro	male second boy
Natsu	summer	Gentaro	fountain first boy
Yasu	easy	Kameshiro	tortoise first boy
Cho	butterfly	Kangoro	examined fifth boy
Tora	tiger	Sadashichi	stable seventh boy
Yuki	snow	Kaitaro	shellfish first boy
Waka	young		
Ito	thread		
Taki	waterfall		

If the girls are not of the lower classes it is customary to put *O* before the name as an honorific prefix, and in every case *san*, a contraction of *sama*, after the name, this being a title of respect, not only coming after the name of a person, but also used in a spirit of playfulness after names of animals. It takes the place of *Miss, Mrs.* or *Mr.* You will hear them speak of *baby san, cat san.* The prefix *O* is used only before a girl's name. Miss Hana would be *O Hana san.* The boys' names *Taro, Jiro*, etc., meaning, first, second, and so on, are common names, but have in a way lost their significance in meaning first boy, second boy, and so on, just as our family name "Johnson" has lost its meaning of "son of John." Nowadays, Mr. Toyama tells me, the boys are being given a great many new names after the style of Cromwell's time, such as Patience, Hope, Prudence, Faith, etc.

In trying to get the names of mountains Toyama called in two or three students to help him, and it was curious to see how hard they worked to recall the names of even a few. I fairly pumped the information out of them, and some of the words were difficult to translate, especially Fuji, which they finally said meant "rich samurai"; samurai being applied to the men who were permitted to wear two swords in feudal days. The character for mountain is called *yama*, the name of mountain in Japan, or after the name of the character in Chinese. To-day, in China, the character is called *shan* except in one province, where it is *san*. Toyama speaks and writes English perfectly, and yet he found it difficult oftentimes to give the exact English equivalent. The following are a few of the names which he gave me. It will be seen that many are names similar in meaning to our names for mountains: —

Mountain names

O Yama	Great mountain
Nantai san	Male body mountain
Hakusan	White mountain
Kabutoyama	Helmet mountain
Shirane	White peak
Tateyama	Erect mountain
Kirishima yama	Foggy Island mountain
Nokogiri yama	Saw mountain

Nokogiri is equivalent to the Spanish *sierra* and from Sacramento the Sierras resemble the teeth of a saw.

For the names of dogs, colors are used, red, black, white, etc., and the dogs seem to know their own colors! The common names for horses are "Harukaze" (spring wind); "Kiyotaki" (pure waterfall); "Onikage" (devil's shadow). Some of the rivers have names which signify "rapid" river, "rhinoceros" river, "large well" river, "heavenly dragon" river, and many others. Their wrestlers, who are highly esteemed, have such names as "Thunderbolt," "Seashore

Breeze," "Plum Valley," "Deviled Face Mountain," "Boundary River," "Morning Sun Peak," "Small Willow," etc. Their vessels or boats, unless they are quite small, also have their peculiar names.

In drawing a mountain, it is said, artists of every nationality always exaggerate the slope; that is, the mountain is represented much steeper than it really is. Certainly the Japanese artists err in this way; at least a few weeks' experience, which has covered only the cheapest illustrations on fans, advertisements, and the like, would show this to be the case, as the drawings of Fuji are always grossly exaggerated. It occurred to me that I would ask the students in the next room to draw from memory the slope of Fuji. This magnificent mountain has been in sight across the Bay, and from morning till night has been the one object that repeatedly draws one's eyes. The other night while at supper I made as careful a drawing as possible of Fuji, which loomed up grandly and was very sharp and dark against the luminous sky beyond. Then I cut out the outline with a pair of scissors, and on holding it up to the mountain found that despite my efforts I had the slopes too steep. So I trimmed the paper down and held it up against the mountain until the outline fitted exactly, then went into the next room and asked the students, through an interpreter, to draw as accurate an outline as possible of Fuji. I had provided four sheets of paper with the base-line — the length of my own sketch — drawn. These young men had looked at Fuji a hundred times a day for several weeks and had studied surveying and drafting and knew angles and arcs of circles, etc., and had been specially warned not to exaggerate. Figure 173 shows the results of their efforts with my outline below. They were simply amazed at the discrepancy between their outlines and mine and showed the greatest interest in the trial. Unconsciously they had recalled the steep outlines represented in all the pictures of Fuji they had seen since childhood. It is curious to observe that they all got nearly the same angle. A student brought to me a fan in which the slope was depicted nearly correctly. One can imagine how a man might exaggerate after having climbed a mountain, for it always seems much steeper than it really is.

FIG. 173

On the long beach yesterday the fishermen pulled in a large net with ropes several hundred feet long. It was interesting to see the fishermen and boys, most of them naked, assisting in the work (fig. 174). A heavy swell came rolling in. The men used an ingenious toggle by which they hung to the rope. They had a smaller rope about six feet long having a loop at

one end which they had about the waist; at the end of the
rope a large disk of wood like a big button was fastened.
By a dexterous fling of the button it would twist around and

FIG. 174

form a hold on the net rope. I try to make this clear in
figure 175. The device may be known to our fishermen, but if
not it should be adopted, for it had the firmest grip on the
rope, could be detached immedi-
ately, and quickly adjusted on the
rope again. When the net came in
sight many gathered about it to
see what had been caught. Into
this crowd of naked bodies I

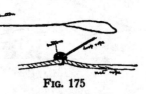

FIG. 175

forced my way and got a bucketful of marine forms. I never.
before knew how tightly a voluntary crowd could squeeze;
they were packed like sardines.

A cluster of fishermen's huts is on the eastern end of the
island and I attempted to sketch a few of the houses, but the

men, women, and children gathered around me so closely that
I had to abandon the effort. Such a jabber as they kept up, and
a child of five spoke as authoritatively as the grown man.
They were evidently disputing as to whose cabin I was drawing.
First, I could hear one name prominent and then, as I added
some new detail to the sketch (fig. 176), such as a big fish basket, there would be much exultant laughing; but as there was

Fig. 176

more than one big fish basket the other claimants had their
turn for a shout. I could stand it only long enough to get three
cabins in my sketch, but it was an odd sight to look through
this long lane of tangle-haired, dark-skinned natives, through
which I had to sketch. One or two leaned on me whereupon
I swore at them in Spanish at which they laughed heartily.

The Japanese write in Chinese characters, of which a good
student may know three or four thousand. These all have
their written form. They also have an alphabet of forty-eight
letters by which they spell out words phonetically, but as I
know little about it, the interested reader may refer to the pref-

ace of Hepburn's "Japanese and English Dictionary." Many of the characters vary only by a dot or a stroke. Professor Toyama had written to the University for nets and the character used was mistaken for rope of which I had enough. Their letters begin in an abrupt fashion; no "Dear Sir" or "Dear Friend." In writing, the brush is held vertically as shown in figure 177.

FIG. 177

It seems curious that the sound of *l* is not known in the Japanese language. One of the most difficult matters for the Japanese in writing English is to distinguish the difference between the sounds of the *l* and the *r* and those who have written English for years will use an *l* instead of an *r*, or *vice versa*. They find the greatest difficulty in pronouncing the sound. I asked Toyama's friend to pronounce "parallel," and it was astonishing to see him struggle with his tongue and lips, all the time intensely watching me to see how I did it, and finally giving up in despair. On the other hand, the Chinese have no sound of *r* and find it just as difficult to pronounce this sound as the Japanese do *l*.

Remembering the comfort I derived from the masseur on my trip to Nikko, and being very tired, I called in a blind *amma*, as he is called, to knead, rub, and pound me. Mr. Matsumura sat beside me as interpreter and I asked many questions. The amma was made blind by smallpox, at one time a dreadful scourge in the country, but now happily un-

known. I asked him if he thought the advent of the foreigner
was a good thing and he answered with animation, "Yes";
and added, "If he had come twenty-five years before, I and
thousands of others would not have been blind." He also
added that the foreigner spends a great deal of money. I asked
him if he could tell the difference between a foreigner and a
Japanese if they were dressed the same, and he promptly said,
"Yes; the foreigner has much larger feet." But suppose the
foreigner had small feet? "Their toes come together," he
said, "and the foot is narrower in front." He was a big, fat,
bald-headed, or rather shaven-headed man, and when he began he immediately took his gown off, apologizing to me at
the same time for so doing. In rubbing they have a curious,
spasmodic jump of the fingers, making a movement not unlike
that made by the dentist's mechanical filler.

I asked my janitor to get me some fresh salt water and he
wanted to know if I wanted it mixed. He has learned to count
to ten in our language, and can say, "fresh water," "salt
water," and "all right." Mr. Matsumura thought it odd to
say fresh salt water, and that led me to ask him what fresh
water was called in Japanese; he replied that they called it
"true water," and the other, "salt water." This seems to be
the best term for it. The Europeans call fresh water "sweet
water," which it certainly is not.

Whatever I am about in my room seems to interest the
curious people in the other rooms, who can look across and
watch my every action. It is hard to realize that all my ways
must be as curious to them as their ways are to me. The first
observation a foreigner makes on coming to Japan is that the

Japanese in certain things do just the reverse from us. We think our way is undeniably right, whereas the Japanese are equally impressed with the fact that we do everything differently from them. As the Japanese are a much older civilized race, it may be possible that their way of doing some things is really the best way.

The desire of the Japanese to acquire knowledge is indicated not only by the way they crowd the hall in public lectures, but by the efforts of young men to enter into service with you, repaying for what instruction they get by helping you in translating Japanese documents or doing menial work about the house. A young man came to my house the other day and asked permission to leave a letter. He had walked nearly two hundred miles from Kaga to Tokyo. The letter was written on Japanese paper in good English script with a brush, a difficult task. The letter is interesting as showing the ambitions of a student in regard to foreign studies and the high estimate he placed on the importance of observing my "scientific actions"!

"Sir: Please excuse me rude words & bad grammar. My name is T. Doki. I am one of the scholars sent from Ishikawa Ken to study in Tokyo. I have determined for many reasons, to study one of the Sciences of Nature. But to do this first of all I must be more or less acquainted with some general sciences such as Phisics, Chemistry, geology, Phisiology. Botany, Zoology & the like. And I have scarcely any idea of those Sciences. The first thing, therefore, I think I have to study is those preparatory lessons & to do this I must have a good teacher. But as I don't like, for several reasons to become the scholar of Tokyo University, I can find no teacher so kind and leisurely as to teach me those lessons.

"Being told that you a famous naturalist, have done much, & are yet anxious to do, good to us. I cannot keep myself without asking you your admission to my following petition.

"As I know well that you are very busy, I wish you will let me live with you in your house as your semi-servant & semi-scholar & at any time you have got less busy, you will explain the difficult points which I find in reading about three or four hours weekly; & thus I can get the advantage, not only of getting explained the difficult points, but also of hearing your scientific sayings & observing your scientific actions. If you will be so kind as to admit my begging, I will willingly subject myself to the following conditions: —

"1st, I will do anything (I can) for you two or three hours every day.

"2nd, I will require nothing but those three which are: first three or four hours of your time every week, secondly *any* food to live on, & thirdly *any* space to abide.

"3rd, I will offer any sum less than three yen, if you will accept.

"Those are not at all the only conditions to which I wish to subject myself, but I will obey any condition as far as it enables me to study those lessons under a good teacher with monthly expense less than three yen. I beg your merciful admission. I beg your merciful admission."

Opposite my piazza is a quaint pile of buildings (fig. 178). Three of these buildings are fireproof ones placed here to be

Fig. 178

out of the way in case the village burns up. If our building
gets afire, however, the entire village will go up in flames, as
the buildings are packed close together and are very com-
bustible.

Matsumura shows a taste for drawing, as most of the Japanese do. Figure 179 is a sketch he made of a child. Notice how

purely Japanese it is in style. One thing that
gives vigor and quaintness to their drawings
is that they always use a brush, and consequently get clear lines of varying thickness
as well as great freedom in their work. The
subjects they select, such as foliage and
figures, are graphically rendered by their
technique. Their figures are all draped in
loose folding robes. The common dress for

Fig. 179

men is a sort of robe gracefully draped, and their hats are
picturesque. Their foliage, the bamboo, bamboo grass, pines,
flowers, etc., are drawn with a strength and dash that render
Japanese drawings very attractive.

Rather poor luck to-day dredging. I returned to try the
cove for *Lingula* and got a fine lot of them, besides some large
Pleurotoma and other things. While out dredging, a sudden
shower came up and I got wet to the skin, but immediately the
hot sun came out and I was soon dried. The Japanese sailors
seem the most timid of all sailors, though they have the repu-
tation of being good boatmen; it is with difficulty that they
can be made to go far from land, and to-day I had to call them
cowards for not going out farther. The fishing boats are seen
in line about two miles out, and when I suggested going out

to Oshima, about thirty miles away, they were aghast with astonishment and laughed incredulously at the idea. While we were dredging, a huge fish came skimming along not far from the boat, his long black fin just showing above the water, and such an excitement! One of the men left his oar, and rushing forward where I sat begged the privilege of chasing it with such earnestness that, though I could not understand a word he said, his imploring manner was unmistakable, and I said "Yoroshii" (all right); and how they flew about! I had thirty-five fathoms of dredge rope out and I expected they would pull the dredge in, but instead they lashed three long poles together and tied the end of the dredge rope to this extemporized float and threw it overboard. I felt some little anxiety for fear the rope would become untied or they would fail to pick it up. Off we went at a lively rate in pursuit of the shark, for such it was. The harpoon consisted of an iron dart loosely affixed to the end of a long pole. The rope was attached to the dart and so, when used, the pole could be withdrawn, leaving the barbed point in the fish. It was curious to watch a school of little fish all huddling to a common centre in fear of the shark — a single scoop of the net would have bagged the whole lot. Such a desperate race! The shark got away, however, and the men turned back and found the dredge float without difficulty. While they were hunting the shark I made sketches of a few fishing boats, but I have not yet caught the right lines and my drawings do not express the gracefulness of the models. In figure 180 the foresail hangs over the side of the boat. When we were coming back a breeze sprang up and a fish pole of bamboo was taken for a spar, a loose sail was run on to it by

loops, and the whole thing hoisted on a pole for a mast, the
lower end of the sail being held in the hand, and with this

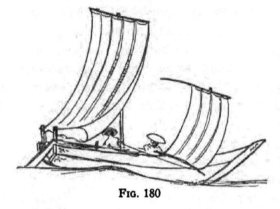

Fig. 180

absurd contrivance we went along at a brisk rate. Figure 181
is the way our sail looked from the boat. Their boats have no

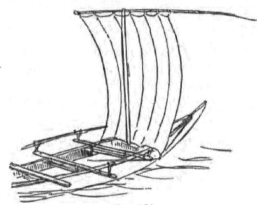

Fig. 181

keel and carry no ballast, and yet accidents rarely happen. If
the boat should upset it would float with as many men as could

cling to her, and the water being so warm and the men as much
at home in the water as the fishes, they could cling to the boat
for days. When we got back to the cove I flung the dredge in
for *Lingula* and got one hundred and fifty specimens besides
other rare objects. Have been hard at work all day on them,
and it is astonishing how many new things are revealed. I had
felt that the North Carolina species had been pretty thoroughly
studied, but this species, though very similar to the North
Carolina one, is more trans-
parent, and I have discovered
a number of new organs never
seen before in Brachiopods.

Figure 182 is a sketch of
our wash sink from the outside. The idea of a spout
never occurred to the builder,
so this projecting portion is
built out in order that the
water may run away freely.

FIG. 182

I have lived on rice, sweet
potatoes, egg plant, and fish for two weeks. I would give all
my old shoes, and new ones too, for a good slice of bread-
and-butter, a bowl of bread-and-milk, or any other good
thing you are enjoying at home.

The teacher of the village called on me and said in a formal
manner, "How do you do?" — with an accent that indicated
his limited knowledge of our language, and afterwards he confessed that his knowledge of English was limited to the saluta-
tion and "Good-bye." It was a little comfort to feel that I

knew more of his language than he did of mine, but not much more. Last night I made a call on the people of an inn just opposite the place at which I first stopped a few weeks ago. I had made their acquaintance in hunting up a more desirable place where the view of Fuji was better. Despite the fact that I had gone farther up the hill to live, they always bowed to me just as amiably as before. I found the family very busy; four of them were settling up the accounts for the day, counting money, entering items, etc. They were on the floor, of course, the desk being like a low stool at which one of them was kneeling. It was too dark to make any sketch, for the Japanese house is poorly lighted. I could not help observing the kindness of the Japanese to children. Here were four men busy with accounts, examining bundles of bills, counting money, etc., and in the midst of them a little boy, perhaps six years old, was sprawled out on the floor directly in front of the desk sound asleep. They had to reach over him for certain things, and yet not one disturbed him by giving him a shake and sending him off to bed. They offered me a drink of saké, and one of the clerks brought to me on a dish two peaches nicely peeled, but they were very green and hard as brickbats. After the first bite I complained of being sick and rubbed my stomach in pantomime fashion, which they promptly interpreted. While I am writing this I can see two domestics across the way leaning over a piazza rail eating peaches. The fruit is so green that I can actually hear them as they tear off the bites. They clutch the peaches firmly in their hands as if they were eating the hardest of apples.

The more I see of these gentle people the more they remind

me of a set of overgrown, good-natured, kind-hearted, laughing children. In many ways they are childish, in precisely the same way that our children are childish, and some of the resemblances are striking. In lifting a load or doing any arduous work they grunt and make a great noise with their mouths in a tone which seems to say, "See what a big thing I am doing!" The other day Mr. Matsumura took an oar and in sculling hissed through his teeth and puffed just as a boy might, as if he were doing something very smart. In some ways they resemble in their behavior the children of our country and in others they differ very greatly. Their self-composure, or rather reticence, in grief reminds one of the North American Indian.

Figure 183 is a sketch of a household shrine; the rows of cups on a little table are of brass and are filled with boiled rice, red in color. In the right-hand lower corner is a sweet potato and a sort of turnip supported on four wooden legs like a pig; in the middle are two rice loaves; also a plate of peaches; and if some of their ancestors died of cholera morbus, the plate of peaches might be a suggestive offering to make, though hardly a pleasant reminder. In the middle of the shrine

FIG. 183

was a beautiful figure of Buddha. This cupboard was in the dingiest of shanties.

This morning I went down to work on my *Lingula*, but so

little sleep did I get last night that I gave up from sheer inability to keep awake; so I came back to my room and had a long nap as refreshing as a short and unstable hammock could afford me. To-morrow it will be just three months since I left home, and with the exception of a few nights at a hotel and at Dr. Murray's I have not known the luxury of a bed. Part of the time I was on a sleeping-car crossing the continent, seventeen days in the narrowest of berths on a steamer, and since then in the hammock or on the hard mats with all sorts of makeshifts for pillows.

So far I have seen no barbers' shops. The barbers are itinerant and carry with them a brass-mounted box with drawers for razors, etc. (fig. 184). This is made of some dark wood with brass devices and reeks with oil and pomade. The shears are like our sheep shears and the razors are long, thin strips of steel entirely unlike the Chinese razor. You will see the hone for the razor below; the drawers were filled with pins, strings, bits of hair, etc. The wooden funnel above held sticks that seemed like skewers to hold the hair in position temporarily; the curved piece of brass hanging from the edge of the funnel is to hold the fine hair shaved from the face; the barber scrapes the razor on its edge. I saw one of the students being shaved; and though I have mentioned the fact that they shave the faces, I was not prepared to see the barber actually shave the eyelids, not shaving off the

Fig. 184

eyelashes, of course, but shaving the entire face, nose, cheeks, eyelids, and all. There is great discomfort in attempting to sketch on the street in such a village as this; the people, young and old, cluster around you keeping up a continuous chatter.

My head fairly rings with the noise and novelty of everything connected with a singer or story-teller who used a huge shell as a resonator. The sketch I made of him (fig. 185) is a fairly good like-ness. He came into my room from across the passage at the request of the students, who noticed my interest in the sounds he was mak-ing. He kneeled down in front of the low, table-like chessboard and kept up the most

Fig. 185

lugubrious sound through his shell, much like that which might be made in imitating the bleating of a calf, but in a regular sequence of notes which I managed to catch; at intervals he coughed and strained, and in drawing in his breath made a sound like a person in deepest grief. While he was blaring through his shell he held in his other hand a curious clicking sort of ringer made of some metal mounted on a wooden handle; the metallic end moved back and forth not over half an inch and made a feeble sort of click. After keeping the sound up for a while he put his trumpet down and recited

in the same tone he had used in singing, and gradually dropped
into narrative, interrupted now and then by chanting and
melancholy sounds made through the shell. The
Japanese students would burst into laughter at
portions of his recitative. I paid him ten cents for
his performance that I might more closely examine
his shell and the little block of wood and fan-shaped
ferule with which he emphasized his story by sharp
raps on the table. Seeing my interest in them, and
grateful for the good pay he had received, he gave
me the blocks and rapper. Figure 186 shows one
of the implements of a story-teller.

On my way to Tokyo a large number of soldiers
came up on the train, and when I got to Tokyo I
found the streets filled with troops coming from the

FIG. 186   southern war, the Satsuma rebellion. On the steps
of the station were a number of officers, a handsome, intelligent-looking set of men, reminding one of German officers.
I saw a large body of soldiers, possibly a regiment, marching in two files on both sides of the street, and to my astonishment and alarm my jinrikisha man, instead of turning
out to one side, followed another jinrikisha between these
two columns and through the entire length of this body of
troops. I got a chance to see the men, dark, sunburned
faces, dark blue uniforms trimmed with red, short leather
caps with a white horsehair plume; officers handsome, some
of them looking like mere boys, but fearless fellows, sons of
samurai. What greatly surprised and pleased me was the fact
that in not a single instance was a laugh or a word thrown

at me. They were marching along in fatigue fashion; some had their pieces at support arms, others at their shoulders, and yet a more quietly disposed and orderly set of men I never saw before; as a matter of fact they were all gentlemen and behaved as such.

In making a call to-day I had the pleasure of passing through a part of the city new to me; it was a most picturesque part — such massive stone walls and wide moats! It was an interesting sight to ride along a smooth road and have in view for a long distance these stone walls rising in a curved slope to a height of forty feet, literally covered with lichens, and on the crest of the walls pines and other trees of great size flinging over their gnarled branches and growing as wild and undisturbed as in the midst of a Maine forest. Here and there through this fringing forest, or on some corner of the wall, quaint old Japanese structures with ponderous roofs were seen. These were painted red or black and were possibly barracks for soldiers in times past. In the moats from which the walls arose was the most luxurious growth of lotus; such masses, indeed, that the water was hidden, the pink blossoms, a foot in diameter, and the beautiful leaves standing up or floating on the water. There were places where the lotus was not growing, and here the reflections of the wall and trees were wonderful. We crossed such odd bridges and went through the most extraordinary gateways, and all this wonderful scenery stretched for miles.

After this delightful ride I went to the University and found that the authorities had allotted to me a number of convenient rooms for my work — two large rooms for a museum and a

lecture room, and in another part of the grounds three long
rooms for a laboratory. In paying my salary for July, my
contract beginning July 12, I was not only paid the odd cent
due, but six tenths of a cent, giving me six little copper coins.
I was told that in all their accounts they get down to tenths of
a cent, and I had to give a receipt for the amount. It is a
curious fact that you find yourself haggling over the fraction
of a cent, and others have confessed to the same experience.
The word for "change" — that is, the money one receives
after paying more than the amount of the bill — is called
tsuri, which means also to fish or to angle.

I wish it were possible to make a decent sketch from memory
of the curious bull teams one sees occasionally. I have at-

Fig. 187

tempted it in figure 187. A single bull is driven in a two-
wheeled cart and the shaft is a wooden loop which goes over
the back and rests on the neck. You will notice a large awning
of straw matting suspended from the cart protecting the beast
from the rays of the sun. The feet also are protected by straw
sandals which are tied on. One sees by this the care bestowed
by these Buddhist pagans on their dumb beasts, and one

cannot help recalling the corresponding treatment of these creatures in Catholic Spain.

Getting my food supplies together, I started again for Enoshima. A week in a primitive fishing village is all right, but when the visit extends for nearly two months it becomes somewhat in the nature of a pilgrimage. Arriving at the village I supped at a place where I had spent the first night, and I invited the family, who had been so kind to me despite the fact that I had gone to another inn, to come to my room and I would show them some curious things under the microscope. My pantomimic conversation was apparently understood. Expecting and waiting for the landlord and his immediate family, I was overwhelmed to see not only these people, but all the servants and children of the house and even people from the other side of the street. However, I did my best and with a Beck's binocular showed them flies' heads, spiders' legs, tiny shells, and the like, and the astonishment they expressed, the low bows and "arigatos" were most amusing. And well they might be amazed! They had never before heard of a microscope or a spy-glass. If they had ever seen an object magnified, it might have been through a burning-glass, though I have never seen one in Japan. Doubtless they have them, as the Chinese use them. This has been one of the treats to-day. The other was in getting acquainted with a dear little Japanese boy, the only one I have seen thus far who seemed attractive. He was not afraid of me as most of the children are, and it is a novel experience for me to have the children afraid. This morning I invited the little boy with his father and mother and servant to the laboratory, and it was charming to see the refined and grateful way in which they expressed their interest in the microscope and other things. The father exchanged cards with me and Matsumura translated. He was an officer connected with the Japanese Treasury Department.

Last evening I had a curious experience at cards. The students came in to see me, and one knew enough English to understand my question when I asked if they knew how to play whist. Some of them thought they could, so I managed to get some chairs, cleared off my circular table, and after the hands were dealt found that they knew hardly the value of the cards. It bothered them to separate the knaves and queens. My question was misunderstood; whist and cards being synonymous terms apparently. They immediately took interest in the game, which, of course, was preposterous, but I did enjoy the good-natured and courteous boys. The chairs seemed to hurt them, and after a little while they were on their knees in their chairs just as they sit on the floor.

To-day a bright and handsome fellow, Matsura by name, came to me as a special student from the University. With Matsumura and the cook with two kerosene lamps we made a visit to the cave, and with the lights made quite a collection of cave crickets and other insects. They were all twilight forms, such as one might find under stones or old logs.

FIG. 188

The odd ways in which they decorate their oiled paper umbrellas are interesting. In some cases the umbrella is painted black with a space in white around the periphery representing the new moon (fig. 188);

flowers and curious designs, also Chinese characters are seen.

Last evening the heavy sea had washed away the farther end of the temporary footbridge which had been built from the island to the mainland. It seemed strange enough to see these tremendous rollers come sweeping in when the weather had been calm and pleasant. The storm had occurred perhaps five hundred miles away and the heavy commotion had just reached the coast. The waves kept up a roar all night.

To-day I noticed a new hanging picture on the post, and turning it about I found the old picture on the other side. Skillful artists are these people, to utilize a thin, cedar board, six inches wide and five and a half feet long, for a picture. To paint a spray of bamboo in a landscape, so that it produces the effect of looking through a narrow opening, requires skill in selecting a proper subject.

The economy of work in a Japanese household is shown in the way of chamber-work. For instance, in a public inn of many rooms the work is easily done by one or two chambermaids. There are no beds, the guests sleeping on the mats; the bedding is a wadded comforter; the pillow a little cushion stuffed with buckwheat hulls, covered with thin Japanese paper and tied on a light box of wood; the toilet is performed out of doors. The comforters are gathered up in the morning and hung over the balcony rails for an airing, and afterwards piled away in some recess or closet; the light, boxlike pillows are gathered up by the armful, carried downstairs, and the soiled pillow-case, in the form of the simple sheet of paper, is taken off and a new sheet added; or, when there are a dozen sheets tied on at once, the soiled one is removed and the work of the day is done so far as the chamber-work is concerned.

Figure 189 shows two maids in the act of replacing the papers on the pillows.

Figure 190 shows a sketch of two boats. The farther boat is known as a "junk" and is much larger than rep-

FIG. 189

resented in the sketch. The boats, as before mentioned, are never painted and all have the uniform grayish wood tint. The boat seems to be joined together by iron rivets of some kind, and the heads of these rivets are sunk below the level

FIG. 190

of the wood and the space plugged with wood, the hole being square. The forward end of the boat has a hole in it from which the water runs when it is dragged up on the beach stern foremost.

A letter from the University requested my attendance at

nine o'clock Monday morning to consult with the other instructors in regard to the programme of studies. It was my intention to go up Sunday noon, but Mr. Hamilton and a friend of his having come down expressly to see the laboratory, and Mr. Hamilton promising to help me pack the bottles of rare objects, they induced me to stay till evening and then walk to Yokohama, seventeen miles, which would have taken us five hours. When evening came, however, great squalls of wind detained us till ten o'clock, as we hoped it would clear up. It did not clear, but, if anything, the wind increased in violence. We started over the narrow bridge knowing that the end had been washed away; the waves tore underneath in fearful fashion. At the end we yelled for a boat, though it would have been hard for any boat to have kept afloat. We thought of wading, but the idea of a walk of seventeen miles with shoes full of sand and water compelled us to turn back to try again at three o'clock in the morning, with jinrikishas to take us to Yokohama. My English friends were at the inn near the water, and they insisted upon my stopping with them that we might start together. I was up and down a dozen times, first to stone some dogs that were barking in concert, then to select a fresh place on the floor to get out of the hurricane which forced the rain through the storm shutters. In going downstairs I saw the family by the dim light of a single candle asleep on different parts of the floor. The room was black with age and smoke and in appearance was like the hut of a savage. The apartments for guests upstairs, though bearing the marks of age, were much better. With very little sleep and having the first cold I have had since being in Japan, we were ready at three o'clock and started, having for breakfast one slice of toasted bread and a cup of tea. I had to carry my handbag, a large package of delicate specimens, and my big sun hat, which I could not keep on my head in the wind. The wind came in what are called typhoon squalls, and the waves dashed up between the boards and over the boards of the bridge. If it was difficult to cross the bridge before, it was now almost impossible, for many more of the boards had been washed away. The bridge swayed and at times we lay flat and felt for a board ahead, for it was absolutely black. We could not hear one another for the noise of the wind and waves, and we were wet to the skin with salt water, but fortunately the water was warm and the air hot. How I ever got over with my luggage is still a mystery to me, for I literally crawled the entire length by inches, and when we reached the end the waves were dashing by, three feet high. We shouted in unison for the jinrikisha men, who had been waiting in the storm for us, and finally they heard us and struggled out through the waves. With great difficulty we got on to their shoulders and with staggering gait they managed to dump us on land instead of into the water. Then came the long ride through the silent villages, with the houses tightly closed by the wooden screens, dogs asleep in the roadway, and the roar of the wind whistling through the groves of bamboo. In one village through which we passed a watchman was going his rounds with a drum which he beat at intervals four times to indicate it was four o'clock. The sunrise was magnificent; such brilliant reds I never saw before. It is curious that in these high gales the heat is oppressive; we were in our shirt sleeves the entire distance. At 6.30 we reached Kanagawa, a station beyond Yokohama, and I boarded the train there for Tokyo, finally reaching the University in time for the meeting. I started back for Enoshima at three o'clock with the sun broiling in its intensity.

Before reaching Fujisawa I saw many people all nicely dressed going along the road. The little girls and even some of the older ones had on bright red undergarments, making a pleasing change from the uniform color of indigo blue. When we reached Fujisawa the place was filled with people. Down the steps of one temple came a troop of forty or fifty men dressed in white, with curious brown paper hats, resembling liberty-caps, on their heads, bearing on their shoulders a huge affair resembling a miniature temple, and ahead a drum was being beaten with slow, monotonous strokes in threes. Something was evidently going on, so by pantomime I indicated to the jinrikisha men that I wanted to stop to see whatever it was. Thereupon they turned down a side street, where I slowly meandered through crowds of children and grown folks and toy booths, the whole presenting the appearance of a fair. A theatrical performance of some kind was in full action. A man vigorously beating a drum was loudly calling attention to something which appeared to be a collection of carved figures arranged behind him. Not knowing that the admission to the show was a tenth of a cent, I put down two cents, whereupon the man thanked me profusely and gave me a ticket to admit me, the ticket being a piece of wood a foot long! The "show" was in a curious kind of a tent with a little stage about seven feet long, and a small audience stood directly in front of it. The people are all so short here that I must seem like a giant to them: at all events, I could see over the heads of all of them as if I had been on stilts. It was somewhat annoying to have the audience gazing at me instead of at the stage and to hear the suppressed "Ijin-san," meaning "different people," equivalent to "Mr. Foreigner."

On the stage two children came out together, one dressed like a kangaroo and jumping about like one, the other in the guise of a little fat man with a mask more grotesque than I ever saw before, the whole figure reminding one of John Gilbert's drawing of Falstaff. The little girl must have had her legs bent to appear so short. They danced about for some time, to the delight of the children.

After enjoying the novelties of the show for a while I continued my ride to the beach, which we reached at eight o'clock at night. The waves were still raging in tumultuous lurches, and there were a dozen men gesticulating and doing their best to make me understand something. It was quite dark, and with some difficulty I discovered that where the bridge had ended at three o'clock in the morning was a huge fragment of a wreck and the bridge was gone! I tried to get a boat, but the men informed me, by a very easy gesture of the hand, that the boat would upset. I look back with shame at the rage I got into. At least a dozen men had collected, twenty or thirty naked fishermen, some smelling strongly of saké, all gesticulating and trying to tell me something in loud tones, and I yelling "Enoshima" and pointing to the island so inaccessible to me. I was shouting, because when people do not understand you unconsciously fancy that they are deaf.

They were animated by the same impulse. Finally I threatened to walk back to Yokohama and walked away from the beach some distance, and, completely tired out, impatiently waited for the tide to go down. I finally got across perched on the shoulders of a man, and was amazed to find that the bridge had entirely disappeared. When I got to the house I learned that the bridge had been swept away directly after we crossed; in fact, it was being swept away at the time we crossed. It was certainly a narrow escape.

My landlord had so outrageously overcharged my English friends the day before that, as soon as I got to the inn, I immediately packed all my things and went to another place farther down the street. My two Japanese also went with me and I induced Dr. Veeder, who had come down to see me from the University, to go too. Tachibana, who has the next best house, and who has always treated me very kindly, was glad to take us in.

CHAPTER VIII

LIFE IN TOKYO

August 28. Very busy packing to-day. The janitor was sick, the special student also, so the work devolved on Matsumura and me. The jinrikisha men we had engaged volunteered their assistance, as they always do, so I got them to chop straw, though with the varied skill of these people they would probably have packed better than we could. Wednesday morning we started with five jinrikishas. The boat, loaded with cases, dredges, etc., and the four men, could not get off until the next day, and so the rest of the packing was left to the janitor. The specimens too delicate to pack I placed in large, shallow baskets; a large, delicate branching coral was arranged resting on a cushion tied to a board; the cook held this in his lap the entire distance. Each of us had a basket of specimens and the rear jinrikisha carried our luggage. Figure 191 gives a faint idea of our appearance as we

Fig. 191

started for Tokyo, a ride of over thirty miles. We kept rather close together, and it was interesting to see the impression our appearance made upon the natives. They would glance at the first one curiously, look at the second one, stare in amazement at the third, and laugh in astonishment at the sight of all of us holding such curious-looking objects in our laps. We concluded to stop in Yokohama for the night. We came to Tokyo the next morning with our precious corals and other objects in perfect condition. Friday morning the boat arrived and I saw the contents safely loaded on two drays, pushed and pulled by three men, and finally unloaded in the rooms assigned to me at the University, the nucleus of a museum — the first zoölogical museum in Japan. I hope to get it on a good foundation before my contract closes.

Now that I am through with Enoshima the experience has gone like a flash. I have spent six weeks in that little crowded collection of houses, with people overworked and at it from four o'clock in the morning till midnight, with an overwhelming amount of work to do in providing for the crowds of pilgrims thronging in upon them, all Japanese with an occasional foreigner for the night. The visitors seem to demand four or five meals a day, and are constantly calling for tea, coals for their pipe, hot saké, etc. Children of all ages were swarming everywhere; yet, living among them in the closest proximity, I did not hear during my whole stay there a single cross word; babies cried, but mothers laughed at them, and when they were in actual distress sympathetically stroked their ventral region. A pleasant smile always greeted me from all, and though I chased their barking dogs through the single street and occasionally threw stones at them, they looked amiably upon my behavior as the eccentricities of a foreign barbarian and laughed! Now this is paganism — to be kind and obliging, courteous and hospitable, generous with their food and their time, sharing their last bowl of rice with you; and whatever you may be doing, — collecting, pulling up a boat, or anything else, — jinrikisha men, or fishermen, always ready to lend, or rather to give in abundance, a helping hand.

Speaking of dogs, you ask for the name of dog and the answer will be "Kumhere." Many think that is the Japanese name for dog, whereas the name has been adapted from the English and American who, in calling a dog, say, "Come here!" "Come here!" — and the Japanese in these parts have supposed that the word represents the English name for dog, which in Japanese is *inu*.

There is no end to the tasteful ways in which the tiny gardens are arranged or to the graceful designs of the fences and the rock paths. The other day, in going through the villages in the early morning, I noticed many of the people washing their faces at the wells or at the end of the house, and cleaning their teeth also; and this among the lower classes. Moreover, these people usually rinse their mouths before drinking.

In the temple at Enoshima are preserved many relics which the priests show you with great reverence. Among these were pieces of armor many hundreds of years old; a metal mirror, five hundred years old, belonging to some great daimyo of that date. The priest brought out a large piece of a hard substance which he said was wood turned into stone. An examination of it showed it to be a fragment of a lower jaw of a sperm whale, and this I told him. The look he gave me was to the effect that I was a poor fool to doubt him; and as he went on explaining the various relics his rapidity of speech, due to the fact that he had uttered the same sentences a thousand times in explaining to others, caused Matsumura some difficulty in translating. Finally he came to an oblong box which he opened with great care and disclosed the shriveled remains of a common Japanese snake, and lying loose in the box were two small black objects which he said were its horns! Of course this was an impossible creature, and the merest glance at the objects showed that they were the mandibles of a large beetle, and so I informed him. He replied without the slightest hesitation, yet with a dignity and positiveness that was delightful, that he had written authority for the statement, and that settled the question. So the Buddhist priests are like the religious devotees of the rest of the world, attempting to combat facts by written authority.

With the absence of all hoodlumism, rowdyism, vandalism, and alcoholism one wonders where all the criminals come from, when one meets in the street, as I did to-day, a band of prisoners chained together, dressed in a sort of orange-colored cloth, with policemen armed with iron rods the size of a light walking-stick. They were a hard-looking set, and certainly, if there is any truth in the criminal face and expression, they showed them quite as distinctly as a similar class at home. From my limited experience, if I had been told that this small band comprised every known criminal in Japan, a nation of over thirty millions, I should hardly have doubted the statement.

Yesterday I engaged a jinrikisha man by the month and find it very convenient. He comes at 7.30 in the morning and is on hand all the time. My first trip with him was to visit the Industrial Exhibition, just opened at Uyeno Park, about a mile from Kaga Yashiki where I live. Arriving at the park we went up a broad avenue lined with stately trees, and on each side of the roadway were little temporary booths, or shops, with displays of porcelain, lacquer, and other Japanese objects for sale. On Sunday the tickets of admission are fifteen

FIG. 192

cents; on all other days seven cents. The entrance was under an imposing old gateway with turnstiles as at the Centennial at Philadelphia. Large one-storied wooden buildings were arranged in an irregular quadrangle; the Art Building was a permanent structure built of brick and stone. Figure 192 is a rough sketch of the entrance to Horticultural Hall, a wooden building one hundred feet long. Within was the most marvelous display of dwarf pines, cherry and plum trees, and flowers of all kinds, and the bewildering "coquetries and charms" of the Japanese gardener. The pines are made to assume the oddest shapes. Figure 193 is an illustration of one of them. The twigs are tied to bamboo frames, like disks, every twig being patiently tied to the frame. There were many other grotesque forms too difficult to sketch in my limited time. The moment I made the slightest attempt to

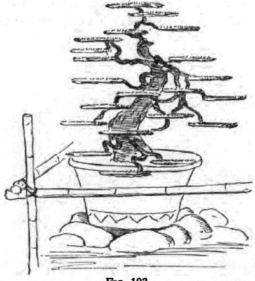

Fig. 193

sketch, a crowd of Japanese gathered close about me watching every line I made. I had barely finished the sketch when a polite and well-dressed Japanese official came up to me and said, in perfect English, "I hope you will excuse me, but no one is allowed to make sketches without the consent of exhibitors." As I had come expressly to sketch, this rather nonplussed me, but gathering my wits I immediately resolved to write an article for a home periodical and told him that I was

preparing an illustrated article for an American magazine to
show the wonderful character of this national exhibition. This
seemed to please him, and he then asked me if I was doing it
for commercial purposes. On informing him that I had never
raised a pine tree or any other tree in my life and had no idea
of doing such a thing at this late day, he requested my card,
and it was with some satisfaction that I gave him one upon
which was written *Dai Gakku* (Great University). His manner
changed instantly, and where before I had been regarded as a
suspicious character stealing designs, I was now at least somebody, and he would lay the case before the Director. In the
mean time I hurried through the buildings making all the
sketches I possibly could, not knowing what decision the
Director might make.

Figure 194 is a sketch of a long table with ten girls on a side
reeling silk from the cocoons. What an attraction this would
have been at the Centennial, these girls in their native dresses
and their gentle behavior! The process of reeling was very
interesting. I had supposed a single thread was caught from
the cocoons and unwound. The cocoons, to the number of
thirty or forty, are put into a shallow pan of hot water, and
with a brush, which you will see at the corner of the table,
the cocoons are soused up and down in the water until the
fibres get loose and adhere to the brush; then all the fibres that
are caught are reeled off together, and as one after the other
breaks it is caught up again. A steam pipe keeps the water
hot and above is a shaft containing the reel.

Watching the people — and there were hundreds — the
recollection came to me of the Centennial with its hordes of

greenhorns, munching gingerbread and peanuts, laughing or talking loudly, tumbling against one and otherwise misbehaving. Here without a single exception everybody was easily and charmingly polite, and if by chance any one collided with you,

Fig. 194

a profound bow was made and a courteous "Go men na sai" (Excuse me) expressed his apology. Most of the people removed their hats on entering the buildings; many of them had no hats to remove, two out of three being bareheaded, having fans or umbrellas to protect them from the sun.

The artistic way in which they utilize worm-eaten wood, planks that have evidently been under water and blackened by age, has already been mentioned. In a huge flower box made of this material was a tangled pine. A flower-holder may be

made from a piece of a decayed stump upon which is affixed
a pearl dragonfly, little bronze ants, or a spider's web made of
silver threads. Such surprises in design and material one
finds nowhere else. On a dark cedar board with the grain
rubbed down and conspicuous, in a frame perhaps two feet
long, was a section of bamboo with a flight of sparrows. The
bamboo was of yellow lacquer and the little birds were made
of some kind of metal (fig. 195). Another panel of old cedar

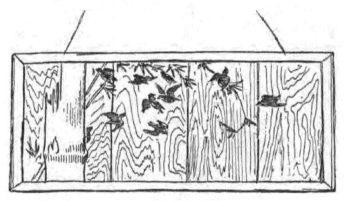

Fig. 195

(fig. 196) had in one corner a hanging flower-holder of bamboo
with a spray of grapevine made apparently of metal, the ten-
drils threads of silver, the leaves and fruit in high relief, of
lacquer probably, but made to resemble copper, silver, etc.
These were ornaments to hang on the walls. No words can
describe the grace, finish, and purity of design; these and
other exquisite productions of the Japanese show their great
love of nature and their power to embody these simple *motifs*
in decorative art, and after seeing these it seems as if the

Japanese were the greatest lovers of nature and the greatest artists in the world. They think of designs that nobody else would possibly dream of and then execute them with a strength and naturalness sur-
passing belief. They select the simplest subject and create the most surprising fancies. The marvelous feature about their pictorial and decorative art is the way

FIG. 196

they use for motives of decoration the commonest objects, pine, bamboo, and other forms. For centuries these have been the inspiration of the artist and ten thousand changes have been rung on these prosaic subjects, not only pictorially, but in metal, wood, and ivory, and all the way from a veritable depiction of the object to the most imaginative and conventional.

No civilized nation on the face of the earth exceeds the Japanese in the love for nature in every aspect. Storm or calm, mist, rain, snow, flowers, the varying tints of the seasons, placid rivers, raging waterfalls, the flight of birds, the dash of fishes, towering peaks, deep ravines — every phase of nature is not only admired, but depicted in unnumbered sketches and kakemono. A realization of this keen love for nature is shown in the fact that the directory of the city of Tokyo has among its prefatory chapters a guide to places where the varying aspects of nature may be seen to the best advantage.

In riding along a shore road in Harima we overtook a party of pilgrims on their way to some shrine. Though it was a very hot day, a stiff breeze was blowing from the Pacific tempering the air and causing the waves to pound the beach with tremendous rollers. The crowd ahead, numbering thirty or forty, filled the entire road, chattering and singing. Being in no hurry we jogged on behind. Suddenly from the sea came a huge eagle with mighty flaps and alighted on a low branch of an oak directly over the road. With ruffled feathers he settled down to rest with no evidence of fear of the noisy crowd approaching. How an Occidental would have longed for a gun! It was delightful to see these men whip out their rolls of paper and brushes and make rapid sketches of the bird from different points of view. As these groups of pilgrims represented various trades and occupations, these sketches would be utilized later in decorating lacquer, fans, or in carving a *netsuki*, or modeling a bronze eagle. After a while the crowd moved on, we following; the eagle remained on the branch till we were out of sight.

So few years have passed since the Restoration that I was astonished, in going through the Exhibition, at the progress which has been made in the manufacture of objects which only a short time ago the Japanese were importing. In one building were displayed surveyors' instruments; large trumpets; foreign clothing; beautiful dresses; boots and shoes, some of them quite equal to ours; trunks; chairs and furniture of all kinds; soap; hats; caps; matches; and some machinery, though not much. The Naval College exhibit was a revelation: large cables, ropes, pulleys, and all the rigging-gear of a ship; and above all a beautiful model of a man-of-war, fourteen feet long and perfect in every part; also a model of a drydock. There were many photographs, and all were artistic. The Japanese Hydrographic Survey exhibited beautiful engraved maps of the coast after the style of our Coast and Geodetic Survey. In another department were ploughs, harrows, and agricultural implements of all kinds; and on large tablets were mounted in an artistic manner the useful productions of Japan, such as rice, wheat, and all growing food products. The school apparatus seemed to include every device used in the laboratories: clocks and telegraphic instruments, telescopes, microscopes, philosophical apparatus, electrical machines, air pumps, etc., made by this wonderful people. One object made me extremely covetous, and that was a perfect human skeleton, made of ivory, just a foot high. The marvel of it was that the bones down to the phalanges were made separately and wired together; the hands would turn, the arms twist, and the legs were flexible. The cartilage that unites the ribs with the sternum was made of yellow horn and looked precisely like cartilage as one sees it in a mounted skeleton. The lower jaw moved, and it really seemed as if the teeth moved in their sockets.

The metal-work, figures, clasps, and pins made for foreign sale, were all remarkable for execution and design. A silver bronze with figures four inches high (fig. 197) represented a man on a rugged cliff throwing an immense rock to a man below, who catches it on his shoulders, and pine trees, and all delicately wrought in silver. The sketch does no justice to the energy and strength of the figures.

FIG. 197

I am fairly settled now at No. 5, Kaga Yashiki. Figure 198 is a rough sketch of the house I live in; built by the Japanese and supposed to be in foreign style. The hasty pen-and-ink

FIG. 198

sketch does it no sort of justice. The massive tiled roof, wide piazza, quaint Japanese carving over the doorway, and the front yard with palms, big banana plant, bamboo grass, and rosebushes in bloom make it very attractive. Inside, the rooms are spacious. The one I occupy for a writing-room or library is thirty feet long, eighteen feet wide, and fourteen feet high. It is the parlor of the house, and the dining-room leading from it is closed by folding doors. The floors are carpeted with straw matting relieving the desolation of the unfurnished condition. It is lonely enough at night: the rats tear around overhead, and the ceiling being made of thin boards papered they make a tremendous noise; the floors crack with the change of temperature; an occasional earthquake makes the roof creak; and by midnight a person is prepared to take his oath that he hears stealthy footsteps on the piazza. However, I am in a pagan country where house-breaking, pocket-picking, etc., are unknown; in fact, I feel a great deal safer here than I should in my quiet town of Salem.

Coming up through one of the back streets to-day, — and they all seem like back streets, — I saw some sort of bread baked in the form of salamanders (fig. 199) and other curious creatures made for the children. I was told that in some parts of Tokyo they make candy in the shape of toads, worms, spiders, and other revolting things for food. The imitation is perfect, and the game is to see who can eat them without faltering. I have heard that dinners are given where infinitely more disgusting things are

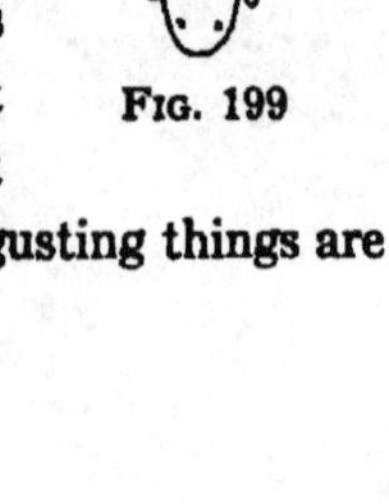

Fig. 199

made of candy, jelly, etc., all good to eat, but requiring an overwhelming effort for a squeamish stomach.

The children in the streets are now seen with long bamboo poles, and with them they chase the dragon flies, and also tie strings about the bodies of these insects and grasshoppers, fasten the strings to the poles, and fly them as they would diminutive kites.

I went to the Exhibition again this afternoon and realized the comfort it was to walk through the crowds that throng the place without having to hold on to your pocketbook, and to feel that you could leave your umbrella beside a bench and find it there an hour later. You see no signs, "Keep off the grass," "Look out for pick-pockets," etc. I hope to visit the place twice a week to make a study of its art treasures. To-day I noticed more particularly the wonderful character of the work in lacquer: the various kinds of lacquer and the effects produced, the overlaying with gold, pearl, and the exquisite taste shown in the subjects selected. Tablets made to hang up as decorative ornaments (whether to use in their houses or made for export I did not learn) were beautiful. On a jet black lacquer tablet was the full moon rising out of the sea. The moon was literally a silver disk, though the reflection in the water was, curiously enough, gold-tinted. It is such violations of truth in many forms of Japanese art which irritate us, though I have not yet seen the new moon turning the wrong way in Japanese drawings as it is so commonly seen in our pictorial art. Now this tablet appeared perfectly black as one glanced at it hanging on the wall; the jet-black surface represented a dark night; the moon was marvelously rendered and hung low down and was partially obscured. A close scrutiny revealed a shore with a few boats hauled up and three large junks afloat, and at one side a distant shore and low mountains on the horizon. It is the reserve, simplicity, and yet audacity these artists show, that is so wonderful. Who would think of details in black on a black background! A jet-black crow on a jet-black *inro!* It is unthinkable, and yet it is only one of hundreds of things the Japanese delight to do. The tablet represented night, and night it was.

There were beautiful wreaths, cherry blossoms, thorns and little flowers in colors, all made out of porcelain; old Dresden and Chelsea products of a similar nature look weak and putty-like in comparison. There was a plain ivory fan on which were marvelously wrought a few lacquered figures; price, $90; a screen, upon which was painted a snow scene, was $95; a metal vase; price, $600. (I learned afterwards that these were all

FIG. 200

made for foreign sale.) In looking over the prices appended to most of the goods it was interesting to note that even the tenth of a cent was put down. The currency is yen = dollar;

FIG. 201

sen = cent; rin = one tenth of a cent. The rin is a little copper coin about as big as our old silver five-cent piece. There were two carved chairs, made, of course, for foreigners, and the price was marked 8 yen, 33 sen, and 7 rin! A person ought to save money with such delicate divisions as these. Here was a tablet (fig. 200) entirely in metal, bamboo frame and all. It was two feet long, the tablet resembling type metal (I have since learned that the metal was probably a com-position known as *shakudo*, an alloy of copper and gold). The dragon-fly in high relief was of silver; the flowers, grasses, and leaves, stand-ing one behind the other, were made of gold, silver, and gold bronze. It was most exquisitely wrought; price, $135. Many other tablets were equally remarkable. In one a bas-ket of shells was represented in low relief, — a few shells had fallen out of the basket; the shells were so perfectly done that one could even recognize the species. In another was

FIG. 202

a spray of autumn leaves. The various designs in relief made of crape in different colors were all true to nature. There was

a set of ten hanging ornaments, made of cedar wood, upon which were mounted beautiful little designs; one of mushrooms is shown in figure 201. The price of the set was $1.30. What amazes one in this work is the originality in all designs, their truthfulness to nature, and their grace and charm. We admire the lifelike etchings of grasses by Dürer, the wild bits over which we become enthusiastic; in the Exhibition one sees the work of a hundred Dürers whose names are but little known. The larger screens, in lacquer and gold and color, representing clumps of bushes in a forest, bamboo groves, and landscapes, were marvels of beauty. The subjects were altogether too elaborate to sketch and only those of the simplest nature were drawn. There was

FIG. 203

a fish piece on cloth, painted in color in bold strokes, which was marvelous for the graceful grouping of the fishes (fig. 202). One of the most striking objects is shown in figure 203; it consisted of a disk of oak with grain in high relief. It was about as big as the head of a barrel. Upon this, near the periphery, was a bull in black metal; a boy resting upon his back in an attitude of amazement at some inscription written in the middle of the disk, his mouth open, and the whole pose that of astonishment. The dress of the boy was cut out of a piece of pearl, and the hand and face with a rope over the neck of the beast were of gold. It was unique and beautiful.

September 8. It is delightful weather and the fresh and invigorating air braces one as it does at home. I am becoming more familiar with Japanese ways which are as different from ours as the behavior of a cat full of fun at times is from that of a frolicking dog. I begin to know my way a little better in this vast city and feel quite at home; the bewilderment and novelty have worn off in a measure, yet this gives me more chance to observe old things more carefully and to grasp new things better. A ride through the streets and to the University, back and forth, again and again, is always a novel and delightful experience. You are sure to see something new and you never tire of the old: the low and queer-looking houses; the odd signs and fluttering awnings; children running across the path of your jinrikisha with their long sleeves flying; women with their highly dressed hair and always bareheaded, the older women waddling like ducks and the younger ones scuffing along; women nursing their children in the streets, in the shops, and even while riding in the jinrikishas; peddlers of all kinds; traveling shows; restaurants; stationary and peripatetic hawkers of fish, of toys, of candy; pipe-repairers; shoe-menders; barbers with their ornamental box, — all with different street cries, some like the call of a strange bird; blind men and women strolling along the street blowing whistles; two old women and a girl, with cracked voices and a cracked guitar, singing; a bald-headed man with a bell who prays in front of your house for a tenth of a cent; another man reciting stories with a laughing group about him; jinrikishas rushing by in every direction and their contents always interesting; here a jinrikisha, drawn by two men, with a dignified officer in uniform; another with two tired-looking chaps sound asleep, their heads dangling against each other; another holds two women each with a child in her arms; another a woman with a large-sized child in her lap, the child holding in her hand a half-consumed sweet potato and tugging away at the maternal font for the milk to go with it, — all these sights are bewildering and absorbing. Enormous loads on two-wheeled drays are pulled and pushed by men with their vociferous accompaniment of grunts, "Hoi saka hoi, hoida hoi." Everybody walks in the streets, for there are no sidewalks, — handsome-looking little boys are seen on their way to school, or a group of highly dressed little girls with powdered faces riding in jinrikishas bound for some gathering, — and all the while such a clatter of wooden clogs on the hard roadway and a continual hum of voices. People profoundly bowing to one another; the interminable shops lining the streets, all open from side to side and all the activities fully exposed; the umbrella-maker, lantern-maker, fan-painter, seal-cutter, every craft being practiced in open daylight, all seem like a grotesque dream, and all these multifarious activities and crowded streets are dominated by an atmosphere of gentleness, politeness, and natural good breeding. The thought continually reverts to the undeniable fact that this is pagan Japan, where animals are always so kindly treated that you have to step out of the way or over hens, dogs, cats, and pigeons, and even the black crows, which at home are the wariest of birds, here are so gently treated that they flock to the city by thousands.

At the University the work on the shells and other marine forms is progressing finely. I am mounting on tablets and labeling for exhibition the different species of shells. This morning when moving a tray of shells I ran against a partially opened door and spilled some of them, whereupon I used emphatically a good old Saxon expression which is unfortunately and erroneously put in the category of profane words. My assistant smiled at my petulance, and as I had been told that the Japanese did not swear I asked him if something was not said at such times to relieve the tension on the brain. Yes, he confessed that they sometimes used an expletive. Now, I thought, I was to get a swear-word in Japanese of which I had at times felt a need. He gave me a word meaning vexing or vexatious! — probably the equivalent of our expression, "Plague take it!" and that was the extent of Japanese profanity! Sometime after I dropped a little pottery teapot; it did not break fortunately, and nothing was said in the way of an expletive, but I asked my assistant what the Japanese would say in the way of an exclamation, and all I got was an address to the teapot meaning, "How impolite you are to leave so unceremoniously without saying good-bye!"

In watching carpenters at work it is alarming to see a man hewing a beam standing on it with his naked feet and bringing down his razor-like adze in vigorous strokes within half an inch of his naked toes (fig. 204). Apparently they rarely cut themselves, as I have examined many for the marks of scars, or the gap for missing toes, and in only one case have I found a scar, and when I called the carpenter's attention to it he smiled and showed me another big one on his leg, pointing to his adze and smiling again.

FIG. 204

Figure 205 is a sketch of a man in the market cleaning sweet potatoes. The tub is half full of them covered with water. The two long round sticks are tied together in the middle and the man turns the ends in the tub by simply moving his arms back and forth. One immediately observes in the market how thoroughly cleansed are all forms of ground vegetables, turnips, radishes, onions, etc.

FIG. 205

The wood engravers are interesting to watch, to see the rapidity with which they slash away, cutting on the side of the grain and not on the end as with us. In engraving seals, however, they cut on the end of the grain as in our wood engraving, and they probably use the same wood that we do, as it looks like boxwood. Everybody has a seal, and when you buy anything the receipted bill is signed with the seal in red. The Chinese character is written in an ancient style much as we would use for similar purposes Old English letters. Figure 206 represents a number of these seals collected at random. Most of the books are printed from blocks the size of the page. The copyist writes the page on thin, translucent paper which is pasted face down on the block, thus reversing the characters which show through. The engraver with quick movements of the hand cuts through the paper and into the wood with a sharp-pointed knife, which is clutched in the hand and drawn inward. After the outlines of the characters have been engraved gouges are used to remove the intervening wood.

Fig. 206

In one small room opening on the street were seven engravers at work, four in one row and three in a row just behind. These men sat in the usual manner on the floor before tables a foot high working away with people watching them and often getting in their light.

The wood-turner is an equally curious sight in the way he works his wood. The lathe is a simple shaft over which a belt is wound several times, the ends, having loops, are held by the turner's feet. The turner sits at the end of the lathe and moves his legs up and down turning the shaft back and forth, and on this rude and primitive device the wood-turner makes the most delicately fitting

Fig. 207

nests of boxes and other objects (fig. 207). In another case a boy was pulling the band back and forth while a man was turning some metal object.

With a friend I made another visit to the great temple at Asakusa, the first visit having been mentioned in earlier pages of the journal. Walking from Kaga Yashiki, the distance may be a mile, but there were so many things to look at on the way that it took us two hours to get there. I bought in a second-hand bookshop some dashing sketches of animals, etc., for a cent apiece. It was interesting to see the main avenue to the temple lined on both sides with booths stocked with children's toys. The broad steps to the temple were occupied with children playing with their dolls, making mud cakes and playing their games. The temples are open for worship seven days in the week from morning till night. Back of the temple are long galleries neatly fitted up, in which one may shoot at targets with bow and arrow. In one place was an animal show of pigeons, porcupines, monkeys, and other animals. A very clever-looking monkey was on a pole, to the top of which he would climb and haul up a bucket by a rope to which he had clung while climbing the pole. When he came down I shook hands with him, and he drew my hand to him and finally got both feet into the palm of my hand and rested them there contentedly for a few minutes. The touch of his hand was precisely like that of a child's, warm and slightly moist, and the finger lines would make a similar mark and probably vary individually as with our hands. From the monkey show we went to a wax-figure show. Never at home have I seen in painting or sculpture such energy and passion as was shown in these figures; men with the most infernal faces. One piece especially was a most hideous-looking figure, a ragged and deformed old beggar crouched in a cart and being dragged by another beggar equally shocking in appearance. There was also a wax-figure theatre in which the figures were made to caper about. In one scene was a princess who was changed into a fox with seven tails, but to watch the old man who related the story about the performance was as much of a study as the mute figures on the stage, and the orchestra with such a thumping and alternation of time was unlike anything I had ever heard before. The princess sat on a sort of throne, her head moving slowly and a number of figures, all life-size, with expressions of expectant fear and horror, surrounded her. Suddenly the throne parts in the middle, the princess tumbles apart and disappears and up comes a gigantic fox with seven tails which hovers over the stage, bending its head and gnashing its jaws in a most threatening manner. The fox was remarkable for its resemblance to a fox. Not being familiar with the folklore of Japan the various figures conveyed no meaning to me, but the vigor and expression showed that the Japanese artist is as great in sculpture as he is in painting.

There was also a wrestling bout in full blast, and we went in for an hour. It was much more interesting than the one I saw before; the wrestlers were younger men and not so fat, and the contests were most exciting and there was some lofty throwing. The preliminary movements of the men were very amusing, especially the slow and ridiculous way in which, with hands on their knees, they would lift first one leg and then the other and stamp their feet on the hard ground, then crouching to each other start for a clinch, only to be stopped by the umpire, for what reason I could not see, and begin the performance all over again. I could have watched them the whole day.

In a smaller temple we saw a curious object of devotion, an immense wooden affair richly carved and painted, ten or fifteen feet high, which rested on a shaft in the ground. With some strength this could be rotated by certain beams sticking out of the side against which one pushed. The casket contains the Chinese library of a famous Buddhist priest, and devotees come in to turn it. If it turns easily their prayers have been answered, and if with difficulty it is doubtful. Here is a

FIG. 208

prayer gauge that all of Tyndall's arguments could not avail against! I have tried it, as is shown in figure 208.

In riding through the streets one notices the crowds in front of the picture shops, which are bright in color from the war prints. The Satsuma rebellion furnishes themes for the illustrators. The pictures are brilliant in reds and blacks, the figures of the officers in most dramatic attitudes, and "bloody war" is really depicted, though grotesque from our standpoint. One of the pictures represents a star in heaven (the planet Mars), in the centre of which is General Saigo, the rebel chief, beloved by all the Japanese. After the capture of Kagoshima he and other officers committed *hara kiri*. Many of the people believe he is in Mars, which is now shining with unusual brilliancy.

I have lately become interested in the household art of Japan: that is, domestic art, the making of objects for the

house that parallels the work at home of pictures painted on
birchbark, pressed seaweed, leatherwork, shellwork, and the
like. For originality of design and nicety of execution these
people beat us out and out. A book on the subject would certainly be of interest to our people, and if time only permitted
I would collect every kind of an object of this nature. In the
kitchen one sees a variety of buckets, shallow ones and deep
ones, all having the generic features of two staves opposite
each other running up a foot or more from the rim and a transverse piece forming the handle. These various forms of buckets
have their special uses. The tubs also vary greatly; there are

Fig. 209

low tubs, like figure 209, used as foot tubs,
and other shallow forms are used in the fish
market. It will be observed that some of the
staves project slightly beyond the bottom rim,
thus holding the tub off the ground. In the Exhibition, hanging
up among the choicest lacquers, bronzes, and porcelains, is a
shallow foot tub ornamented with the most exquisite inlaid
work of different woods. It is an odd conceit to select a tub
for decorative purposes, and what surprises us in the work is
the startling novelty of design, material, and purpose. Jarves,
who was the first one in America to write on Japanese art
in a sympathetic and appreciative manner, especially notes
these attributes when he says, comparing it with the European:
"It is more subtile, intense, varied, free, and truthfully artistic
in decorative expression; more abounding in unexpectedness
and delicious surprises, in æsthetic coquetries and charms of
æsthetic speech intelligible to every degree of culture." [1]

[1] J. J. Jarves, *A Glimpse at the Art of Japan.* 1876.

A friend has found in an obscure part of Tokyo a basket-
maker who fabricates little hanging holders for flowers in the
shape of insects, lobsters, fishes, etc. I hunted him up and
secured a number of specimens. Figure 210 is in the form of

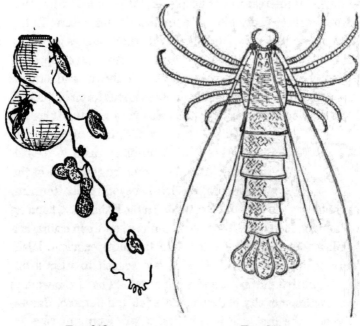

FIG. 210   FIG. 211

a gourd with vine. The leaves, and flat surfaces in others, like
the wings of insects, are made of a matting. All other details
are true basket-work. A loop behind allows it to hang from
the wall, while inside the object is a segment of bamboo to
hold water. Figure 211 represents a crayfish; figure 212, a
carp. The sketch does no justice to the plump and bending

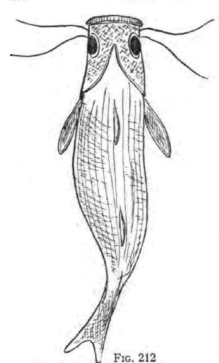

FIG. 212

body of the carp and the graceful swing of its tail. Figure 213 represents a grasshopper, fairly good, but even here there are the right number of legs springing from the proper region of the body. Figure 214 is a dragonfly, fairly good also. Figure 215 shows curious objects to represent in basket-work, but so perfect in form that a mycologist might almost determine the genus. These straw objects were six or eight inches in length and were very low in

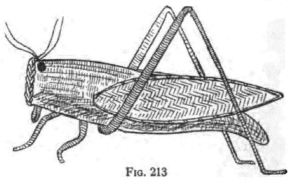

FIG. 213

price, — ten or fifteen cents. The interest attaching to them and to all work of this nature is that the Japanese never make a mistake in the details of structure of animals represented. Insects have three pairs of legs; spiders have four; higher crustaceans, five; and all springing from the right

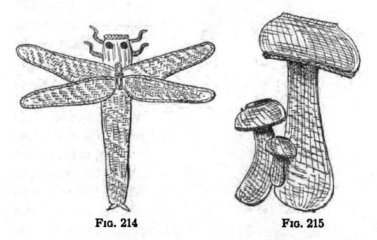

FIG. 214   FIG. 215

regions of the body. It is their love for nature and their keen observational powers that enable them to do these things correctly. Many of these designs are symbolical.

Coming up from the station I noticed a great crowd in the street, and saw on one side a booth, something like a band-stand, where a pantomime was being acted. Such extraordinary gestures were made and such curious masks were seen that I watched it as eagerly as the crowd. The orchestra in quaintness beat the Chinese orchestra in San Francisco, but agreeably lacked the ear-splitting blasts of the trumpet. I held my jinrikisha back at the side of the road and endeavored to make a sketch of the show, but such a crowd of people were looking over my shoulder, and others fairly hiding the object from view, that I only got an impression of the scene (fig. 216). The lanterns hanging from the poles were dark red.

The toleration that these people have for eccentricities in dress or behavior is a charming trait. A native may dress as

Fig. 216

he pleases and no notice is taken of him; if he is markedly odd
in his appearance he may excite a smile, but not a taunt nor
other demonstration from the boys — a strong contrast to the
intolerant behavior of men and boys at home. The considerate
treatment they accord to every one is also a notable trait in
their character. At home we walk rapidly along the streets
bent on business or we ride in closed cars and see but little that
is going on; here I have always had a clear view, whether
walking or riding, and I have been incessantly watching everything from the moment I first landed in the country and have
recorded every feature and incident. Now, I have never seen
a cripple or ragged person or uncouth dress derided or shouted
at.[1] The story of the little boys who were eaten up by a bear
for calling names and making faces needs no parallel story
in this country of kindness and good behavior. Quite a number
of the Japanese officials often appear in our dress and some of
the Japanese professors also, at times, dress in our costume,
yet repeated inquiries fail to find that any of them have been
taunted or spoken to or even noticed. I tried to fancy what my
experience would be if I, dressed in the graceful robes of a
Japanese, had ventured to appear on the streets in our cities,
or even in country villages. The attempt that some of the
Japanese make to appear in our costume is often most ludicrous. I saw a fellow the other day in a dress-coat almost big
enough to go round him twice, a tall hat which came down to
his eyes, with a wad of paper crammed in to hold it on, and white
cotton gloves many sizes too large. His appearance was like a

[1] The other day I read in a New York newspaper the account of a poor old man
actually snowballed to death by a lot of hoodlums. How such deviltry as this would
confirm the Japanese opinion that we were barbarians!

Fourth of July burlesque. Figure 217 is a rough sketch of him. He was a shabby-looking fellow and evidently did not belong to the higher classes. At the opening of the Exposition here

Fig. 217

one saw individuals dressed in our clothes in the most extraordinary way. One man had a suit altogether too small for him. The waist-coat and trousers did not meet within three or four inches and strings were used to tie them together. A good many were in full evening dress with the trousers tucked into long-legged boots which came to the knees. The oddest-looking travesty was another man, also with a dress-suit, the coat tails of which nearly touched the ground, while bright red sus-penders came outside his waistcoat! In respect to cloth-ing, the Chinese are much more dignified in adhering to their native costume, which, like the native costume of the Japanese, is more comfortable than ours. I had the greatest charity for them, however, when I recalled the attempts of our people to dress à la Japonaise.[1] As to their own dress I have noticed at the University that, while some of the Japanese professors appear in our clothing at times, they told me that on extremely hot days and on very cold days their own cloth-ing was more comfortable, but that in the laboratories their sleeves were constantly in the way.

At Enoshima I had a Japanese gown made for me, tied with an *obi*, which looked to me quite grand. It came down to

[1] One of these attempts we saw later on the stage in the *Mikado* of Gilbert and Sullivan, and it appeared equally preposterous to the Japanese.

within three inches of the heels; I asked Toyama if it was all right; he smiled and said it was not long enough, it should be two inches longer. Upon pressing him as to how it looked I found it had the same appearance to him that a countryman in our country might have to us with his trousers three inches too short! In other words, it looked "green." Thus their dress, careless as it looks to us with its loose folds and rather girlish appearance, has its precise lines and proportions. With the exception of China there is probably no country in the world where more thought or care is bestowed upon dress than in Japan. Official rank and station, material and color, design, form of knot, and other details are rigidly adhered to.

In Tokyo, and more especially in Yokohama, are many Chinese following their trades of shoemakers, tailors, etc. The men dress in their native costumes, and it is odd to see two or three of them fluttering down the street in beautiful gauze-like robes of blue with tunic-like breeches below and embroidered shoes. Although living among the Japanese, who do not like them, they are never molested. Within a year or so the two countries have been on the verge of war, and yet, while not amalgamating, they live together peaceably. The Chinese are treated in a Christian manner, as, indeed, they are in the eastern and middle United States, but the unchristian and brutal way in which the Pacific Coast States, and particularly California, have treated them only emphasizes the belief among the Japanese that we are barbarians. San Francisco, with its Protestant and Catholic churches, mission schools, and other good agencies, seems utterly helpless in affecting public opinion. It is depressing and hopeless to touch on these matters involving the missionary question and other agencies at work with the heathen abroad. But enough of this.

FIG. 218

The form of the axe with which wood is cut is very heavy and apparently as serviceable as ours. The blade is transverse to the handle as in the adze (fig. 218).

The sweet-potato cleaner I have since noticed belongs to a shop where they boil sweet potatoes, and children flock to it for a hot luncheon of one potato. The furniture of the shop consists of two immense kettles, a dozen baskets of sweet potatoes, nicely cleaned, and a little board for a counter on which are displayed a number of potatoes steaming hot. These places are scattered all over the city. It would be a good idea if a similar shop could be started in the poorer quarters of our cities. The Japanese sweet potato is rather tasteless, but evidently nutritious.

The grapes have come, light green in color, round in form, very juicy, with a grape, and slightly acid, flavor. They do not seem quite ripe, but doubtless they are very pleasant to eat when one is thirsty, and they are very cheap, a big bunch costing only two or three cents. Wherever the grapes are sold the fruit is always displayed in an attractive way: a few boards are placed together vertically and covered with some

FIG. 219

evergreen shrub, little wooden pegs stand out from the green upon which are hung the bunches of grapes (fig. 219). If the grapes are in a basket they rest on a cushion of evergreen. The fruit shop has other fruits in their season. After a lecture at the University the other day, my throat being dry, and having a long dusty ride before me, I endeavored to eat some grapes while riding through the streets. No matter how slyly I slipped a grape into my mouth the Japanese would notice it, smile, and probably comment on the strange habits of the barbarians.

Among the charms of the country are the restaurants and tea-houses. The waiters are all girls, so gentle in their behavior, so neatly dressed, and in every instance with their hair gracefully arranged. Figure 220 shows the prevailing style of hair-dressing. Sometimes one sees the folds of the bow standing vertical, with the larger fold above.

Fig. 220

In a vast city like Tokyo, with every street and lane crooked and narrow, it is almost impossible to find a place even with the most explicit directions. When Professor Chaplin and I endeavored to find the man who made the curious flower-holders of basket-work, it was a good two hours before we found him with the jinrikisha men doing their best. In our quest we came to a long flight of wide and steep stone steps, from the top of which we got a fine view of the city. It was marvelous to look across this great city and see the shipping in the

Bay of Yedo; not a chimney, not even a haziness: a marked
contrast to our smoke-begrimed cities. Of course there was
no wind, as on windy days it is very dusty and everything is obscured. On top of the abrupt hill which we ascended were a number of low sheds where one could sit
and admire the view and be served with tea by prettily
dressed girls. I induced one to permit me to make a sketch of
her head; thanks to her assumed or real diffidence she turned
her face away, and so I got an excellent sketch of her hair,
which is given in figure 220.

CHAPTER IX

UNIVERSITY WORK

September 11. The regular work of the University began this morning at eight o'clock with a meeting of the faculty, Dr. Hamao, the Vice-Director, presiding. Apologizing for the absence of Dr. Kato, the Director, whose mother was very ill, he proceeded in a slow and hesitating manner to make a few introductory remarks and expressed the hope that the term might be a pleasant one for both the teachers and the students. In the afternoon the senior Vice-Minister of Education gave a reception to the foreign professors of the University at the Educational Museum at Uyeno Park. It was an interesting gathering. The Medical College is officered by Germans; the School of Language has French, German, English, and Chinese teachers; and our branch of the University has four or five Englishmen, eight or nine Americans, a Frenchman, two Germans, and a number of Japanese assistant professors. The Japanese with few exceptions were in our dress, but the Chinese teachers were in their own costume, for they never change. The museum is a large, handsome, two-story building with a wing; a large library was in one of the lower halls and a long and spacious hall was filled with an extensive and interesting collection of educational apparatus from Europe and America—modern schoolhouses in miniature, desks, pictures, maps, models, globes, slates, blackboards, inkstands, and the minutest details of school appliances abroad. Despite the

fact that every object was familiar to me, it was a most interesting museum and a kind that our larger cities at home
should have. What a wise conception of the Japanese, entering as they were on our methods of education, that they should
establish a museum to display the apparatus used in the work.
Here was a nation spending nearly a third of its annual budget
on education, and in contrast Russia spending a half of one
per cent on the same department. On the second floor was a
museum of natural history, and with the exception of the
fishes it was rather poor; the fishes, however, were beautifully
prepared and mounted. There were nearly a hundred guests
present at the reception, including the wives of a number of
the teachers. After promenading through the various halls
we were led into a large room, where were spread refreshments
in the shape of pyramids of ice cream, cake, sandwiches, fruit,
and other food, with masses of flowers arranged by the only
people in the world who know how to handle them from sprout
to death. The affair would have done credit to the best cater-
ers at home, and in this well-ordered pedagogical museum,
with the elaborate lunch and all arrangements, one stood
bewildered and asked himself, "Are we in Japan?"

The Japanese officers, with Dr. Murray and whoever cared
to volunteer, served the various edibles, and it was interesting
to watch the Japanese when they passed the plates to a lady
and gentleman sitting together, offering to the man first
and then, recalling their instructions, instantly passing to
the woman. The absence of that deference and courtesy to
women, so universal in our country, though much less so in
Europe, is very marked here. In entering a carriage or jin-

rikisha the man will enter before his wife; in walking along the street the wife lags behind, at least four or five feet; and in various ways one observes the inferior position of women. Even when the Japanese, returning from abroad, would like to follow foreign ways, the wives would be embarrassed if they did. It would be as if our women, recognizing certain advanced ideas of dress or of customs (such as riding astride a horse), should still adhere to the old ways to avoid being conspicuous. This fact I was told by one of the Japanese professors. The Japanese women accept this condition meekly, for that has been the custom from immemorial times. The only thing that can be said in extenuation is that the Japanese women have far larger liberties than the women of any other Oriental nation.

On the day I began my lectures the Vice-Director of the University brought in a boy about fourteen years old who was to be my servant. Already I have found him very useful. He helps in the laboratory cleaning jars, scouring shells, and cleaning my blackboard every morning. To-day I set him at work assorting a lot of odd shells to see what he could do, and he managed to separate the genera and species very well; I also sent him off to collect some fresh-water shells and he brought back quite a collection of them. His dress consists of a sort of blue frock that several years ago had done service as a student's uniform, no uniform now

FIG. 221

being worn; for breeches he wears a pair of knit woolen drawers; his head is covered with a perfect mop of black hair, dry and clean. He was amazed and abashed when I asked him to stand while I sketched him (fig. 221). When I enter the room he gives me a bow that would certainly break my back if I attempted it.

I gave my first lecture September 12. The lecture room is in the second story of the building. It is furnished with a big blackboard, a desk with a number of drawers, and a large case in which I have a collection of objects to illustrate my lectures. There are a number of preparations in papier maché, illustrating the digestive organs of various animals; also models of nerve centres and other apparatus that will work in well with the course. The class is divided into two divisions of forty-five pupils each, so each lecture has to be given twice, which is somewhat exhausting. I am in love with my students already; it is a delight to teach such good boys, all greedy to learn. Their attention, their courtesy, and their respectful demeanor is an inspiration. Most of them are rationalists and a few may be Buddhists, so with these conditions I anticipate a delightful experience in presenting Darwinism pure and simple. Especially noticeable is their alert recognition of my drawings of various animals on the blackboard. These young men are sons of samurai, some of great wealth, others poor, but all modest and polite to one another and very quiet and attentive. Each one has jet-black hair and dark eyes and all are dressed in bluish-colored clothes, the hakama so like a divided skirt that it seems as if I had a class of girls. There is one large room, known as the professors' room, with neat straw matting, chairs, a large table upon which are the Yokohama morning papers, a few magazines, and the usual hibachi. Here one may beguile himself while waiting for the lecture time. During the forenoon a servant brings in a tray with cups, and a pot of delicious tea, which is refreshing. The members of the faculty are all pleasant men. The general officers of the University consist of a director, two vice-directors, curator, treasurer, and clerk, all extremely polite and attentive, and nothing could be more agreeable than my association with them and the position I occupy. Whatever I want in the way of apparatus is instantly secured for me, and the cases of which I am making the plans will be constructed at once.

At my house in the Yashiki the jinrikisha man whom I have hired by the month runs errands for me and is ready to do anything I can make him understand. The wife of another jinrikisha man, a rather plain, black-toothed creature (a hideous disfigurement of married women, who purposely take as much pains to blacken their teeth with some stain as we do to make our teeth white), though faithful and honest, comes in every evening to do the work of a chambermaid, washing my towels, blacking my shoes, etc., for the princely sum of three dollars a month. I have the whole house to myself, and I can scatter things from one end to the other. Rigid instructions have been given to the woman not to touch a thing on the tables or on the floor, and she obeys. It is rather lonesome here evenings, but I have so much writing to do that at every spare moment my pen is at work.

Figure 222 is a sketch of a Chinese shoemaker repairing my boots. In Tokyo and in Yokohama the Chinese find ample

employment in pursuing their various trades, and as tailors
and shoemakers they are very successful. There are very good
photographers among them and, of course, laundrymen. I
have had already a suit of clothes made by a Chinese tailor

FIG. 222

and a stout pair of shoes by a Chinese shoemaker at a much
less cost than at home.

This afternoon I visited the Industrial Exposition again
with a letter from the Director of the University to the
Director of the Exposition asking permission for me to sketch.
While I am permitted to sketch the building I must get permission from the exhibitors for the privilege of sketching their
objects. Mr. Kato is endeavoring to get me a letter which I
can show to the exhibitors; in the mean time I managed to get
a few more sketches, but with so much personal annoyance
from the interference of officials, who are doubtless obeying
instructions, and from the people crowding around me to see
the sketch, that I finally gave up in despair and left the

grounds. During the last hour I was there an officer followed me about apparently in the most careless manner, but watching me closely to see that I got no sketches. For the fun of it I led him a great tramp in and out through the alcoves and from one building to another. During this time I managed to make a few sketches, one of which I had longed to get. This object was a beautiful panel to hang against the wall. It was in a simple frame painted a dark red and was a study of morning-glories and other plants done in lacquer and other

Fig. 223

material on four planks of cedar, worm-eaten, with the grain rubbed down. It shows a waning moon in polished brass, the leaves in dark bronze, the flowers of the morning-glory in white-and-blue glazed pottery (fig. 223). The work is all in relief. Conceive for a moment making a design like this with blades of grass worn and ragged at the edges. The Japanese seemed to enjoy it, and it certainly was a most beautiful and fascinating object.

The very first time I rode to Tokyo, a few days after I landed, I noticed from the car windows in a railway cut through which we passed, a deposit of shells which I knew at

once to be a true Kjoekkenmoedding. I had studied too many
shell heaps on the coast of Maine not to recognize its character at once. I had waited for months for an opportunity to
visit it, fearing all the time that somebody would get there
before me. Dr. Murray, the Superintendent of Education, was
the only one to whom I told the nature of the deposit. Now
with matters started in my work at the University I made
arrangements to examine the deposit. First I had to get permission from the director of the railway to invade the property;
this I got through the Educational Department. Soon a letter
came from the principal engineer of the railway, as follows: —

To all platelayers
&c, &c, &c,

Allow the bearer (one of the professors of the Educational
Department) accompanied by his pupils to walk along the line
and examine any works they may wish, on Sunday, 16 inst.

They will keep clear of the trains and in no way interfere
with any of the works.

L. ENGLAND,
Principal Eng. &c, I.G.C.

With Mr. Matsumura and two of my special students I
started early in the morning, carrying a small basket but no
implements with which to dig, as from the letter I knew we
should not be allowed on the line with shovels and picks. We
rode to Omori, six miles from Tokyo, and then walked up the
line half a mile to the embankment. In the mean time I told my
students what we should find — ancient hand-made pottery,

worked bones, and possibly a few crude stone implements, and then gave a brief account of Steenstrup's discovery of shell heaps along the Baltic and also the shell heaps in New England and Florida. When we finally reached the place we began immediately to pick up remarkable fragments of ancient pottery and the students insisted that I must have been there before. I was quite frantic with delight and the students shared in my enthusiasm. We dug with our hands and examined the detritus that had rolled down and got a large collection of unique forms of pottery, three worked bones, and a curious baked-clay tablet. As there has always been a great interest as to the character of the aborigines of the country, and as this subject has never before been studied, it is considered an important discovery. I shall prepare a general paper for the "Popular Science Monthly," [1] and then more carefully work up some memoir.[2]

Monday, September 17, was a national holiday and a holiday at the University. I wish it were possible to record with pen and pencil the strange experiences of the day. I inquired of my students if anything of interest was going on, but could ascertain nothing definite. I did, however, find out that on this day there would be some important services with music at the temples. A beautiful temple in Uyeno Park would give us an opportunity to witness the ceremonies, and we loafed about in the crowd watching the people and forgetting our impatience in the presence of so many novel sights. The music in the big temple was to begin at ten o'clock. In com-

---

[1] Since published in *Popular Science Monthly*, January, 1879.
[2] Since published by the Imperial University, Tokyo.

pany with Dr. Murray, Professor Chaplin, and a Japanese
interpreter I stood in the broiling sun with a large crowd that
had collected. The temple resembled the Nikko temple, not
so magnificent, though extremely beautiful; within, the same
polish and brilliancy of gilt and ornamentation. It was so open
that from the outside everything going on within could be
distinctly seen. I got a good seat on the edge of the upper step,
where I could see the musicians, for I was naturally more interested in the music than in the services of the priests. I
learned from my students that each temple had its parish, or,
in other words, a church membership, every one professing the
faith belonging to one of the temples. The balcony outside
seems to be the sitting place for the worshipers, as, of course
they all sit in the customary attitude with legs bent under
them. The congregation of thirty or forty worshipers rather
obscured our view, the broad spacious temple floor being
reserved for the services and ceremonies of the priests. At ten
o'clock a big drum began to beat, first slowly and then with
rapidly increasing strokes, whereat the crowds flocked into the
temple yard, said their prayers at the foot of the broad flight
of steps, rubbed their hands, and flung their coins into a big
box which always stands in front of each temple. A contribu-
tion box is never passed around. Its counterpart is a big box,
four feet long or more, resting on the veranda or ground, with
transverse bars angular in section, an inch apart, forming the
upper face of the box, so that a coin thrown at it is bound to
slide into the box, and this is in service night and day. A man
going along the street offers up a devout prayer, tosses his
money at a distance of ten feet or more from the box, and

goes on. The box is often missed, and coins of low denominations are seen scattered about the balcony. It was curious to see a very old man dressed in our costume devoutly praying, at the same time rubbing his hands in an imploring manner, as they generally do in the attitude of prayer. Dr. Murray sent his interpreter to the rear of the temple to see if the authorities could be induced to allow us to go inside, giving him a dollar to assist his efforts, and he soon came back, having got permission for us to enter. So back of the temple we went; and, taking off our shoes, we were shown a place at one side corresponding to the position occupied by the musicians on the other side — a place which even the members of the church did not occupy. It was embarrassing, for hundreds of Japanese in crowds outside were curiously gazing at the novel sight of three barbarians conspicuously kneeling in such a place. The priests, all chastely dressed in purple, green, and other kinds of gauze robes, keen, intelligent-looking men, were going through their solemn ceremonies. The floor of the temple was one sheet of polished black lacquer and reflected the light like a mirror. How keenly I watched everything! The musicians interested me greatly: there was a flute, a small reed pipe, and two curious-look-ing instruments with tubes of bamboo standing vertically from an oval base. This instrument, called *sho*, is held in the two hands and blown into from the side, as in the sketch. There were also a

Fig. 224

tiny drum and a big drum each standing on a four-legged

support, and a flattened bell in a frame. Figure 224 is a sketch of the musicians. It was impossible to catch any air or strain. The music sounded weird and solemn. The sho kept up a continuous note, or rather a humming sound, which varied slightly, and the other instruments came in at

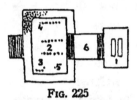

FIG. 225

intervals. The plan of the temple is shown in figure 225. It consists of a main hall, a short corridor with a short flight of steps descending to it, and a similar flight ascending to an inner hall. No words can describe the carving, elaborate decorations, and intricate details of the interior of these remarkable buildings, nor will I attempt it. In the sketch, 1 is the inner temple with tables upon which the food offerings were placed; 2 represents the position of two rows of priests; 3 represents our position; 4 the position of the orchestra; 5 represents the son of the leading priest, who was a great daimyo before the Revolution; and the little dots on the balcony indicate the members who were attending the services. After a long strain by the musicians the rows of priests, who had been kneeling, stood up; the two highest in rank walked in solemn step into the inner temple, two more descended the short flight of steps and stood in the passageway (6), two others stood where the priests had been kneeling, and two others stood behind us. Their head-coverings were of two kinds, one a ceremonial, black silk, bag-like affair, flattened on the sides and worn by lower officials (fig. 226); the other (fig. 227), a ceremonial device worn by daimyos. It was flattened sideways, was black, lacquered, and perched on the top of the head with an overhang behind. The ceremonies consisted in bringing in trays in which were food offerings to the departed shogun. Before bringing in the trays the priests tied a broad band of white paper over the nose and mouth so that their breath would not fall  upon the offerings. The trays were of light wood, natural, of course, square and shallow with the corners squared off. These trays rested on unglazed

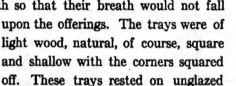

FIG. 226

FIG. 227

pottery stands of light red. The food offerings consisted of rice in two flattened balls, one upon the other, fish, vegetables, rice cakes, etc. These were in shallow plates of the same pottery material as the stands which supported the trays and were six or eight inches high (fig. 228). They were brought in as follows: a priest in the main hall would bring in one in his two hands, approach another priest, who would bow very low, and then take it; the first priest then made the same kind of a bow; then the second priest would carry it to a third priest, who bowed in the same profound manner, and having taken it would bow in turn. When the fourth priest had received it, he carried it with slow and measured step down the stairs to the

FIG. 228

passageway and passed it to the priest stationed there with the same dignified bowing; then the last priest ascended the flight of steps, offered it to one of the priests near the table in the inner sanctuary, who passed it to the second

one stationed there, and he finally placed it on the table in
a certain position. These last two priests were ex-daimyos.
As there were at least twenty of these offerings, all accompanied with the same solemn and profound obeisances, the
ceremony took a long time, though it was interesting throughout. During the whole time the orchestra kept up its weird
and mysterious music, and the crowd outside seemed to divide
its attention between this ceremony and the curious but intent
barbarians.

The musicians and all were on their knees and we sprawled
out the best we could, though it was very hard on the legs;
but the sight was indeed interesting. After the ceremony was
over the congregation on the balcony arose and walked across
the temple floor and down the flight of stairs to the passageway, and the priests courteously invited us to follow. Outside
the temple was a narrow table upon which were light wood
stands in the form of square trays resting on square boxes.

In the trays were unglazed
dishes holding food offerings
of various kinds, and on the
ground in front was a larger
tray. One is impressed with
the plain wood trays, tables,
and other furniture in this
land of beautiful lacquer. The
method of Shinto is to use

Fig. 229

this unpainted and unlacquered wood and unglazed pottery (fig. 229). The priests gave each of us a cup of saké, the
most delicious I ever drank. The cup was of unglazed pot-

tery with the crest of the Tokugawa family in relief in the centre; also two rice cakes, a red and a white one, with the same crest impressed upon them, the Tokugawa family being patrons of the temple; and so we had joined in the communion of the Shinto faith. Our missionaries would consider that we had been idolatrous, but so long as the priests had been liberal enough to invite us we could be as free from bigotry as they.

After these novel experiences we visited again the Industrial Exhibition, which is near by. The naval band, composed entirely of Japanese, had been trained in our school of music, with our instruments and uniforms. Had we not seen their faces we should have supposed them to be Occidentals. The Japanese leader led with his baton swinging modestly, and nearly all the members of the band beat time with their feet in an almost imperceptible manner. You will wonder what my opinion was of their playing. The fact, so marvelous, that the Japanese, with instruments and music so remote from ours, should be able to accomplish so much, makes one favorably prejudiced in judging of their performance. The swing and blare of the trumpet is always inspiring, even if done poorly; yet, critically, I must say that their performance of most of the pieces was like the playing of simple music by an ordinary country band at home. To one with no ear for music it would sound very well; the air was full of sound; but any one with an ear could hear discords and recognize the faulty time. The solo bugle parts were given with a freedom that was admirable; they would often hurry, but would get back all right. In the overture to the "Calif of Bagdad," the part which goes up higher and higher was played to perfection. I have as yet heard nothing in Japan that we could regard as music from our standpoint, and so the performance of our music by Japanese was as startling to me as if a North American Indian should suddenly be able to produce an Inness or a Bierstadt. Among other pieces were the beautiful Danube Waltz, Grand Fantasia of Meyerbeer's "Huguenots," selections from Gounod's "Faust," and others of a similar type, all arranged in the simplest manner.

In riding through the streets one notices now and then a shop sign in our language, to attract the few foreigners that may go by and to look rather "swell" to Japanese who have learned English. Here is one I saw on a tailor's shop: "The place build for making dresses according to the fashion of different countries." This is simple compared to some that have been published in English papers.

In watching children on the street their habits and behavior seem more and more like those of our children. When you first see them in their odd costumes, the hair shaved from the heads in so grotesque a style, and with their curious gait as they clump about on their wooden sandals, you identify them as children, but from another planet. They fly kites, spin tops, make mud pies, or cakes, also make little rag babies, and curious objects some of them are. I have seen one child run up to another from behind and clap her hands over the other's eyes and hold on until the right guess is given; they ride on one another's backs, play battledore and shuttle-cock, and they play a game similar to our jackstones. I have never seen them play marbles, for they have none; or ball as we play it, — though they pat a ball to see how many times they can make it bounce from the ground, — nor race with one another, though you see them playing counting-out games, blind man's buff, and a number of games in which they stand in a row or march around in single file. The mothers play "creepy mouse" with the children as we do, only it is "creepy fox." They seem specially fond of playing around the foot of a large tree, making little paths in the sand, and sticking up little things for houses, temples, bridges, etc. I have often seen in a house a large shallow dish holding water in which was an old tangled root, a few little plants growing on it, and pathways winding about, bridges spanning some chasm, with here and there a little toy house. These things are bought in sets, and young as well as old seem to enjoy the simple and diminutive landscapes. It is the enjoyment of these apparently infantile pleasures that has given us the idea that the Japanese are essentially an effeminate nation, and yet in their fight with the Formosan savages and in the late Satsuma rebellion they showed the fiercest courage and fighting valor.

It is a pleasant sight to see people walking together, often holding hands, and the women and children usually do so. A grown-up daughter and her mother or grandmother, in nine cases out of ten, will hold each other's hands as they pass along; fathers always hold their children's hands, and if anything of interest is going on, will hold the children high on their shoulders to see the sight. From the reticent way the people behave we imagine they have no sentiment; they were supposed never to kiss; and it is a rare sight to see a mother kiss her child; even when she does she scarcely does more than snuggle her nose in the child's neck. I asked Professor

Toyama to tell me frankly if people or lovers never kissed. He said reluctantly, "Why, yes, but never before other people or in public"; and so far as I could learn from him nothing seems coarser or more ill-bred to a Japanese than the sight of Americans, or English, kissing their wives good-bye at the station; a matter that with us means nothing more than an affectionate good-bye or welcome. We have only to realize how some of our customs — such as dancing, for example — appear to them to understand how some of their customs which are equally innocent appear to us. Toyama told me that the oddest sight to him, when he came to America to go to the University of Michigan, was to see people at a railway station bidding good-bye and kissing all round, and school-girls flying to each other; but for men to commit such an act was the height of absurdity to him.

To-night some sort of a festival is being celebrated. I have been standing on the street for an hour watching the crowds,  who were hilariously looking on at a pantomime which was being played on a temporary stage erected for the purpose. While enjoying it along came two carts dragged by children holding light-colored paper lanterns. The carts were rude two-wheeled vehicles built up roughly with boards and packed full of

Fig. 230

children beating drums, screaming, and laughing as only children will. The framework above was elaborately deco-

rated with paper figures, colored cloth, and a liberal supply
of lanterns. As the cart went by in a crowd I was only able
to get an idea of its appearance (fig. 230.) A few men went
along to steady or to direct the cart. It was an enlivening
sight, the children swarm-
ing like ants, everybody
laughing and shouting.
Japan is certainly a paradise for children, and the
charm of it all is that in
every gathering of this sort,
and at all times, the older
people join in the sports.
The children have their *matsuri*, or festival, rigging up
a little cart with lanterns
and dragging it through
the streets in imitation of

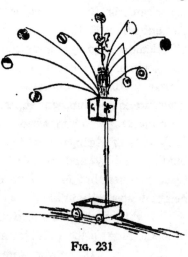

FIG. 231

FIG. 232

the larger cars. Figure 231 is a sketch of the children's attempt at getting up a matsuri car, and they
were having as much fun out of it as if they had
been dragging a big car. The lanterns pendent
from bamboo poles were of the brightest colored
paper, and as they dragged the cart along everything was dancing and jiggling. On the street were
children with long bamboo poles, on the ends of
which, cut out of paper, were large butterflies
which were made to flutter when the children were
running against the wind (fig. 232).

September 21. The markets are getting full of fruit. A species of persimmon, bright red in color, is delicious; the grapes are ripening; and the pears, though apparently unripe, are prettily displayed piled in triangular form in shallow tubs lined with evergreen (fig. 233). Everything in the market

FIG. 233

looks clean and is displayed with much taste: the onions shine, the turnips are white as snow, so thoroughly are they scoured. After seeing a market here you are never able to forget the condition of things that are brought to our markets at home.

In company with two friends I saw three Japanese dancing girls, whom we had engaged beforehand, one of them quite pretty, the other two very plain. We had two rooms, the sliding screens being removed between them, and candles arranged to throw light upon the girls, one of whom danced while the other two kept up a continuous twanging on a guitar-like affair. The dancer walked around in a monotonous way, the body swaying, the head, the arms, and the legs assuming various attitudes. It seems that the selections have various names, and the gestures are intended to represent rowing a boat, gathering flowers, and the like. A folding fan was twirled, opened, and closed to accompany the various attitudes. The dresses were of beautiful silk crape. While this was going on, the maids of the house brought up, first, sixteen hard-boiled eggs, for three of us, and afterwards fish, lobster, cake, and other things, enough for a dozen hungry persons, and we had just risen from a hearty dinner. Of course we could not eat a particle of food, and I inwardly groaned to think of the precious moments I was losing on the various matters that absorbed my time, and was glad when the show was over, though ethnologically the exhibition was very interesting.

September 22. 'To-day and yesterday I have been hard at work writing up an account of the Omori shell heaps and making drawings of the pottery found there. There are so few books to consult in this part of the world that it is difficult to write on any subject of a scientific character.

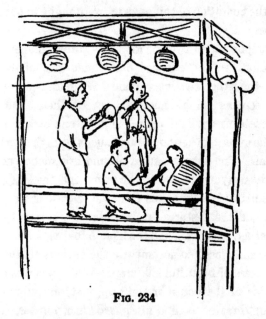

Fig. 234

On the day we visited the temple there were a number of stages erected along the road leading to it, and on these stages were men performing with a big and a little drum, a bell, and a flute. These men play hour after hour without showing the least fatigue. I listened in vain to detect a strain of what we regard as music and gave up in despair; I not only could not understand the music, but was equally ignorant of what it was all about. Figure 234 gives an idea of the appearance of these musicians. One has on his head a towel folded in such a way as to resemble a bonnet.

FIG. 235

Figure 235 is a sketch of one of my special students sorting specimens. The tousled hair is due to the fact that before the Japanese adopted the simple sanitary method of dressing the hair, the head was shaved on top and a queue was worn. They find it very hard to part their hair or to make it lie down properly after years of shaving. I made this sketch in order to show the Japanese dress, which is hard to describe. It will be observed that the sleeves are sewed up part way, and this makes the only pockets he has, one in each sleeve. He has a foreign undershirt; otherwise his arms would be bare. Before three hundred years ago the Japanese wore tight sleeves like ours; even two hundred years ago the sleeves were very close, so Mr. Kashiwagi told me. The skirt is really a voluminous pair of trousers opened at the sides; on the back is a stiff piece standing erect, and only samurai are privileged to wear this garment.

Fig. 236

Daughters of samurai may also wear the same garment when they go to school, thus insuring them a little more respect and consideration. Figures 236 and 237 are sketches of young boys belonging to the Preparatory School, where they learn English before entering the University. I often watch them out of the windows in my laboratory; they are handsome, manly little fellows, all so gentle and polite in their demeanor, and they look at you so kindly that you feel at once sympathy and affection for them. You never seem to

Fig. 237

see expressions of malice, contempt, or disdain. I do not mean that they may not have such expressions, but I have never seen them.

Since the Exhibition has been open I have visited it seven times and have managed to get a few sketches every time. Figure 238 represents a girl in the act of doing up her hair. It was life-size, carved out of wood in high relief, and was extremely graceful, the drapery being colored. It was difficult to sketch in the

FIG. 238

midst of a crowd, which was, nevertheless, a placid sea compared to a similar exhibition crowd at home. A flower- or plant-holder (fig. 239) is an ingenious piece of work and one of some little difficulty to construct. It will be seen that the three staves forming the lower bucket are extended to enter into the structure of three smaller buckets above, and these three in turn contribute a stave to form an upper bucket of the same size. The wood was so

FIG. 239

white and clean that the whole object was perfection itself.

Figure 240 is another bucket for flowers, much smaller, but
following the same idea in construction; it was
about two feet high and a most dainty object.
The smaller bucket on the right was oval in
shape. A flower-pot made of porcelain, at least
three feet long, with blue decoration of pine running across the side, and containing a dwarf
pine, was a striking object (fig. 241). A curious

FIG. 240

device quite new to me was displayed in one of the alcoves at

FIG. 241

the fair. There was a large bamboo frame
on which were stretched two sheets of a
very fine netting, or muslin; at all events,
a kind of cloth that you could see through.
These were about an inch apart, and on
one was painted a foreground of dark trees and a middle
ground of distant hills; on the other netting was a strong
sketch of the great Fuji. It was made to look distant on
account of the netting through which you looked, and the

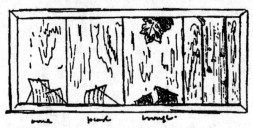

FIG. 242

illusion was perfect. Another of these wonderful framed decorations I managed to draw, and a sketch of it is shown in figure
242. It was made on the base of a rotten and worm-eaten

cedar, the grain conspicuous, and was as dainty an object as one could imagine. It was three and one half feet long and a deep red frame enclosed it. The design consisted of the trunk of some tree, or possibly a grapevine, with one leaf showing. It was made of bamboo, green in color, and probably of lacquer. The three vessels, only the sails of which show above the frame, were made respectively of bone or ivory, pearl and bronze, or bronze lacquer, all in relief. The sails were made of narrow strips of cloth laced together, the lacing delicately carved, and the whole design illustrated well the conceits of the Japanese artist. There was also a lacquered cabinet, of

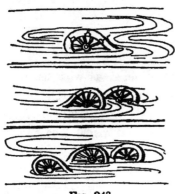

FIG. 243

exquisite workmanship, with three drawers and the oddest motive for a design that I ever saw, consisting of wheels carved out of ivory and half submerged in swirling currents of water (fig. 243). It will be observed that the wheel is not perfectly round. This was to heighten the illusion that the water was tearing by at a great rate. The hubs of the wheels formed the knobs by which the drawers were drawn out; but who but a Japanese would think of a decoration for a cabinet of drawers of half-submerged cart wheels twisted out of shape? It is no wonder that the world goes wild over Japanese decorative art. I must state here that I have not yet learned anything about the mythology and folklore of Japan. I am too much absorbed in present things to find time to look backward, but doubtless many, if not all, the motives of decoration so mysterious to us refer to some well-known story or myth of the Japanese.

In figure 244 are given two forms of shovels and a hoe. The cutting edges are slightly curved inward and this insures the cutting of roots in digging, whereas in our shovel and hoe, rounding the other way, the roots are liable to slip off sideways. In the shovels the

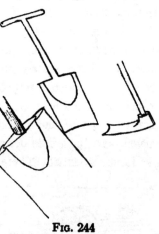

FIG. 244

wooden handle, instead of being riveted as with us, runs into grooves in the metal. In figure 245 is shown a serviceable form of hoe used on roads. The handle is of bamboo about three feet long, light and strong, and the body of the hoe is basket-work connecting with the handle by a bail with an edge of iron. The workman holds the iron bail firmly at any angle he wishes in digging or scraping, and

FIG. 245

a mass of dirt can be instantly dumped by letting go the bail. The basket-work of the bail makes it very light.

CHAPTER X

ANCIENT POTTERY AND THE SHELL HEAPS AT OMORI

To-day Dr. Murray, with his interpreter, and I visited the shell heaps at Omori, taking with us two coolies to bring back whatever we collected. A short walk from Omori station brought us to the place, and we began immediately to dig, the coolies with their hoes and we with trowels. In the course of two hours we had dug down an immense mass of stuff, quite filling the deep ditch beside the track and getting a good many fragments of pottery and other things. While eating our lunch, feeling dirty and hot, we told the coolies that unless we dug the stuff back again we should be arrested, and they immediately set to work, and not only cleared out the ditch,

FIG. 246

but hoed it all back again up the embankment, smoothed it down perfectly, and set out a number of small trees and bushes; indeed, there was no evidence that we had disturbed anything. I have never learned of the condition of the place after a good downpour of rain. I was fortunate enough to find two perfect pots and one rude stone implement at the top of the deposit; also three horn implements and one of bone.

For the last few days I have been making drawings of the

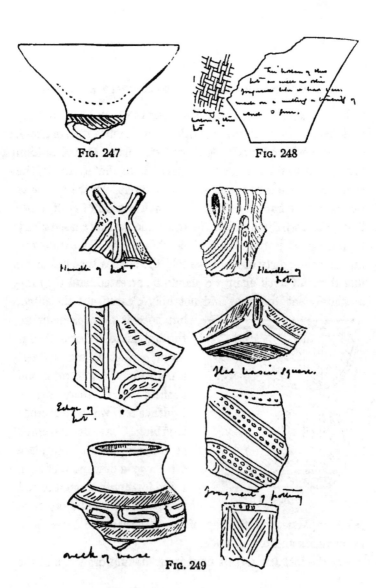

Fig. 247

Fig. 248

Fig. 249

fragments of the pottery, and the diversity of ornamentation is remarkable. All the pots and fragments are drawn half-size unless otherwise marked. Figure 246 was found at the bottom of the deposit. Traces of bright red cinnabar were found on the inner side of this piece; outside it was black and burnt and the interspaces were cord-marked. Figure 247 represents a bowl with black walls, the base being gone; figure 248, another

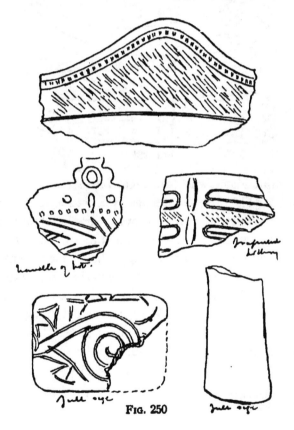

Fig. 250

bowl, the base marked with matting of simple weave; figures
249 and 250 show other pieces, some of them rims, handles or
knobs. The two pieces at the bottom of figure 250 represent
a curious clay tablet and the only stone implement; figure
251, the bone and deer-horn implements. I am told by Jap-

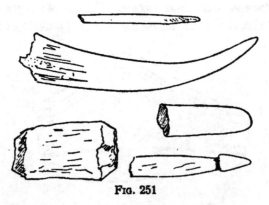

Fig. 251

anese antiquarians, who take great interest in the matter,
that nothing like these objects has ever been found in Japan.
As the University has a number of lithographic stones I purpose to draw whatever we may get and the University prom-
ises to publish any memoir I may make on the subject and
send it to various societies abroad. I hope in this way to start
a set of scientific publications, which may be sent in exchange
to institutions, and thus build up a scientific library. With
this material I have started a little room at the University as
a beginning of an archæological museum.[1]

Mr. Fukui came in last night to see my drawings, and I had

[1] This was the inception of their large archæological museum and their publications which already comprise many volumes.

a long talk with him on Japanese customs. He explained everything I asked about as far as he could, and I learned a great many new things. The samurai class, of which he was one, were the retainers of the daimyos, lords of the provinces. They represented the highest class, and until within a few years were permitted to wear two swords; a short one thrust inside the inner fold of the band which goes around the waist and the long sword stuck into the outer fold of the sash. By an edict of the Emperor, the wearing of swords was prohibited; no Occidental nation has yet had the faintest appreciation of the sacrifice made when the edict was obeyed out of devotion and loyalty to their sovereign. The big sword used in the two hands was to fight with, the smaller sword to finish the work of the larger sword. Mr. Fukui told me about the feudal practice of executions, a few of which he had witnessed. The professional executioner was selected from the Eta class, the lowest social group, — outcasts, in fact (the Government has lately abolished the distinction). The executioner inherited the clothes of the victim, so he was very careful to pull the dress down from the neck and up from the knees, as when the condemned was kneeling, with the head thrust forward, the keen-edged sword would not only go through the neck like a flash, but would even cut the knees; and but for the solicitude of the executioner the clothes would be ruined!

The samurai used to come together once a year to examine their blades. The name of the maker is cut on that portion of the blade which fits into the handle, the handle being held by a little wooden pin. These were really guessing parties, and the determination of the maker of the blade had to be made by an examination of the blade alone; the color of the steel, the depth of temper, the curious wavy lines made by the union of the steel edge with the soft iron into which it is welded. After all had recorded their guesses the handles were taken off the swords and the signatures read. In handling the blade they use the long sleeve of their outer garment to rest it upon, never permitting the hand to touch the blade; in drawing it from the scabbard the cutting edge must always turn toward the holder. Mr. Fukui explained to me a number of courtesies observed in regard to the sword, which was called the "Soul of the Samurai," but I did not get the information clearly enough to record.

I had repeatedly observed that young men in the street were never accompanied by girls unless it was a father with his little daughter. The girls are always seen alone, or in company with other girls, or with their mothers. Rarely do you see a young man bowing to one of the opposite sex. I asked Mr. Fukui bluntly how many girls he counted among his acquaintances, or knew well enough to invite them to go to the Exhibition with him. He laughed at the idea, and admitted that he did not know a single girl. I could hardly believe it, and told him, much to his astonishment, that at home young men invited girl friends to drive, to picnics, concerts, boat sails, and the like. He was frankly amazed and said such social manners were unknown in Japan. When he calls to see a friend, if by chance a sister or daughter is present, no matter how well he may have known her when she was a child, the girl politely bows and retires, and if by chance they meet in the street she holds her parasol or umbrella down and he turns his head away. He told me this was the custom among the lower samurai; the upper samurai bow politely under similar circumstances. Afterwards I asked Professor Toyama if his experiences had been the same and he confirmed all that Mr. Fukui had said. Said he, "I do not know a single young lady"! It is only within a few years that the husband and wife have been seen walking in public side by side, and that only in rare cases, by radicals who approve of foreign methods; nearly always when you see a husband and wife walking in the street the wife is from five to ten feet behind her husband; and a husband and wife riding together in a jinrikisha is an embarrassing sight. Professor Toyama said, "When I see such a sight the man turns red in the face, and if he does n't, then I turn red in the face." He said such men are called by a name which signifies "long hair in the nose"; for a man who has long hair in his nostrils is supposed to be led about by his wife, or, as we say, "henpecked," a name as strange to them as their name for henpecked is to us. My Japanese informant is now twenty-two years old and I asked him if he intended to get married. He said, "Certainly." "But," I asked, "how can you find a wife if you have no girl friends among your acquaintances?" He said the affair is always arranged by friends or "go betweens." If a man signifies his desire to be married, his family or friends find out for him some desirable mate; he communicates with the family, expressing a wish and asking permission to call, and sees his possible future wife for the first time. If they are apparently agreeably disposed, the information is conveyed in some way, and he does not see her again until the wedding. "But," I asked, "how do you know that she is not indolent, quick-tempered, or something of that sort?" He said these matters are carefully inquired into before betrothal. He also added: "In the American way of approaching the subject, the girl always appears different from what she really is; she dresses to allure and behaves to win; while in our way, which we think infinitely better, matters pursue an even course without emotion, but with consideration for the future happiness of the parties." However absurd or unromantic this method appears to us, the divorce rate is much lower than with us. In Japan, within my limited observation, the married people appear to be happy, smiling, and contented. With this rigid separation of the sexes socially, the boys and girls of Japan lose a great many innocent and happy experiences. When we recall the picnics, candy parties, and other parties at home, amateur theatricals, sleigh rides, boating, coasting, and similar gatherings, it seems as if our social ways in that respect were far better, even for the girls. I am not sure about it, as my point of view in many things is repeatedly changed by my experiences here.

Last Monday I gave a strong lecture on Evolution, and now the class expresses an impatient desire to have a course on the subject, but I shall not have time to prepare it until I get back from America in the spring. A student from another class came to me to-day and asked permission to attend my lectures, and so far the students seem much interested. Certainly I have never had students pay stricter attention; this, however, would be natural, as they are listening to a strange language and that spoken somewhat rapidly.

The one-storied block of houses, with four or five tenements and front doors opening on the street, is a recent idea here. Before the Revolution in 1868 this form of house was not known, the tenements in the city were built like the yashiki, in a square, facing inward, with one big gate used on ceremonial occasions, and at each side little entrances through which the people daily passed. The Kaga Yashiki, where we live, has an imposing gateway which I have never seen open, and some distance from it a little entrance, closed at night, with a gate-keeper close by in a little room, who, knowing the people living within, would let us in late at night. The present mode of building is more economical and will be the method in the future. Each house has a little garden bordered by a light bamboo fence.

There is a small portion of the city set apart for foreigners, and no foreigner can have a residence outside this limit unless he is a Government officer; as the Imperial University is sustained by the Government the instructors are regarded as Government officers and are privileged to reside in any part of the city. In the Kaga Yashiki, four miles or more from the foreign concession, we are in the midst of Japanese life pure and simple. I often go out of the yashiki gate (where there is always a gate-keeper) and wander up and down the thoroughfare, or into side streets, to enjoy the many odd sights — the little low shops, the front entirely open in the daytime, and the stock of goods in some cases moved out and spread on the ground. I have often waited fifteen or twenty minutes for the shopkeeper, who may have gone off for half a day. I have taken something from the little shop-like shelves and carried it in to the shopkeeper next door to ask him to tell the absent man that I wanted it. I could have run off with a pocketful of small articles with the greatest ease.[1]

In figure 252 I give a rough sketch of my room, which is a long, high-studded room, a drawing-room, in fact, thirty feet

FIG. 252

long, back of which is the dining-room, separated by folding doors and which I now use as a bedroom. The table, or desk, with student lamp, I use for my journal and correspondence; the next table I use as a catch-all, though somehow or other the other tables catch a good many things that do not belong to them. The farther table, the round one, I reserve for my shell-heap work and a few memoirs relating to the subject; the desk in the corner contains all my scientific notes and the

[1] Such honesty might be found in our country villages, but in our large cities never, while the above experience, repeated many times, was in the vast city of Tokyo. In this allusion to one of the many phases of the honesty of the people one must remember that in our cities, outside thermometers are screwed to the wall, dippers are chained to the fountain, and so common is the pilfering of soap and towels from public conveniences that devices are invented such as a fluid soap, its receptacle screwed to the wall to guard against this mean and petty stealing.

special work I am doing on the Brachiopods, so I move my lamp from one table to another as necessity requires. In this room I write night after night undisturbed by a single caller; outside, absolute peace and quiet reigns; indeed, the only sound that reaches one's ears is the distant sound of some high notes of some one slightly exhilarated by saké; for these people, when in that condition, seem inclined to sing instead of to fight, as is the common impulse with the Anglo-Saxon and the Irish, and particularly the Irish.

I saw a curious article for sale the other day in the form of a curved bamboo with a large wooden ball affixed to the end. I gave up the puzzle and finally asked the man what it was,

Fig. 253

and he smilingly showed me by holding the loop over his shoulder and moving it back and forth, literally pounding his back with the ball (fig. 253). This pounding is supposed to be good for rheumatism, and one often sees children pounding with both their fists the back of some old person. This simple contrivance enables one to do it for himself, at the same getting a certain amount of exercise.

In presenting paper currency objection is always made if the edge of the bill is torn ever so slightly. The result is that but little torn currency is seen in circulation; in fact, none at all except some bill torn slightly at the point of folding. The paper is thicker and seems smoother than ours, and though somewhat soiled, the bills are always whole and never present the worn and dirty condition of our bills. It may be that the poorer classes never handle so large a piece of money as a bill, but the cleanly habits of the Japanese would also account for it.

In figure 254 is the roughest sketch of the zoölogical laboratory of the University where my special students work. Besides this room, which is a long, narrow apartment, I have

Fig. 254

two more on the other side of the passageway. Figure 255 is a plan of the main University building. The frontage on the street must be nearly two hundred feet; from the main building three wings run back, between which are two long, low buildings, one story high, connected with the wings by a narrow passageway, on the railing of which I made the sketches of boys (figs. 236, 237). I have one of these long buildings. The room marked (1) is my lecture room upstairs, and beneath this is a hall, twice the length, which I am to use as a museum. Besides this building there is a handsome hall

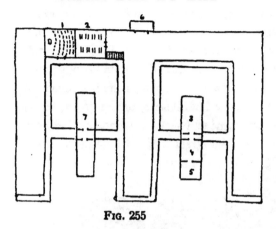

FIG. 255

by itself, a library building with many other buildings for mining and smelting ores, dormitories for the students and others, forming a little village by itself, there being several hundred students with a host of officers, under-servants, laborers, etc.

The Asiatic Society of Japan has invited me to give the opening address at their meeting October 13, and I shall speak of the Omori pottery, and the evidences of an early race in Japan.

Saturday afternoon there was an autumn meeting of the Tokyo Athletic Club made up almost exclusively of Englishmen who are attachés of the British Legation. A number came from Yokohama, representatives of the Athletic Club there. The games were held on a large parade ground near the Imperial Naval College, a broad, flat field, and as I stood there I could hardly realize that I was not at home about to witness a baseball game. It was a beautiful day, as all fall days are

in Japan. There were some sixty or seventy men as contest-
ants, and intermingled were a number of Japanese, and in a
pavilion were a few ladies. It seemed so homelike and natural;
but this illusion was immediately dispelled upon looking about
and seeing the dense crowds leaning against the ropes, all
Japanese, all bareheaded and of all sizes, babies on the backs
of little children and women; and such chattering as they kept
up! A brick wall along the street had a fringe of Japanese
lining the top (fig. 256), as unlike home in appearance as

FIG. 256

anything could be, and yet betraying the universal curiosity
of man, shared also by his nearest relatives, the monkeys. The
native brass band belonging to the Marine College provided
the music and played very well. In the medleys the strains of
"Yankee Doodle" and "We won't go home till morning," etc.,
were reminders of home. The sports consisted of foot races,
hurdle races, jumping, throwing the hammer, three-legged
races, etc. It was a great rest and change for me and most
enjoyable.

On our return to the yashiki Dr. Murray had a carriage
with two horses and I followed behind in a jinrikisha;
though the horses went off at a smart trot my man easily kept

up with them, and though the distance was nearly five miles the
man did not show the slightest fatigue. The endurance of these
men is always a matter of interest to a foreigner. In riding
behind the carriage I had an opportunity to realize what a
novelty the carriage and its occupants were, for everybody
turned round and stared at it. After the carriage passed I
saw two little girls bowing to one another in the manner of the
English ladies they had seen, with the head moving a little
sideways in perfect mimicry, and the other day I saw a
woman make a motion of smoking a cigar by pursing the lips
as I rode by, though I was not smoking.

Sunday I took my sketching-block and started off expressly
to sketch the shop signs, of which there are so many different
kinds. In our country we have a few which are everywhere
familiar; the mortar for an apothecary, a North American
Indian for a tobacco store, a watch for a watchmaker, a long-
legged boot for a shoemaker, and a few others. Here every
kind of a shop will have its symbol in the form of some huge
carving or covered framework. Over every shop is a light
though permanent wooden
awning, and most of the signs
hang from a straight beam
which runs out from the main
roof and is propped up on this
awning; some of these supports have a little roof built
over the sign, either to protect
it or to add to its importance. Figure 257 represents the
sign of a grocer's shop or a sugar shop, a huge bag of paper

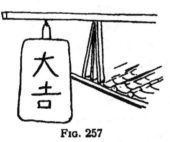

Fig. 257

painted white with the characters painted black. Figure 258
is a large tassel of hempen strands and indicates a place

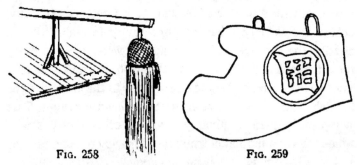

FIG. 258   FIG. 259

where one may buy rope, netting, and the like. Figure 259 is

a very common sign, made of
a plank, two or three feet long,
painted white with the shopkeeper's name upon it in black,
and represents the pattern of a
Japanese stocking. Figure 260

FIG. 260   FIG. 261

is a standing sign on the ground, and the ornamental symbol in high relief shows where brushes may be

bought. Figure 261 represents a
place where rice cakes are sold; the
cakes are thin and look like huge
wafers. Figure 262 indicates where
an eye doctor may be found; the
sign is black with gilt writing and
brass mountings. Figure 263 is an

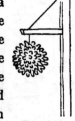

FIG. 262

odd-looking sign; it is round, made out of thick   FIG. 263
paper and painted white, and is about a foot and a half

in diameter; it is the invariable sign for a confectioner's store, the sign representing in an exaggerated form the Japanese sugar plum; our sugar plum has similar

FIG. 264

prominences, but very small ones. Figure 264 is also an odd sign, and when I sketched it I had no idea what it represented. A curious rattling sound of pounding was heard, and looking into the shop I found two men beating gold leaf, and on the sign are represented two leaves of gold. Figure 265 is the sign of a candle shop, the candle in white on a black ground, in relief. Figure 266 resembles a large six-cornered box with a fringe of black hair hanging from the bottom of it, indicating a shop where artificial hair may be bought, for I saw wigs for sale inside. Figure

FIG. 265

267 is a seal-cutter's sign; it always stands on the ground. Nearly everybody uses a seal, and they have the most compact and ingenious contrivances to carry a seal with its red pigment in the smallest possible compass; they stamp

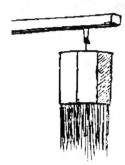

FIG. 266

FIG. 267

their bills, receipts, letters, etc. The seal-cutter's sign, meaning stamp, is very common, and I learned my first

Chinese character by observing the resemblance a portion of it bore to a capital P in stamp. Figure 268 is the universal sign of a money-changer or broker. It is a round disk of wood with a smaller circle cut out on either side, and is a conventional form signifying money. Figure 269 indicates a comb shop, and this comb was about three feet long.

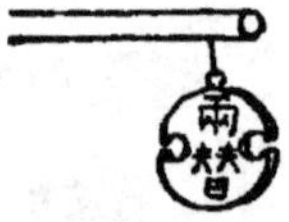

FIG. 268

Figure 270 not only represents an umbrella shop, but a modern foreign umbrella, their own kind, made of oiled paper, was very heavy and particularly clumsy and the people took readily to our form, and it is quite commonly seen on the streets used as a parasol as well.

FIG. 269

There are many more kinds of signs, and I hope to get them in my wanderings round the city, but you may imagine how odd the streets appear with these large and conspicuous objects of various kinds projecting from the front of the shops. These shops are rarely over one story, unpainted or painted black, so that they appear dingy, and the signs are rarely anything more than black and white.

FIG. 270

You can thus realize what a striking object in the gray street is, for instance, a girl walking along dressed for company, her hair black and shining like their beautiful lacquer, her sash, or obi, strikingly brilliant in color, with face whitened with powder, bright red lips, and the whitest of stockings and the cleanest of sandals. These touches of color in the midst of a gray street with quaint signs are particularly conspicuous, and at intervals compact displays of

blue-and-white porcelain and yellow fruit give the streets
an appearance that is always fascinating. Added to all these
novelties are the various street cries of peddlers who sell fish,
men who mend pipes or tinware, junk-dealers; and to-day, I
heard an extraordinary cry from a fellow who sold ladders.
When I get home remind me to give you the newspaper
dealer's cry and the ladder cry.[1]

The peddlers of candy often have a little exhibition of some
kind to attract children in order to sell them candy. Once or
twice I have regarded them as something akin to our hand-
organ men, and have given them a few pennies, whereupon
they have offered me a handful of candy, which, if there were
no children about, I have refused with thanks, knowing too
well that it would be flavorless and insipid. I met a peddler
lately who imitated the cries of a crow, pig, goose, and calf,
and did it to perfection. I made a sketch (fig. 271) of a good-
natured old man who, to draw a crowd of children, had a form
of glass cut into a number of facets and looking through it
many images could be seen. He had a number of these in
handled frames which were given to the children to look
through while he danced about and made all sorts of funny
motions; he also had some bright-colored paper butterflies on
sticks and these he would twirl. In a box was his candy to
sell. I sat in my jinrikisha while I sketched him, and had only
time to get the old man and one child, but when you look
at the sketch imagine a crowd of children with mothers looking
on. When he saw what I was about, he laughed, but kept up
his antics, and the children laughed too. When I finished my

[1] Alas, they are all forgotten!

sketch, which was made in a hurry, as many were staring over
my back at the drawing, I gave him two cents, for which he
thanked me with a very low bow and gave me a dozen sticks
of candy. I saw a mistake had been made, and that he was not
dancing for money; however, the candy was declined with

Fig. 271

thanks. Then he offered it to the jinrikisha man, who would
not take it, and so he reluctantly put it back in his box and
went on performing and dancing in the happiest spirit. Suddenly a bright thought occurred to him and he opened the box,
took out a handful of candy again, and, making a motion
to me, said something in which I understood the words for
"present" (*shinjo*), "children" (*kodomo*), and "you" (*anata*),
and gave it all to the little ones about him; the children accepted it and smilingly thanked me. A few days after, I met
the old man performing on the street and he thanked me
again, and this, by the way, is a custom that surprises you.

You buy some trifle in a shop, and passing the place a week after, the shopkeeper recognizes you and thanks you again.

Saturday was the day appointed to name a child of the Emperor who was born last week, and all the shops displayed the national flag, a great red disk on a white ground. It gave a very gay appearance to the long streets.

A ride along the great moat which surrounds the castle is very picturesque. Before the Revolution the Shogun dwelt within the enclosure, which is surrounded by huge stone walls slanting to the water of the moat, which is like a wide canal. There are now many buildings within used for Government purposes. The roadway bordering the moat is smooth and level and runs for a mile or two, as it encircles the enclosure, turning at times as it follows the moat and bringing into

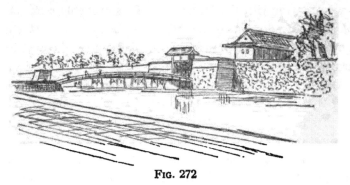

Fig. 272

view new bridges and Oriental-looking buildings perched high on the walls or just inside (fig. 272). Strong old gateways are seen at intervals, and the walls made of large blocks of stone are solid and massive, appearing more massive with their great slope to the water of the moat. Around the top of the wall is a fringe of ancient pine trees in whose branches are perched hundreds of cormorants, while in the broad moat at certain places the lotus grows luxuriantly, and when in bloom, with its great pink flowers is a charming sight. In the water flocks of wild ducks, geese, and other birds are seen in their migration. Nothing illustrates more strongly the gentle character of the people, or I might say of the boys and young men, than the appearance in the midst of a great city of flocks of wild birds which make themselves perfectly at home in the parks and ponds. To see a similar sight in our country one has to go to some wild place in the South. In the yashiki where I live, foxes are occasionally seen.

A favorite subject for decoration for lacquer cups and hanging pictures is a carp, or a carp ascending a waterfall. It is always drawn with the tail curved. It is probably a sketch of a fish ascending rapids, or falls, to deposit its eggs. It is a symbol for aspiration or persistency, and is a lesson to boys to aspire to higher positions.

On May 5 there is a national festival for boys, and I was told that families in which a boy had been born during the year were privileged to fly, from the end of a long pole, a huge fish made of paper or cloth, the mouth distended by a hoop by which it is suspended; the wind, which blows most of the time, dilates the fish, and the creature sways in the wind in the most natural swimming attitudes. It is a curious sight all over the vast city to see these fish, some ten feet in length, swaying and flopping.

I made an interesting call on an artist named Shorin who came from Kyoto to paint some flower pictures for the Exhibition. He lives on a street that leads off from the Hongo. I passed through a little gate in a fence and found myself inside the enclosure of an old samurai. The severity of the garden was almost Quaker-like in its simplicity. It was the finest private house I had thus far seen, and nicer and cleaner than the others, if that were possible. The room which opened on a wide veranda was severe in its simplicity, with the dark cedar ceiling, the natural wood showing everywhere, the cleanest of straw mattings, in one corner of the floor a few books neatly piled, and the ever-present box with its live coals. A few simple pictures completed the furniture and adornment of the room. Such a room is the ideal for the student. Let one recall the usual room at home, with the infinite variety of objects to distract the attention in the daytime and many things to tumble over in the dark, all of which must consume the time of somebody to dust and clean. The artist met me with the deepest bows, and then quietly showed me his sketch-books in which were hundreds of drawings of dragonflies, grasshoppers, cicadas, snails, frogs, toads, birds, etc.; all drawn so lifelike and simply. In one book with a lot of flowers were sketches of the dresses of a prince in whose retinue Shorin had been during feudal times. When I retired he made a bow that nearly took my breath away. I have seen many bow with head touching the mat, yet his head remained for a few seconds as if he were in deep prayer. The Japanese sit on bent legs and in the bow the back must be horizontal to the floor and not elevated behind.

As I came away I noticed at the end of the veranda a pretty device: a large bamboo hanging down notched at the lower end, on which hung a bucket of water, and just above, a shallow bamboo dipper hanging from a peg. Conveniences of this nature for rinsing the hands are found in every house (fig. 273).

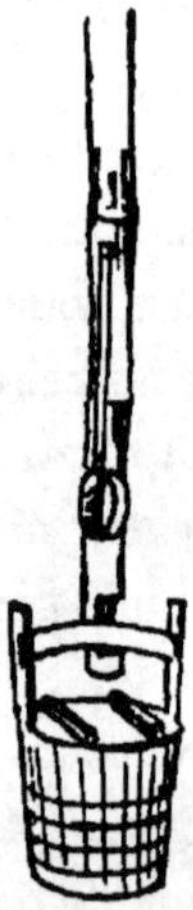

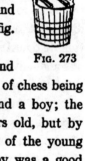

In the street one often encounters an itinerant musician who walks slowly along thrumming a samisen and singing in a low, absent-minded kind of way. He wears an enormous straw hat resembling a shallow basket; his clothes, though much worn, are clean and are marked by hundreds of patches. These people go from house to house singing in a tremulous voice which seems to be fearfully cracked, and the singer is very old and worn and frightfully plain (fig. 274).

FIG. 273

At the side of a street and on the ground I saw a game of chess being played by a young man and a boy; the boy was not over ten years old, but by the starts and exclamations of the young man I judged the little boy was a good match for him. A number stood around watching the game, and by squatting down on the ground, apparently watching the game too, I managed to get a hasty sketch of the players (fig. 275).

FIG. 274

On my way to the college I get a view of Fuji nearly seventy miles off; it is a perpetual source of delight. To-day the air was remarkably clear and Fuji stood out with a new dress of snow. It was magnificent, so soft and clear. The mountain was covered a third of the way down with snow and the west-

FIG. 275

ern slope was covered still farther down, indicating from which direction the snow-storm had come.

On my way back from the University there is a long hill to climb, and I always get out and walk up. In one shop there are four monkeys chained to a roost. One may buy for. the tenth of a cent some parched peas or slices of carrots in shallow wooden trays on the end of a long stick. People stop for a minute to feed the monkeys, and I keep a handful of small coin in my pocket and every day have some fun with them. I found that the monkeys could catch the peas when tossed to them even from the middle of the street; they catch them as a boy catches a ball, with two hands, and no matter how quickly I tossed the pea they never failed to catch it. They seem to know me now, and if I plague them by holding the tray just beyond their reach they frown at me and make awful faces and jump up and down on their perch, thumping down upon it with their feet, and literally shaking the light wooden structure of the place. A big, cross old monkey who is kept imprisoned in a cage will grasp the bars and shake away furi-ously out of sympathy. The more I study them the more I recognize their human ways of doing things. They pick up

minute objects with the thumb and fingers when I should have
to use delicate forceps.

At right angles to the University as it faces the street is the
entrance to a residence of an old daimyo, a yashiki, in fact.
The buildings are very old; the gables, the heavily tiled roof
and ponderous ridges and solid gateway are typical of the
architecture of these august residences. The structure on
the roof is a recent addition for ventilation. The place is now
being used for a school (fig. 276).

Fig. 276

I will not repeat here the sketches which are reproduced in
my "Japanese Homes," but I cannot refrain from referring to
figures 33, 34, 35, and 38, in that work, showing the appearance of the street through which I pass every day. The houses
are mostly one story. As I walk by, from one house comes the
sound of a squeaking voice accompanied by a samisen or koto;
the next house is evidently a private school where the children
are learning the Chinese characters and shouting their names
at the top of their voices; such a Babel! In the next house
some one is reading Chinese classics and making that sing-

song drawl that must be heard to be appreciated. The thin
structure and open condition of the houses may be understood by the ease with which all sounds are heard outside.

At the Tokyo Museum I have seen some prehistoric pottery
found in Yezo supposed to be ancient Ainu pottery. A few
pieces have some resemblance to the Omori pottery, but it is
much thinner and all is cord-marked.

In a few instances in this journal I have recorded slight
earthquake shocks. Others have occurred, but I was either
riding in a jinrikisha or walking and did not feel them. To-
night, however, we have had a rouser. I had just sat down
to supper with Professor and Mrs. C. when the shock began.
We all recognized it instantly, and the Professor said, in a surprised manner, "It is an earthquake!" So I begged them to
remain quiet to appreciate it, but I never thought of timing
the duration till it was all over. I wanted to experience the
whole thing. It was a series of lateral vibrations and might be
compared to the movements in the cabin of a steamer just as
she is getting under way. As it continued, Mrs. C. turned
pale and left the room to look after the children, who were
asleep; the Professor put his hands on the table as if to get
up, but the oscillations becoming fainter he remained. I saw
a physicist afterwards and he said the earthquake lasted a
minute and a half with vibrations at the rate of two and a half
a second. This imperturbability on my part was not due to
any special bravery, but because I had not been long enough
in the country to realize the danger. I had been told by old
residents that the time would come when an earthquake
would be anything but agreeable to me, but thus far it has

been an event of the keenest enjoyment. Only a few evenings ago Mr. Fukuyo was with me to spend the evening and he told me of the great earthquake in Tokyo, twenty-two years ago, when sixty thousand people lost their lives by the earthquake and the conflagration that followed. He said his father ran over the tops of prostrate houses for a long distance hearing the agonizing cries of people buried in the ruins. The moment this earthquake occurred I thought of the account that Mr. Fukuyo had given me, yet did not feel the slightest alarm; on the contrary, it was an enjoyable experience. It was not like the explosion of a powder mill nor a hurricane that made the house shake, but the solid ground itself was shaking like a big dish of jelly, and we were being shaken with it. Not a breath of air was stirring, and this rendered the disturbance all the more noticeable.

To-day I lunched with Professor E. He lives in a Japanese house on the brow of a hill from which a good view of a portion of the city is obtained (fig. 277). I made an attempt at a sketch, but it was too intricate to get in more than a suggestion of its appearance. The building to the extreme left and in the distance belongs to the War Department, as does also the one with the high cupola on the hill. You will observe the entire absence of chimneys and church spires, the general level of the roofs, with now and then a tall fireproof building, or *kura*. The absence of smoke is observed; indeed, no sign of smoke or white, cloud-like steam is anywhere seen. The artificial heat of the house is secured from a few bits of charcoal partially buried in ashes and held in a pottery, porcelain, or bronze receptacle. The people do not seem to mind the cold as we do. It is now cold enough to wear a light overcoat, and yet these people are flying about in their thin kimonos and with bare legs, as they were in hot summer.

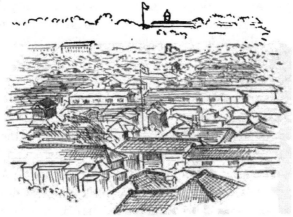

Fig. 277

The dread word has come that Asiatic cholera has broken out in Yokohama and Tokyo. The foresight and thoroughness of the Government is remarkable. The vast city covers an extent of territory three times that of New York City and there are said to be fifty or sixty thousand jinrikishas, every one of which is compelled to carry a box of chloride of lime. Every morning a servant passes through the corridors and entry-ways of the University sprinkling carbolic acid water on the floors and mats; every Government officer, native and foreign, receives a small vial of cholera medicine made by the regular formula of laudanum, rhubarb, camphor, etc., with a paper containing printed directions as to when and how to use it. Mine was in terse English.

The Imperial Gardens have often been described and I will
not attempt it; they resemble the wilder parts of Central Park
in New York, but are more natural and beautiful, with large
mounds and hills, deep ravines, waterfalls tumbling down
over rocks that seem natural till an examination shows you a
conglomeration of faults, synclinals, anticlinals, and a viola-
tion of every principle of geology, and then you realize that
the whole mass has been built up from a level plain; big rocks
for this purpose have been literally brought a hundred and
more miles. At the side of this mountain brook was an irregular flight of stone steps, lichen-covered, which led to the top,
where a rustic summer house tempted you to sit and admire
the view from the top of this artificial hill. To your surprise
you find extending from the summer house for a long distance
what appears to be a beautiful lawn. The existence of such a
feature you gradually realize is impossible; leaving your seat
to examine the puzzle you first encounter little bushes, six
inches high, and then, as you descend a gradual slope, are
bushes a little higher. As you continue, the height of the bushes
increases; you come to small trees, but all are trimmed off at
a perfect level above. When you reach the bottom of the
hill you pass into a forest of great trees, the tops of which have
been trimmed to a common level with the rest. The garden is
three hundred years old, and so there has been ample time to
accomplish these wonderful features. It would be useless to
attempt a description without sketches, and sketches of such
scenery are quite beyond me, though I did get an outline of a
gigantic tree whose roots and branches were almost intermingled (fig. 278). A large bamboo grove was remarkable

for its beauty. There were no flower beds, but quaint stone bridges, paths, summer houses, huge wistarias trained on horizontal trellises, and the like. The place is open to visitors on Saturday only and special tickets are required; and, according to the usual contrariness of Japanese customs, you give up your ticket when you depart and not when you enter.

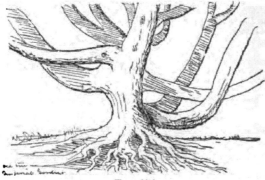

Fig. 278

The other morning I made a sketch of the main gateway of Kaga Yashiki (fig. 279). We do not use it in going to our houses within the walls, but use a smaller gate nearer to where we live. The roofs of the gateway are heavily tiled with massive ridges. The woodwork is painted dark red, while the iron facings, bolts, etc., are black. It is a picturesque sight, and I always take a good look at it when I pass, as I do every morning. The wall surrounding the yashiki is very thick and is made of tiles and cement and rests on a solid base of stone with a gutter or channel separating it from the road. The top of the wall is capped with roofing tiles, as shown in the sketch.

FIG. 279

Saturday, October 6, 1877. I gave my first lecture in a course of three on Evolution to-night in the large college hall. A number of professors and their wives and from five hundred to six hundred students were present, and nearly all of them were taking notes. It was an interesting and inspiring sight. The platform was large, with a rail in front; the seats were arranged on the main floor and rose like steps on the sides of the hall. A good blackboard was provided, and on the right of the stage was a little circular table containing two trays, on one of which was a decanter filled with water, out of deference to the foreigner, and on the other, a teapot of steaming tea (fig. 280), this being the customary drink for a speaker in Japan; physiologically it may be better for the throat than cold water. The audience seemed to be keenly interested, and it was delightful to explain the

FIG. 280

Darwinian theory without running up against theological pre-
judice as I often did at home. The moment I finished there
was a rousing and nervous clapping of the hands which made
my cheeks tingle. One of the Japanese professors told me
that this was the first lecture ever given in Japan on Darwinism or Evolution. I am looking forward with interest to
the other lectures, for I shall have objects to illustrate the
points, though the Japanese are quick as a flash to interpret
my blackboard drawings.

The students interested in botany and zoölogy came together the other day at my suggestion and formed a biological
society. The members are exclusively Japanese and most of
them work in my laboratory. A number of meetings have
been held, and thus far the communications made would be
considered appropriate in any of our older
societies at home. These are sometimes
given in English, always so when they are
written, but when given verbally they are
in their native language, though it sounds
odd to hear the freedom with which the
English words are used when they have no
Japanese equivalent. They all
dress in native costume which
is always so graceful in appearance. The members illustrate
their remarks freely on the blackboard, and as most of them are
born artists, the outlines are re-
markable for their accuracy. Preparations of specimens gen-

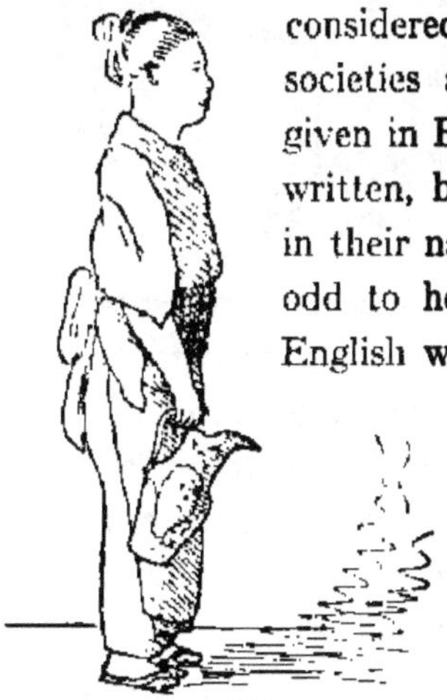

FIG. 281

erally accompany their communications. It is hoped that a journal will be published for exchange with societies abroad.

The sketch (fig. 281) represents my chambermaid, painfully plain in the face, lips partially open, exposing a row of polished black teeth. She is holding in her hand a pitcher as hideous as herself, made in Japan, but for foreign use, the Japanese using no pitcher of any kind.

FIG. 282

Every day something new turns up in the way of street jugglers, musicians, peddlers, and acrobats, but no beggars. Figure 282 is a rough sketch of a strolling group of three poorly dressed people. One held in her hand a curious device of bamboo with glass which I supposed was an ornament of some kind; another, a woman, twanged a samisen; and the third held a square box and continually and rapidly declaimed something. I followed the group for some time, but nothing happened; then overtaking them, I gave the man a cent and the performance began at once. The man, taking the object, which looked like a rude imitation of a sprig of flowers, held the lower part of the bamboo rod to his mouth and blowing in and out produced a peculiar clanging sound not entirely unmusical. On examining the bell-shaped device I found that a film of glass extended across the mouth of it and that the sound was produced by the pushing in and out of the glass diaphragm. Having done this for a while he put the end of the bamboo against his throat, and by some movement which I could not understand managed to make the diaphragm sound. After that he lifted a long-stemmed pipe, and after smoking a few puffs, placed the end against the throat and smoked away just as vigorously. It was a great puzzle, as it seemed impossible that he could make the skin move in and out with sufficient vigor to smoke; he must have had concealed under his clothes some kind of a bellows that he could move with his abdomen. I noticed that he had a cloth tied closely about the neck, probably concealing the tube that led to the abdominal bellows. It was a clever trick and the crowd seemed greatly puzzled by it.

Speaking of jugglers' tricks, I passed a shop the other day in which were for sale various objects for conjurers. Hanging in front were two devices to arrest the attention and advertise the place. One consisted of a sheet of tissue paper, ragged and torn, suspended by a string, and hanging from the lower edge of this paper was a stone nearly a foot in diameter. Either the stone was an artificial device as light as a feather, or a framework of wire meandered through the sound portions of the paper, though no evidence of such a support could be detected in the translucent sheet. The other device consisted of a horizontal rod of wood suspended in the middle by a cord which ran to the ceiling; on one end of the rod was apparently a large stone and on the other end a light Japanese lantern. Here again the lantern must have been heavily weighted or the stone was artificial, for the rod was horizontal.

I visited a wood market to-day and found that firewood was often used for large boilers and also in stoves. The wood, instead of being sold by the cord, or in large masses as with us, is tied up in small bundles of six sticks. I saw a large pile of these little bundles of wood. They were sold at the rate of one dollar for twenty bundles. The wood was good and was cut about twice the length of the wood we use at home for stoves.

It is a never-ending source of enjoyment just to walk along the street of shops — one continuous stretch for miles of shops with a frontage of fifteen feet, or less, and only ten feet deep, though behind the back screens the family live. There is scarcely a change in these proportions, and yet every conceivable trade is carried on limited to these dimensions: lantern-makers, confectioners, barrel-makers, carpenters, joiners, blacksmiths, and all open wide to the street. There are no large workshops, and little or no demarkation between the artist and the artisan. Each master made it a point of honor to instruct only such apprentices as were likely to do him credit, and even to this day the good artists and artisans are generally known as being the pupils of such and such a master until they in their turn attain fame. It occurred to me that here was an education for the children — to see the method and manner of making the objects they are familiar with: as they saunter along the street they often stop to watch some artisan making a lantern or carving wood. Our children at home have often told me that they have never seen melted iron, or red-hot iron, or the manufacture of anything. In many of the shops the lightness of the stock is surprising; one might buy out the entire contents of a shop for a few dollars, and yet the slight profit on occasional sales seems sufficient to support a family. The sketch (fig. 283) represents a black-

FIG. 283

smith's shop. The man is in a squat position all the time. The anvils are of very small size and the objects he is making are of diminutive proportions. Figure 284 is of a shoe and umbrella shop. It would have required a long time to draw the elaborate tiled roof, and I did not attempt it. The basket of umbrellas is seen at the left. Notice the stone to which the corner of a curtain is tied to keep it in position; the long piece above is in the nature of an awning. Sandals and wooden clogs are seen within.

Sunday afternoon Professor Chaplin and I walked through the streets for miles, coming across something new all the time. In one place a man had grasshoppers for sale as an article of food, the insects having been either boiled or baked. I

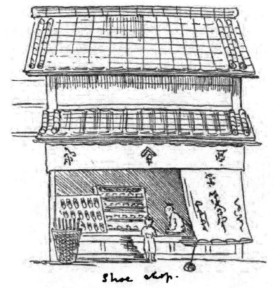

Shoe shop.
Fig. 284

ate one and found it very good, tasting like a dried shrimp. The grasshoppers looked precisely like our common grasshoppers, and there is no reason why they should not be eaten with us. In one place the laborers were repairing the street, and the contrivance they have for lugging dirt and stone was interesting. A large, coarse matting, square in shape, with looped handles from the corners, is laid on the ground and the dirt is shoveled upon it as

Fig. 285

shown in figure 285; when a sufficient load is collected a pole is thrust through the loops and two men lug it off on their shoulders, the matting suspended from the pole like a hammock. Wheelbarrows are unknown in Japan and this device provides a good substitute. I have noticed that when laborers are filling or grading the street they have a measure for the gravel. The box is made of large planks keyed to-

Fig. 286

gether, and men drag the dirt as above described and dump it into the box and measure and charge for the amount of road material, for which they have already contracted.

Figure 286 represents street laborers pounding down a place in the street that has been dug up; foundation stones of a house are also pounded down in this way. During the work of pounding, the laborers keep up a curious chant that I can neither imitate nor describe.

An interesting attraction on the street was the sand artist (fig. 287). He was an old man with patched clothing. I wondered what he was about when he got down on his knees and with his hand brushed a smooth area on the ground; a few people and children gathered evidently knowing what was coming. Having swept a sufficient area he took out of a box a handful of reddish sand and, with his hand closed, allowed it to run through his fingers, moving his hand about at the same time and making an outline of a face. He made a fine double line by permitting the sand to run through interspaces between the fingers. A box of white sand was also used. He made a clever drawing, and several small coins were pitched to him from the crowd, for which he bowed his head.[1]

A very common sight to encounter in the streets is laborers dragging on a two-wheeled dray a fruit, or flowering, tree,

FIG. 287

such as a camellia. The trees are often large ones, and the root end is sometimes five or six feet in diameter, bound up with matting. These trees are often in flower or fruit, and yet the Japanese seem to be able to transport them without detriment to the tree which, as soon as planted again, continues its blossoming. The soil is rich and the air damp, which favors the transplanting; a great mass of earth is taken up with the tree, and the Japanese gardener is a past-master in the art. That

[1] I have also seen in London drawings made this way on the sidewalk and for the same purpose — to win pennies from the crowd. The publications of the United States Bureau of Ethnology describe certain tribes of Western Indians making elaborate designs with various colored sands in connection with religious ceremonial rites.

the load is sometimes very heavy is evident when four or five men are seen straining and struggling to pull and push the dray along.

In our walk we passed a wide, open place in which were a number of cheap booths, the frames of which were constructed of bamboo poles, supporting cloth curtains; flags with curious drawings were swaying from poles of bamboo. Figure 288 represents the appearance of these booths. These rude shelters were occupied by all sorts of peddlers with all kinds of cheap things for sale. One man had the painted diagram of a hand and he would tell your fortune; another had spread out before him a board upon which was a pile of clean clam shells — the highly polished species. These were

Fig. 288

used as boxes to hold a brownish-looking substance, which he kept in a large earthen bowl. He offered me a taste of the substance, which was politely declined. There were some curious diagrams on his table, and I endeavored to make out what he had to sell by a study of his pictures. One represented in a rude way the anatomy of a man — about as correct as were the early maps of the world. There were a few other pictures from which nothing could be gleaned, and I was about to

leave when I caught sight of a picture of a long worm, and
that explained the whole thing; he had been offering me a
taste of his worm medicine! In some of the booths, large
enough to hold an audience of fifty, were story-tellers, whose
performance I have described before: the same kind of a triton
shell to growl through, wooden blocks to strike the table with
sharp clicks, and an enraptured audience. It was interesting
to us, but we were not so rapturous, as, of course, we could not
understand a word. The entertainments were evidently for
the lower classes, and the audience consisted exclusively of men
and boys.

The money-broker has an ingenious way of rapidly counting
money. He has a handled tray divided by thin strips into
squares, making ten rows and ten in a row; the strips are of
the thickness of the coin he wishes to count and a tray is used
for each kind of coin. A handful of five-dollar gold pieces, for
example, is dropped upon the tray, which is deftly shaken so
that the interspaces are immediately filled, the coins sliding
over the filled ones to spaces unoccupied. The broker counts
them by tens, and glances at them at the same time to see if
there are counterfeits among them. These devices are used
in the banks and money-exchange offices.

Yesterday afternoon when I left the laboratory I started off
in an opposite direction from that of my house and determined to lose myself, which I promptly did, and for two hours
and a half I roamed, a perfect stranger to everybody, through
long streets and narrow lanes, seeing many odd sights and
novelties. At about five o'clock in the afternoon everybody
seemed to be engaged in sweeping the road in front of his shop

and house, in many cases sprinkling before sweeping; an excellent idea and a custom that would lead to a great improvement to some of our towns and cities if carried out.

On my way back, in one of the streets leading to a temple, a children's fair was going on. Both sides of the avenue were lined with little booths of various kinds and in every instance the objects for sale were children's toys. The booths were attended by old men or old women and the objects cost from a tenth of a cent to a cent. The children were flying about in the happiest spirits, flitting from one booth to another, looking at the pretty objects and making up their minds how they would invest their little coin. One old man had a boxlike stove, the upper surface being of stone beneath which was a charcoal fire. At one side was a large jar containing a mixture of rice flour, eggs, and sugar — a batter, in fact. He would sell this to the children by the cupful and provide a little tin spoon and they were allowed to spread it out a little at a time on the stove, cook it, and then, scraping it off, eat it, or give it to their little friends, or feed the baby perched up behind. One who recalls the delight of getting into the kitchen and scraping dough out of some vessel in which gingerbread or cake had been made, and with a knife scooping out drops of it, patting it down on the hot stove and baking little cakes can appreciate the delight of these Japanese children. Figure 289 gives an idea of this outdoor bakery. The old man's booth was portable; he could fold up his huge umbrella and pack the other things compactly and move to another place. This might be introduced into our cities in regions where children swarm, and with this hint some poor man or woman may do it.

There was another booth, where children could peep through openings and see pictures of some kind, which were being described by an old man. Again I must repeat that Japan is the paradise for children. There is no other country in the world where they are so kindly treated or where so much attention is devoted to them. From the appearance of their smiling faces they must be happy from morning till night. They go to school early in the morning, or remain at

FIG. 289

home to help their parents in the domestic work of the house, or work with their father at some trade or in tending shop. They work contentedly and happily, and I have never seen a sulky child or any personal chastisement. Their houses are so simple that there are no objects to be pulled down, no furniture to tumble over; it is not continually dinned into their heads to get off this, or don't touch that, or to look out for their clothes. Little children are never left alone in the house, but are tied to the back of the mother or one of the older children and have delightful rides, fresh air, and see everything that is going on. The Japanese have certainly solved the children problem, and no better behaved, kinder children exist, and no more patient, affectionate, and devoted mothers are found. However, this is all trite, as every book on Japan has said the same thing again and again.

Last Tuesday I started with a lot of workmen to make a thorough exploration of the Omori shell mounds. I hired the two laborers who went with me before and the University sent four laborers, who work about the grounds, to help me. They all carried hoes, shovels, etc., and an immense square basket to bring back whatever we might find. My two special students, Mr. Sasaki and Mr. Matsura, as well as Professor

FIG. 290

Toyama and Professor Yatabe and Mr. Fukuyo, accompanied me. I also had with me General Le Gendre, a gentleman who is connected with the War Department. He is greatly interested in the subject of the origin of the Japanese. On a later train Dr. Murray and Professor Parsons came to help us and with this large force we dug many trenches and deep channels. The result of our day's work filled the big square basket and I had a freight bill for three hundred pounds in smaller packages besides, while the more precious specimens I carried in a handbag. Figure 290 is the appearance of the workmen returning along the railroad track with the big basket filled with shell-heap pottery. As in our visit before, the workmen hoed and shoveled back the material dug over, filled the trenches, planted bushes and even small trees, and left it about as we found it. They are most persistent workers and never seem to tire. With the addition of this day's work the University will have one of the most valuable collections of ancient pottery in Japan. The collection already arranged in a room at the University is attracting a great deal of attention and almost every day learned Japanese ask permission to see the pottery. It is delightful to observe their intelligent appreciation, their careful manner in handling the objects, and their

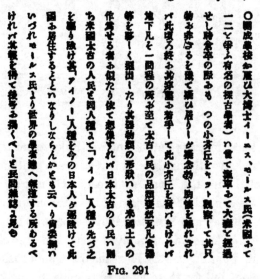

Fig. 291

politeness in expressing their interest. The "Nichi Nichi Shinbun," the principal newspaper of Tokyo, has an appreciative notice of my discovery. Figure 291 is a reproduction of this article.

I present a few figures of some of the curious shapes of Omori

FIG. 292

pottery that we found. Figure 292 is a curious form; a hole in the side indicating either a place to pour from or an aperture in which a tube might be introduced to suck the contents. Fig. 293 is a bowl eleven inches in diameter. Fig. 294 is a foot in height; fragments of a similar rim are not uncommon.

All this pottery is modeled by hand, no evidence of lathe-work having ever been found.

When I arose this morning the air was oppressively warm. For the last week it has been clear and cold and this sud-

FIG. 293

den change of temperature indicated some atmospheric dis-

FIG. 294

turbance. It began to rain this noon, the wind all the time increasing in strength, and in the afternoon it developed into a regular typhoon. It has blown down many of the high fences in the yashiki and done a great deal of damage in the street in blowing tiles from the roofs. About five P.M. the rain stopped, but the gale continued with undiminished fury. At the risk of getting my head broken with flying roofing tiles I ventured on the street to see how matters looked. The shops were nearly all closed, the storm shutters being up: the people stood under the overhanging roofs in front of their shops and were admiring the beautiful cloud effects as the setting sun illuminated the sky. In the street the children had possession of some big, ragged straw hats and allowed the wind to roll them along while they went screaming after them. It is interesting to see how much enjoyment the people seem to take in beautiful scenery. Without exaggeration I see a hundred times as many people in this country enjoying beautiful cloud effects, lotus blooming, the parks and garden, as I do at home. The masses like to trade and barter, but they are keenly alive to the beauties of art and nature.

Mr. Scott was telling me of the scenes which follow a great conflagration here. He says the people that have been burned out always look happy and smiling; he has actually seen people who had fenced in their lot displaying their signs and engaged in cleaning away the embers while the conflagration was still raging through the city. He told me that they have no such institution as insurance, but the merchants always calculate to be burned out on an average once in seven years and so lay by money every year in view of this calamity. Moreover, he learned that the people were very thoughtful and kind and they go out of their way for a while to trade in those streets that have been scourged, and the result is that very little suffering comes from the catastrophe. The fire that Mr. Scott spoke of ran for three miles unchecked.

At last I have had an opportunity of seeing a fair-sized conflagration, some sixty or seventy houses destroyed. Professor Smith, a tall Scotchman with reddish hair and whiskers, — a giant in fact, — came into my house at 10.30 at night and told me that a big fire was raging in the southern part of the city and asked me if I wanted to go. Of course I did, and off we went. We found a jinrikisha at the gate and, hiring two men, we started off at a rattling pace. The fire showed brightly above the low houses and now and then we passed a fireman running toward it. A half-hour's ride brought us to a steep hill beyond which was the fire, so leaving the jinrikisha we ran up the steep and narrow lane and soon reached the crest of the hill, when the conflagration burst upon us in all its splendor. We had passed groups of people gathered about their scant belongings; patient old women with children on their backs, helpless infants on the backs of small children, men and women, all with smiles on their faces as if a festival were going on; during the whole night I never saw a tear or an impatient gesture or heard a cross word. Loud cries were heard at times when the standard-bearers stood in peril of their lives, but I did not see an expression of distress or concern. Smith and I rushed through hedges, over choice gardens, and through low houses that had been vacated until we reached a long street lined with houses on both sides, most of them in flames. I stood under overhanging eaves out of the way of falling tiles and watched the fight. The roofs of the long row of low houses were literally covered with firemen, working like heroes, tearing off the roofing tiles, shoveling off the light shingles, and pulling, cutting, and tearing apart the framework, while, blistered by the heat, several standard-bearers stood on the ridge-poles, saved from being consumed only by the streams of water more often thrown upon them and the firemen than upon the fire. A wide balcony which held four men engaged in their destructive work suddenly fell outward, and down they came into the street, with a crash, on burning timbers and hot tiles, while one of them fell inside the burning building. I thought, of course, that he was lost, but brave fellows rushed in and rescued him; shortly after he was carried by me a helpless lump, whether dead or not I did not learn. From this place Smith and I hurried off to another point, and here we took a hand in the fight. The efforts of the firemen in tearing down one low balcony were so futile that I could stand it no longer, and seizing a long beam I rushed in, tearing my coat and scratching my hands with the nails. No sooner was I exposed to the fire than a pipeman immediately directed his

FIG. 295

stream on me, and a muddy stream it was! I yelled to him to
stop in as polite Japanese as I could muster out of my limited
vocabulary; the pipeman smiled and directly turned the
stream on Smith, who, if I mistake not, swore in Scotch. It
was a satisfaction, however, to see the building go down by

Fig. 296

our united efforts. The amount of courage and misspent efforts
displayed at these fires is amazing; with one tenth the courage
and a little intelligent action a great deal more could be accomplished. The sight of the standard-bearers perched on the
ridge-pole is ludicrous in the extreme. Courageous fellows
they are, and often they lose their lives by remaining at their
perilous posts too long. By this heroic conduct they inspire
the members of their companies to deeds of bravery. I have
understood also that when buildings upon which they stand
are saved the fire companies represented by them receive a gift
of money. Figure 295 is a rough sketch of the fire. Many of the
firemen wore the thickest of padded clothes, and their hats
were like cushions, to protect their heads from the heavy roofing tiles. Figure 296 represents a few of these head protectors.
One of the oddest things about a fire is that the firemen carry
lighted lanterns!

When the fire was under control we concluded to walk back to Kaga Yashiki, and, furthermore, to take a short cut across a large area of paddy fields. We knew the general direction, but soon got lost in the paths. We had overtaken or passed nobody of whom we might inquire; the region was deserted. It was dark, but the stars gave light enough dimly to distinguish the path. At last we saw the light of a lantern approaching and finally encountered a little boy on his way somewhere at two o'clock in the morning. We asked him the direction to the yashiki, and I shall never forget the calm, fearless way in which he held the lantern up to see our faces, both bearded and one of us a giant. His upturned face was absolutely without fear as he quietly told us the direction, nor did he glance back after we had passed.

On Saturday, October 13, I gave a lecture before the Asiatic Society of Japan, in Yokohama, on "Traces of Early Man in Japan." It has never been my fortune to have so mixed an audience before, mostly Englishmen, a few Americans, a few ladies, and in the rear of the hall a fringe of Japanese. Mr. Fukuyo helped me get my objects down from Tokyo, and I had some rare and delicate specimens to handle.

Farewell dinners are in order, as I return to America for my winter lectures. I gave a dinner to my special students at a Japanese restaurant and afterwards we went to the Exhibition, which was for the first time opened at night and beautifully illuminated. The naval brass band gave Occidental music and the Emperor's band, in another pavilion, played its own native music with its peculiar instruments. The native music is utterly indescribable. I listened intently for nearly two hours, much to the wonderment of my friends, and although I have a fair ear for music I managed to carry away only three consecutive notes of an air and these I still have in my head. It is one constant wail of the saddest sounds. The music suggests the desultory whistling of a gale in subdued tones or the natural sounds one hears in the forest on a windy day, with a mountain brook assisting. Some of the instruments are blown continuously, the flutes are all high-pitched, and not a low note is heard except the dull thump of the big drum. The next day I asked one of the students who was with us how he slept after the dissipation of the night before, and he said he did not sleep much, as the "imagination of that luminary came to my mind," referring to the brilliant display at the Exhibition.

A visit to the city poorhouse was sad enough. Here were confined a number of insane poor. It was a sad sight to see these unfortunate people in a long row of rooms barred in front and arranged as wild animals would be in a menagerie. The keepers seemed to look at them with awe. They are treated kindly, but the whole affair is not up to the modern ways of treating the insane. I saw typical cases of dementia and melancholia as I had seen them in the great asylum in Utica, New York. I shook hands with some of them; all spoke to me pleasantly, and there was something inexpressibly pathetic in their quiet "Sayonara" (Good-bye).

The other day I asked Matsura's permission to see his study room, and we went together to a large dormitory in the rear of the University buildings. The students' rooms are arranged in a curious fashion. The dormitories are two stories in height.

A single row of rooms on each story opens on a broad veranda. Each two rooms accommodate seven students, the one below being the study room and the one above the bedroom. Nothing could be more cheerless than these rooms. Cold and barren, they had neither the interest nor comfort of the native house nor the coziness of a student's room at home. A narrow crib for one person only, and seven of these scattered without order about the room, no pictures on the walls, of course; no furniture except the cribs. The study room was a little better, as on the walls were a few brush sketches of some of their pranks. The rooms were very cold, but stoves were being put in. Everything indicated the hardest of study. I asked Matsura if they had secret societies and he said they had societies, but not secret ones, and after a little conversation I got out of him the fact that their herding together led to rough talk or slang; then I discovered that they had nicknames for their foreign professors as students have in America. The oldest professor is known as the "Old Man"; another, who has a square head, is called "Cube"; an English professor who is bald-headed and has reddish mutton-chop whiskers is called "Cuttlefish." Matsura said that parents observed that boys attending the University became brusque in their manners, and they had often discussed among themselves the reason for this change in behavior. I told him that the same abruptness of behavior and the using of nicknames for their teachers were characteristics of American boys attending college. (I did not tell him how we acted before coming to college.) I also told him that the young boy is essentially a savage, and at home he is chided by his parents and sisters; in getting away from these restraints, and with the hurrying to recitations and crowding together, some corners of good manners are rubbed off.

[A large volume might be written on students and student life in Japan. Hazing is never known. The profound respect shown to teachers protects the professor from the trifling annoyances he is subject to in our colleges at home, such as greasing the blackboard, stealing the chalk, and other petty deviltries. The impious behavior of students in our colleges, such as stealing the Bible and hymn-books from the chapel of Princeton University, the crucifying of an effigy of a professor on the cross of Appleton Chapel at Harvard, and disfiguring, torturing, and even causing the death of brother students in hazing, are illustrations of this barbarous and savage behavior often recorded in our country.

There is not a boy in Japan who would not be called a "sissy" if brought in contact with the usual run of our boys. In our country the hoodlum behavior of a boy is condoned by saying "Boys will be boys." In Japan the saying might well be, "Boys will be gentlemen." No feature in Japanese life impresses an American more than the behavior of schoolchildren. Their profound respect for the teacher is universal throughout the Empire. One has simply to recall the records of country schools in Maine and possibly other States, where the boys are so turbulent that a teacher has literally to fight his way before getting control! Some school districts are without teachers unless a man with the ability of a prize-fighter can be found. With the high position of teachers in Japan and the respect for education, no deeper blow could be dealt to a nation than the San Francisco affair, when Japanese children were excluded from the public schools, and I may add that the Japanese, though never forgetting the deep insult, for such it was, let the matter rest realizing the degradation of the community which permitted it.]

I have often wondered why one never sees a long-tailed cat in Japan. They are all of the Manx breed, or at least tailless. The Japanese believe that cats' tails were cut off to prevent them from standing on their hind legs to pull things down to the floor, the cat evidently using the tail after the fashion of a kangaroo in balancing itself. They have an idea that this is a mutilation transmitted to succeeding generations. This idea is paralleled in Cuba, where the ears of a cat are cut off to prevent it from roaming in the cane fields. The sudden showers that fall in the tropics are annoying to cats, inasmuch as the rain gets into their ears, and this they particularly loathe. The result is that cats remain near the house, so that in case of a shower they can make a quick dash for protection.

In the bric-à-brac shops, and there are many in Tokyo, you occasionally see an iron fan, or rather, one with the end frame of iron or sometimes a rigid rod of iron modeled in the shape of a folded fan. I was told that this device was carried on occasions by the samurai class in olden times. In hostile times, when a samurai called on his lord, he had to leave his swords in the hands of an attendant. The custom was to pull the screens slightly open, and through this opening the caller thrust his head, bowing low at the same time, with his hands on the grooved space below; in this groove he would place the fan, thus protecting himself against a possible assassination by preventing the screens from being suddenly closed against his neck. This I was told by an old samurai. The iron fan could also be used, he said, as a weapon of offense or in defending one's self.

One of my general students came to my house to ask me if I had time to look at some insects he had collected. I found he lived only a short distance from the yashiki gate, and so I accompanied him to his house, a neat little place back from the street, with a pretty garden. His room was the typical entomologist's room with nets, boxes, poison bottle, setting boards, and a few books. He had made a fine collection of butterflies and gave me a few; he would have given me the whole collection if I had asked for it. The next day I gave him a large number of insect pins, which pleased him greatly, as he had used only the common pins. A few days after he brought me a little present neatly done up, simple in character, but it showed the kindly feeling, and that is the secret of present-giving, after all.

On Sunday night, October 28, the Japanese professors gave me a dinner in a Japanese tea-house. The place was an agreeable mixture of Japanese and European style, or at least it had one room with chairs and a long table. They were young, bright Japanese teachers at the University, all of them speaking English freely and a number of them graduates of American and English universities. It was delightful to be the only foreigner among them. There were present, among others, Mr. Hamao, the Vice-Director of the University; Professors Toyama, Agee, Enouye, and Hattori. The first three courses were in our style; an omelette with green peas, the most delicious steak I ever tasted, and broiled chicken. I was somewhat disappointed, however, hoping to have a genuine Japanese dinner. The fourth course was Japanese, and all the rest of the dinner was in true Japanese style. They explained to me that, thinking I might not like Japanese food, they had fortified me first with my own kind of food. This was thoughtful, but fortunately I had appetite enough to enjoy thoroughly the remaining courses. Their celebrated fish, the *tai*, a bream, was delicious. There were many things I tasted for the first time. The bulb or root of the lily was an excellent substitute for the potato; there were a number of water plants similar to water-cress; a preparation of fish, like macaroni; the nut of the gingko tree, which I did not like, and a preparation of tea, which I did. This tea was made of a fine powder, served in large bowls, and it was like a thick soup. I understood it was quite expensive and could not be exported, as it rapidly deteriorates. We had a delightfully social time and the kindly feelings of my associates will never be forgotten.

On Monday night Dr. Kato, the Director of the University, gave me a dinner in a large Japanese hall next to the old Chinese college. The Vice-Minister of Education, Mr. Tanaka, as well as the Japanese professors, was present, Dr. Murray, Superintendent of Education, and I being the only foreigners. The long table was decorated with huge bouquets of chrysanthemums. The menu was printed, the food as good as the best places at home could serve, the wines delicious, and all appointments without a flaw. Dr. Murray had warned me that I must be on my dignity, as the affair would be very formal, and so it was. After dinner we gathered about another table where there were cigars, coffee, cordials, etc. A long screen was drawn concealing the table from us while it was being noiselessly cleared by the servants. Even this retirement did not alter the extremely dignified and courteous behavior of all. It got on my nerves, and I made a gentle intrusion by remarking on the similarity of certain games in Japan to ours. This led others to ask if we were familiar with such a trick, performing it with their hands, and I matched it with another. Some one sent for a wafer-like rice cake and showed me a trick played with it. The cake is very thin and exceedingly brittle, and the trick consists in two persons holding the edge with thumb and first finger and each endeavoring to break it by a sudden downward snap of the cake and to retain the larger portion. The nearest game we have to it is the pulling of a wish-bone to retain the larger portion, but this is simply chance as to where the clavicles will break first. I then described other games, and they in turn showed me some new and interesting ones. The game of thumb wrestling was an odd game and they beat me at it every time. The fingers of the right hands are firmly interlocked and with the thumb you endeavor to catch the other's thumb and press it down on the hand; if the thumb is fairly caught, it is impossible to pull it out. To make a long story short, in less than half an hour I had all the guests trying to see how far they could chalk on the floor and various other games. Professor Kikuchi suggested a three-legged race, and Toyama and Yatabe had, one his right leg and the other his left leg, bound together by handkerchiefs. Kikuchi and I were bound up in the same manner, and away we four went across the floor, encouraged by the uproarious laughter of the others. These revels we kept up until midnight. Dr. Murray and I were presented with one each of the huge bouquets of chrysanthemums, and they filled the jinrikisha as we held them between our legs. Dr. Murray again and again expressed his bewilderment as to how I had induced such a carnival of fun; he had never seen such behavior before. I quoted an old Chinese saying that in the four quarters of the world men are brothers. Human nature is about the same everywhere.

When I came to Japan in the spring the rice fields were just being planted, and now, as I ride through the country, the work of harvesting is in full activity. I noticed that the rows of grain and other plants run around the hill in horizontal lines precisely like the lines on a topographical map; this is to prevent the rains from gullying out the soil, a feature that our farmers might adopt with profit. Running through the rice fields are rows of trees which seem to be utilized for tying bunches of rice to the trunks. The rice straw is saved for thatching roofs and for other purposes. Cold as it is the last of October I noticed the harvesting being carried on by men quite naked.

In going along the river the other day I noticed a fine

FIG. 297

two-arched bridge of stone and on the middle abutment were carved in the solid stone four turtles in the most lifelike attitudes (fig. 297).

The steamer is to sail November 5, and I have been in a whirl of farewell dinners, packing, and other duties. One of my students helped me in getting things to the steamer, Mr. Matsumura took charge of my living *Lingula* which I was bound to get home alive (which I did). My colleagues and my dear and faithful students were at the station to bid me goodbye. At Yokohama I spent the night with a friend, and in the afternoon, in honor of the Emperor's birthday, November 3, I saw a remarkable exhibition of day fireworks, consisting of colored smokes and objects floating in the air. Great bombs were thrown up, and as they exploded, radiating lines of sharply colored smoke, yellow, blue, and green, were left, forming various figures in the sky, marvelous in their character and beauty. The night fireworks were equally remarkable, though not so unique. The shipping in the harbor was illuminated with red lanterns, and at intervals a large rocket would whirl up into the air throwing beautiful reflections on the water.

We sailed from Yokohama November 5, encountering the usual storms and meeting the usual queer and interesting passengers, but as all records are personal they are omitted. One experience I must record. Among the passengers was a returning missionary from China with wife and children, all speaking Chinese. I played pease porridge hot with the children, and, learning the Chinese rendering from the mother, we played it with Chinese words. Another missionary who was a fine Chinese scholar explained to me the delicate changes in the inflection of the sound of the word. An upward inflection would mean one thing, while with a downward inflection an entirely different meaning would be indicated. We failed to get the right inflection, or at least I did, and the missionary said it conveyed the following meaning to him: —

Head murky hat

Head murky { Painful / shaky / all the same

Head murky walk

Old time furnace

Then he wrote it in Chinese characters, which I have appended (fig. 298), with the form of inflection, which I did not understand, marked on the character.

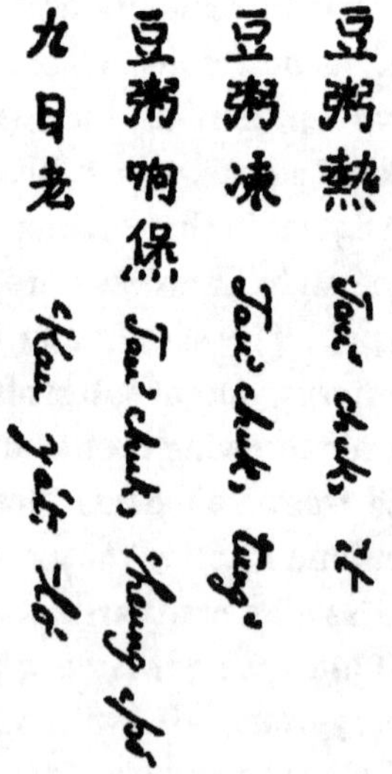

I asked a Japanese to translate "pease porridge hot" into Japanese, writing the Chinese characters in their method of syntax; then I showed this to another Japanese and asked him kindly to translate it into English, and got the following: —

Pea juice is warm
And cold and in bottle
And has already been
Nine days old.

When I came to Japan in the spring with Mr. Metcalf, we had a

豆粥熱　Tou' chuk, it

豆粥凍　Tou' chuk, tang'

豆粥响保　Tou' chuk,' heung fo

九日老　Kau yat lo'

FIG. 298

few days at San Francisco and we explored Chinatown with a guide. We admired the behavior of the Chinese in contrast to the rough hoodlums of the city and agreed that they were a quiet, peaceful, and kindly people. Now, after spending half a year with the Japanese, I again have a chance to study three hundred Chinese on the boat, and the contrast with the Japanese is striking. They appear dirty and rough in their behavior, and while these Chinese in their deportment are far ahead of similar classes in San Francisco or in their country, the Japanese seemed superior to the Chinese in the gentler amenities of life.

CHAPTER XI

May 1, 1878. How strange it seems to begin the journal again and in the same house where I made most of the records before. Our trip across the continent was extremely pleasant, and on the plains I studied the groups of Indians at the stations and was interested to see among them certain resemblances to the Japanese: whether these resemblances betray any ethnic affinity with the Japanese can be learned only after long and careful study. There are certain superficial resemblances: their black hair, the depression of the nasals, and other similarities have led some to suggest a common origin.[1]

To-day, May 5, the boys' festival occurs. I have alluded to this before. I managed to get a hasty sketch of the floating fishes. The wind inflated the body, the fish at the same time swaying back and forth as if ascending a rapid current. A family is permitted to fly the fish if a boy has been born to them during the year (fig. 299).

FIG. 299

It is curious to see a man with a small bundle tied about his

[1] As evidence of these resemblances, in 1884, at Philadelphia, I introduced Mr. Flesch, an Omaha Indian, to Professor Kikuchi, who immediately began to converse with him in Japanese, and he was amazed when I told him he was talking to an Omaha Indian.

neck either hanging over the back or under the chin (fig. 300). They always have with them a square piece of cloth like our

Fig. 300

old bandanna or bundle handkerchief, and everything that the cloth can enwrap is tied up in it. I have seen a man take a bundle a foot long from the fold of his dress.

The country presents an appearance quite different in May from what it did in June when I arrived last year. The rice fields are black, but form a good background for the patches of bright yellow blossoms of the rape from which is derived rape-seed oil. The cherry and plum are marvelous in their profusion and beauty, yet I am told it is too late to see these flowers at their best; the camellia trees, as large as our apple trees, are fairly crowded with blossoms, and each flower is as large and perfect as those we see in conservatories at home; the dwarf maple tree with its little red leaves is a beautiful garden ornament; the leaves remain red for a long time before they turn green; and the fields look like a variegated carpet. Everything is fresh, and it is a constant delight to see the landscape as one rides back and forth from Yokohama to Tokyo.

The various ways in which the Japanese shave their children's heads appear as strange to us as the various ways in which we shave our faces appear to them — mustache and no beard, beard and no mustache, chin shaved with side whiskers, a tiny beard on chin only, or the attempt to join a strip of side whiskers with the mustache to look furious! One is no more absurd than the other.

Figure 301 shows the long plane of a carpenter resting at an angle on the ground, the other end propped up on a wooden horse. The wood to be planed is moved back and forth on the plane and is always drawn toward the carpenter. Here is one of those curious reversals of practice so often alluded to by travelers: the wood is moved instead of the plane and drawn toward the carpenter instead of the other way, and the plane is upside down.

FIG. 301

A lacquer case of four drawers which was shown to me the other day was a curious object inasmuch as there were no knobs on the drawers. A plain black polished surface with the drawers closely fitting; to open one of them you pushed in the drawer above or below the one you wish opened and out it came. A lever device back of the drawers enabled any one of them to be opened (fig. 302).

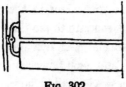

FIG. 302

I saw a man polishing paper. A smooth, convex porcelain disk was on the end of a bamboo pole, the other end of which was fastened to the ceiling, the bamboo being greatly curved, as the ceiling was only seven and a half feet above the floor while the bamboo was ten feet long. This brought great pressure on the burnisher,

FIG. 303

and all the man had to do was to pull the end of the bamboo back and forth on the paper (fig. 303). The devices for doing many kinds of work are so different from our methods that they arrest your attention at once. They utilize power as in the paper-polishing device by the spring of a bamboo. I saw

FIG. 304

two little boys chopping up some kind of nut or bark. The chopper was a round-bladed affair secured in a block of wood from which arose two handles and between the handles was a heavy block of stone (fig. 304). The boys sat opposite each other and simply rocked the chopping-knife back and forth.

May 7. Saw through the college telescope the transit of Mercury. Quite a number were there, including the Chinese Ambassador and his colleagues. It was interesting to see the little black dot against the sun's disk, and in looking at it one could more clearly appreciate the planet's revolution around the sun.

I have already remarked on the curious signs one sees in English. Most of them are amusing, and of the few I have already noticed hardly one is correct. They also make ludicrous pictures for their signs; a dentist's sign showed the dentist pulling a tooth, and the open mouth of the patient and the determined face of the dentist were made as grotesque as possible.

I notice among the lower classes young men walking along with their arms over each other's shoulders. I have never seen girls skip along the path as our children do at home; indeed, it would seem impossible to do it in their wooden clogs.

The general behavior of the lower classes on the street is not unlike that of the same classes at home a few years younger.

I have lately been making plans for showcases for the Museum, a double showcase with an upright case in the middle. It is astonishing how difficult it is for the Japanese cabinet-maker to understand. The building officer of the University comes to me and through an interpreter I explain the sections and elevations; but the smallest details have to be explained over and over again, and after I have done this, the man who is to make the case comes to me and I have to go all over the matter again. Our ways of drafting an object are so different from their ways, and the objects we want made are so unlike anything they have ever made or seen, it is no wonder they are bothered and perplexed as to what we desire.

Within a rod of my house in the yashiki are a well and a stone monument, the latter enclosed by a bamboo fence, tumbling to pieces. In various parts of the yashiki are deep wells, fenced in, high mounds which were formerly beautiful features in some garden, and other evidences of a large settlement when the Prince of Kaga and thousands of his retainers made their annual visit to the Shogun at Yedo. It is difficult to realize that less than ten years ago the Shogun was in power, and that this yashiki and other yashikis in the city were filled with houses in which the retainers, artisans, and servants were quartered, and that at six o'clock everybody had to be within the gates. No foreigner was allowed to live in Yedo, nor could he ever visit it unless he was a high official of some foreign Government, and here we are roaming round the city unguarded and unmolested.

May 15. A startling event occurred yesterday. Count Okubo, one of the Councillors of the Government, was assassinated. He was returning from the Emperor's palace in his coach accompanied by two bettos who ran ahead of the horses, when eight men suddenly rushed upon the carriage, first hacking at the horses' legs so that they could not run, then killing the coachmen and the two bettos, and finally killing the Count. After this the assassins went to the palace and presented a letter of complaint against the Government and confessed their crime. Policemen were immediately summoned, and the assassins were led off to jail, on the way loudly proclaiming their crime. The affair has produced a profound sensation in the city, as such a tragic event has not occurred in Japan for years. Count Okubo was one of the highest officers of the Government, a man of great intelligence and action. It seems, however, that there is much complaint against the Government on account of its extravagance. The men who committed the murders were from the Province of Kaga. The deed was committed within half a mile of the College. A son of Count Okubo is a member of my class. One of the morning papers issued the accompanying supplement (fig. 305) last evening, which was delivered to every one of its subscribers. Mr. Takamine gave me his slip. It is a brief announcement of the tragic event, and I asked Mr. Takamine to translate the characters in sequence literally. Beginning at the top of the right-hand column it reads

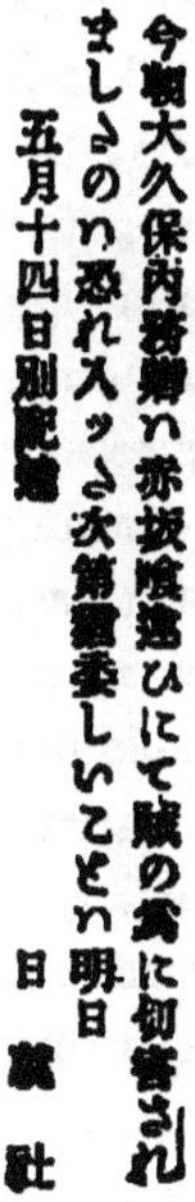

今朝大久保内務卿ハ赤坂喰違にて賊の為に切害され
さしものゝ恐れ入ッゝ次第委しいことハ明日
五月十四日別紙号
日 貳 社

FIG. 305

as follows: "New morning great long keep Interior business minister [grammatical character] red slope bite different in traitor of action by cut killed has been of [grammatical character] terrible yet detailed fact [grammatical character] light day. 5 month, 10–4 day, special distribution reach." Name of paper below on the left. One may realize from this how much scanning one must do to make any sense of it, and the difficulty in reading Chinese characters, even if one knows them all. To construct a sentence out of the following seems difficult. "Red slope bite different in traitor of action by cut killed has been." "Red slope" is the name of the place where the assassination occurred, and "bite different" is a term to designate where the roads intersect. Reading the sentence backward would be our way of constructing the sentence. There are no articles in Japanese, but supplying these we should read, "Has been cut and killed by the action of traitors in different bite of Red Slope." The expression, "yet detailed fact light day," means that in the morning more details will be given. Some of the words in the text are spelled in phonetic characters; other characters represent grammatical expressions which Mr. Takamine could not explain. The morning papers brought more details. It seems the men, who were quite young, were members of a secret society, but became so unruly that they were dismissed. They then came to Tokyo, and the police were warned that they were bent upon some mischief, but it was not known where the blow would fall. After the affair they gave themselves up, were immediately tried, and promptly executed. It is interesting to observe that there was no plea of emo-

tional insanity; no indictment under a wrong initial, and
hence the murderer is some one else and escapes; no trial in
the wrong court; no appeal to higher courts or disagreements
among the jury with the result that the criminal finally goes
free: all so different from the way they manage matters in
our blessed country, which as a consequence has the highest
murder rate in the world.

In the habits of the Japanese one sees a remarkable resemblance to the habits of other nations: as examples, the motion
of the blacksmith, who after every blow rests his hammer upon
the anvil; the shingler, who, in shingling carries the bamboo

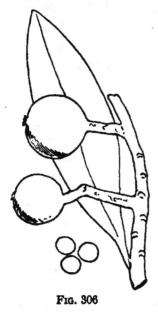

Fig. 306

nails in his mouth and moves his
hand back and forth as rapidly as
in similar acts of our shinglers and
lathers; the Japanese barber, who
in shampooing swings his body
back and forth in rhythmic time,
as you will see the printers do
when they are setting or distributing type.

Middle of May — warm and
muggy — vegetation luxuriant.
Such roses in our garden, — the
darkest, richest reds, blossoms
large and every petal perfect, and
such perfume! Walking along the
street I gather from the walls and
fences a few species of snails.

Last Sunday I visited the Botanical Garden with one of my

students and collected some *Clausilia*, a long, turreted shell, a genus with many species, common in Europe. A fruit called *biwa* is just coming into the market. It is something like an apple in shape, but has a sweet, plummy sort of taste with no suggestion of an apple flavor. It has three stones within, so large as nearly to fill the fruit (fig. 306).

So many matters in the way of work are cheap. A watch-repairer did some work for me for which, had he charged me fifty cents, I should have paid without protest, but he charged only six cents; and my section cutter had a screw bent, to straighten which cost me two cents.

Since the assassination of Count Okubo the high officers of the Government ride along with an escort of soldiers. The more liberal Japanese are thoroughly disheartened by this tragedy, for it seemed a recession to feudal days, when such events took place.

I am directing the building of the cabinets for the collection of shells and fossils. The other day I went to the cabinet-makers to examine a case nearly completed. It was an odd sight to see most of the workmen naked, old men and all. To plane a board they fasten it to uprights (fig. 307), and not a trace of a carpenter's bench or table of any kind is seen. It is amazing to see their

Fig. 307

planes, augers, adzes, chisels, near enough like ours to be recognized as such, but rather rude-looking, with a flimsy little box to keep them in, and then to see the marvelous joints, dovetails, and the superb work they do. One realizes, after recalling our carpenters' brass-mounted chests with polished tools, etc., that it is not the gun, but the man behind the gun, that does the work.

FIG. 308

Fig. 308 shows the newsboy, or rather newsman, as boys are not trusted to deliver papers. He has the papers in a box hanging on the end of a pole and on the other end is a bell which jangles constantly. Having completed his route the bell is removed.

An astronomical observatory is being built back of my house, and in pounding down cement for the foundation, eight or ten men stand on a staging each holding a rope which is attached to a heavy weight. This they pull up and then allow to drop, but in doing this they pause to sing the weirdest sort of a chanty. I heard the same in Nikko last year, and it must be a definite song, but the keenest ears could not carry away two consecutive notes of it. I mean by this that in their music there are no "catchy" motives as in our music. Their music does not strike a responsive cord; one does not recall a single musical phrase; one never hears home or family singing, no college chorus, no groups of men singing or serenading on the street. This is the more extraordinary in that their art, their manners, their love of flowers, their children's games even, all appeal to us. Their singing sounds ludicrous when first heard.

A dinner was given yesterday by the Director of the University to the professors, native and foreign, of the Educational Department. Ladies were not invited to the dinner, but we were allowed to bring them in the afternoon. The garden where the reception was held was built a few hundred

years ago by the Daimyo of Kishiu, and it has been carefully
preserved by the Government for the entertainment of foreign
guests. It may be eight hundred feet each way, but is considered small in comparison with some of the great gardens seen
here. It was impossible to judge its size, so remarkably decep-
tive are the appearances produced by the Japanese landscape
gardener; it seemed ten times as large as it really was, with its
irregular lake enclosed by a rough rock-work border crossed
at various points by tiny foot-bridges; little hills from twenty
to thirty feet high with steps leading to their summits; trees
dwarfed in the most extraordinary forms, others packed together and trimmed in rounded masses; paths of pebbles or
flat rocks, and such odd turns, and at every
point a new view. I attempted a hasty
sketch of it from one point, but it gave
only the faintest idea of its character, so it
is not reproduced. Only a good photograph

FIG. 309

could do justice to the wonderful character of the place.[1]
The oddest conceit for a foot-bridge is shown in figure 309;

the discontinuity of the foot-
path would certainly throw
a man into the water on a
dark night. Figure 310 is a
foot-bridge made of a single
slab of stone, ten feet long

FIG. 310

and four feet wide. Figure 311 is an interesting foot-bridge;
curved beams formed the support stretching from one abutment to the other, and round sticks, three inches in diame-

[1] Some of the bridges have been pictured in *Japanese Homes.*

ter, were laid transversely as a floor upon which was piled
earth; the edges were lined with grass, and in the centre a

FIG. 311

space two feet wide was covered with the cleanest flat
pebbles brought from some
seashore. The entire garden
had been reclaimed from a
mud flat; the hills were piled up; the stones were brought
many miles to make some of the bridges. On one of the
hills are four monoliths (fig. 312), square pillars five or six
feet in height; these were brought from Fuji, sixty miles

away, nearly two hundred and
fifty years ago, and formed
the gates of an old palace. The
garden is called Shiba Rikyu;
Rikyu means "outside palace"; *Shiba*, the region where
the garden is. It is the most
surprising and delightful spot

FIG. 312

I have yet seen in Japan. The buildings on the ground were
of one story as are most Japanese houses, from the Emperor's
palace to the simplest cottage.

. The entertainment in the evening consisted of a royal
dinner of fourteen courses with many kinds of wine. There
were seventy guests present, including General Saigo, who
had just been appointed Secretary of Education. I found him
a bright and charming man looking every inch a soldier.
Beautiful and precious flowers adorned the table; pyramids
of roses three feet high were at each end and in the middle of

the table, and the hall was delicately scented with some perfume. Such a jargon of voices I never heard before; the French,
German, and Chinese teachers from the Foreign Language
School; the professors from the Medical College, all Germans;
and the professors from the Imperial University — English,
American, and Japanese. With-
out exaggeration the table was
as fine-looking as any I had
ever seen at home and the cooking was unexcelled. The cooks
were all Japanese, but taught
by the best French chefs. I
had to come away at 9.30, as
I had a lot of work to do, but
the dinner was not over until
midnight.

Fig. 313

Figure 313 represents a man mowing with a straight-
handled scythe. All the scythes are of this kind.

To-day I tried to find the man who some time ago brought
me a present of cake. I had his address plainly written, but

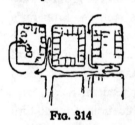

Fig. 314

the diagram (fig. 314) illustrates the
devious route my Japanese man took
in finding the place. I was told again
that there are but few streets with
names: the name applies to a whole
square through which may run a few
other streets. So up and down and
round and round we went before we found the place.

To-day a man came into the yard having potted plants for

sale. We bought fourteen plants, pots and all, and paid one cent a plant. Among them were two beautiful pinks in full blossom, two verbenas, some beautiful geraniums and others.

The Japanese in their adoption of our clothing manage very well with the hat, and even with the clothing, though it is always ill-fitting and shocking-looking in contrast to their own sensible and graceful robes. But the Japanese bootmaker, while making something, the outward semblance of which

 suggests boots, has not yet learned the art of stiffening the ankle. Though you see boots but rarely, when you do see them they are usually run down at the heels. Figure 315 is an accurate sketch of a pair of boots which I saw to-day on a man.

FIG. 315

Mr. Takamine, a graduate of the Oswego Normal School, whose acquaintance I made on the steamer, often comes to the house. He is a charming fellow, and I ask him many questions which he answers very frankly. He was speaking of my boy and how he liked to hug him, and this led to my speaking of the different ways of manifesting affection. Takamine's mother is a fine, intelligent-looking woman with a warm-hearted way about her that is very pleasant, and I asked Takamine, who has been absent for two and a half years, if he did not rush into her arms and give her a good hug and kiss? He answered, after pausing a moment, "No, I could not; it would have been very embarrassing; but I shook her hand, getting hold of the left one, and startled her by the vigor with which I did it, and she thought I was entirely foreignized!"

Then I asked him if he thought the love and affection for
friends and relatives, and particularly for one's children, was
as intense among the Japanese as with us. He admitted
frankly that he thought not, adding that he believed that affection and affectionate demonstrations could be cultivated
and that he had a more tender regard for his brothers since
he had been in America than he had had before.

Returning from the Educational Museum yesterday I
heard the pounding of the temple drums, and taking a short

cut through the woods of the
park came to a curious exhibition on one of the pavilions
that surround the temple.
Two actors came out on the
platform with the most brilliantly colored brocade dresses
and the most hideous masks
it is possible to conceive. One
had on a mass of white hair,
and his mask·was green in
color with gilt eyebrows and

FIG. 316

purple lips; the other had on a ghastly white mask, like
death itself, and an enormous mass of long black hair. They
went through a sort of fight with their swords till the white-
haired devil was vanquished (fig. 316). The Japanese get
up the most frightful-looking masks I ever saw. They are
carved out of wood and are made to represent different characters in a certain form of drama.

A few days ago I was invited to address a native archæo-

logical club on the Omori shell mounds. The club holds its
meetings at a room in the University on the first Sunday of
every month. Mr. Hattori, the Vice-Director of the University, is to act as interpreter. This morning, June 2, I went to
the place of the meeting. The members were sitting around a
big table, each one having in front of him a small vessel of hot
coals buried in ashes for warming the hands and lighting the
pipe. I was introduced to them and they all bowed profoundly.
I gave my talk in an adjoining room, where I had the ancient
pottery spread out in trays. I gave them a general sketch of
the subject: the four ages in Europe as defined by Lubbock,
the paleolithic, neolithic, bronze, and iron age; then Steenstrup's work on the shell heaps of the Baltic; and finally the
Omori mound. It was delightful to have such intelligent and
attentive listeners. My blackboard drawings seemed to please
them. Altogether I don't know when I have enjoyed giving a
lecture more than I did this one.

Professor Kikuchi came to dinner to-night. We played domi-
noes until ten. While we were playing his jinrikisha man
came up on the veranda and spoke through the closed blinds;
he knew nothing about ringing the bell, as the Japanese house
has no such contrivance. He began by saying in a low voice
(in Japanese, of course), "I have a little request to make"; and
then inquired if his master was within. It sounded so odd to
hear him talking there out of sight. I mention this incident
merely to illustrate the natural politeness of the people.

Professor Toyama, who lives in true Japanese style, invited
the family to his home to dinner. Before entering the house we
all took off our shoes and left them outside. This amused the

children, for they had never done it before except to go in wading or to go to bed. His wife and sister waited upon us, and when we had finished they had their dinner. When we first entered the house tea and a sweet sort of jelly were offered us. The dinner was brought in on square lacquer trays, we sitting on the floor and the trays being placed in front of us. It was interesting to see the children attempt to eat the various articles of food all tasting so unlike what they had been accustomed to. I am slowly acquiring a taste for nearly everything, and some kinds of food I like very much. There were two kinds of soup; the first clear like water, in which were a few sprigs of green, and sliced vegetables of some kind; the other like a custard, and mixed with it were boiled eel and egg plant. Next came a kind of omelette, lily bulbs, a white sort of yam, and a long leaf, reddish-green in color, and quite delicious. Vegetables formed the principal articles of food. Toyama's little niece danced for us while her mother played the samisen. The dancing was very pretty, consisting of graceful postures and attitudes. It is really a pantomime, the singer furnishing the subject by words and the dancer imitating by gestures the features of the story.

The work goes on steadily at the laboratory. Besides a bright, intelligent fellow whom the authorities have given me for an assistant and who helps label the collection which I brought from America, I have a boy who sweeps out, clears up, empties the stuff from the dissecting-pans, and when not otherwise engaged goes off into the surrounding country to collect land shells and fresh-water shells for me. This is what amazes one, the willingness and alertness of these people to learn and to help. Mr. Sasaki, a student, told me he hired a jinrikisha and went to a remote part of the city to collect, and his jinrikisha man got interested and collected too, so that they brought back a large lot of material.

Some Japanese friends of John's came to play with him, and little Miyaoka, to whom I have taken such a fancy, came too. I was holding him on my knee listening to his quaint English when, after a while, he put up his hand and gently felt my beard. I made a snap at his hand with my mouth, at the same time making a growling sound like a dog. To my astonishment he made no jump or movement of any kind. At home a child will intuitively draw its hands away as if a dog were really snapping at the fingers. Trying the experiment several times I asked him if his parents ever did such things, and he said no, and did not seem to know what it meant. When I told him that the act represented the snap of a dog, he said that their dogs did not snap. I may add that one does not see any attention paid to a dog, such as petting, and most of the dogs that one sees in Japan are of the wolf variety; they do not

bark but howl. John (my son) is much liked by the Japanese, and his light curly hair is a wonderful and curious sight to them.

I have often noticed the serviceable and economical way in which

FIG. 317

the dirt carts, which are hand carts, are provided with a tail-

board. It is simply a coarse matting hung on a stick like a
curtain, the ends of the short curtain hanging out at the end
of the cart, the weight of the dirt keeping the matting down
while the stick to which it is attached keeps it from dropping
out (fig. 317). The things to commend about
it are the simplicity and cleanliness of the whole
affair. Such simple, practical devices as these often arrest your attention. At the foot of the road
in the yashiki they are making new land. Instead of dragging their dirt carts over the made
land, they carry in all the dirt in mats hung
from poles on the shoulders of two men. At a
distance they look like a swarm of ants.

Figure 318 represents a glass device blown in
the form of a gourd. It is mounted on a board,
and in it goldfishes are kept; it might be used
also for a few flowers.

Fig. 318

Boys in going to school carry their
foreign inkbottle tied by a string and hanging
from the hand (fig. 319). Many small articles
are carried in this way tied by a string with a
loop for a handle. The string is made out of paper
which in most cases is very tough. They cut the
paper into long strips and then twist it and roll
it on their knees, twisting piece after piece together in the most adroit way. Bundles are tied

Fig. 319

up with it and it seems as strong as our linen cord.

An invitation to a dinner at a Japanese tea-house at an
early hour was promptly accepted. We were invited to the

second story, where we had a chance to examine the simple beauties and the cleanliness of the rooms. The hotel, if it may be called so, is in a densely populated part of Tokyo and yet there was room for a garden. In the garden was a large pile of

FIG. 320

rocks so closely cemented together that it looked like a protuberance of a natural ledge (fig. 320). All over it were beautiful ferns, azaleas, and other plants, and on the top a quaint, scraggy pine. There is a cave in the rock, and in front of the entrance, a little pond. Only Japanese were present and we knew most of them; such a happy, jolly set of men — there was hardly a moment that some of them were not romping with my little boy. Besides the Japanese professors there was a newspaper man, and a noble and a fine-looking man he was. All were in the native costumes, much more beautiful for them than our clothing. Mr. Hattori brought his wife, and Mr. Agee and Mr. Enouye brought their mothers. Before the dinner was served, tea and a delicious confection enclosed in some gelatinous substance were offered, a sharp-pointed stick being served to eat the latter with. Square, mat-like cushions were placed in a line on the floor with a square hibachi in front of each.

The cushions in summer are of straw; in winter, of cloth padded with cotton. The dinner was excellent, and gradually I am getting accustomed to Japanese food. I recall the lily bulbs, boiled in sugar, and the young ginger shoots salted. An enormous dish of Japanese vermicelli was brought in and passed around. A large colored flower, made out of slices of some kind of a turnip, appeared so natural that I thought it must be a genuine flower (fig. 321).

Fig. 321

The Japanese show their artistic skill in devising such decorative features for the table; their food is always served in an attractive manner, and even the eatables they peddle on the street show this same art. While we were at supper two girls with samisens made their appearance, and two smaller girls, beautifully dressed, with curious forms of drums. One girl held two hour-glass shaped drums, one under the left arm, while the left hand held the other by its tightening cords over the right shoulder. These were struck with the right hand, first one and then the other, the rim being struck with the ball of the hand and the fingers bouncing on the drumhead. Each drum had a different sound. The other girl had a drum of our type resting at an angle as in the sketch (fig. 322). This was struck with round sticks. With a deep bow they began and emitted the

Fig. 322

most curious music I have yet heard, and altogether unfathomable. The two with the samisens sang in low, plaintive voices while the drummers would break in at times with a short squeak that sounded as if made by a very small infant. After the singing came the posture dancing by the two little girls. From certain attitudes and expressions John thought they felt proud; for at times they would make a peculiarly contemptuous sort of face. The whole performance, with the beautiful dresses and graceful movements, was always interesting, but utterly unintelligible, as we knew nothing about the story they were acting and much of the acting was conventional. Some gestures suggested rowing a boat, swimming, cutting with the swords, and other movements. The variety of ways in which they twirled their folding fans was remarkable. After this ended, two little girls not over three years old, very pretty and clean, approached us in the sweetest manner. John tried to get near them, but they became so frightened at the appearance of a little boy with light curly hair that they both burst out crying and had to be taken away and calmed.

After this we were treated to a juggler's show. First a boy came in bringing various devices for the performance. He wore a black lace head-covering that reached below his shoulders such as the supernumeraries wear on the stage. Then came the juggler, a man of fifty, who made a long speech enumerating the things he was going to do. He then placed two chopsticks on the mat some distance in front of him and made them dance and caper for a while; then, borrowing a lady's long hairpin, he made that dance in the same manner, and asking for my cigar-holder, he made that skip about. He rolled up a bit of paper in the rude shape of a butterfly and with his fan kept it fluttering in the air; another butterfly was made and he kept the two in the air, even making them alight on a box on his head. Of course these objects were held by the most delicate silk fibres, but they were invisible and the trick was very ingenious. Many of the tricks were the purest sleight-of-hand, as when he took one of the butterflies and rolled it into a pellet and with the fan in his other hand apparently fanned out of the pellet hundreds of little bits of paper all over the room; then with a fling of his hand he tossed out a dozen long coils of paper ribbon, gathered them up in his hand in a mass of festoons, and set them afire, and suddenly from the blazing mass opened a big umbrella. These tricks were all done with great rapidity and skill. Afterwards he came near us and made objects mysteriously disappear and performed other sleight-of-hand tricks. Such a jolly time the Japanese had; they entered into the spirit of the thing like children, laughing heartily. Mr. Enouye then made a short speech of welcome, to which I had to respond. We got

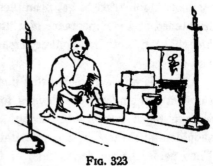

FIG. 323

home near midnight, the children tired enough, and my head swimming with the strange sights I had seen. Figure 323 gives an idea of the juggler.

June 15. There was a flower fair at a temple not far from the yashiki. The sides of the road were lined with little temporary booths filled with toys of all sorts, flower hairpins for children,

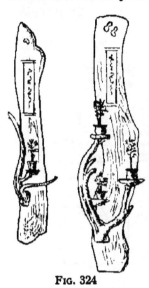

candies, and cake, and the road was fairly encumbered with flowers in bunches, in masses, and of all kinds. A good-natured crowd was passing back and forth, and when John got out of the jinrikisha and walked about he was followed by an admiring crowd of Japanese, men and children. At one booth were hanging devices for holding diminutive flower pots with plants growing and strips of paper with poems written on them. The objects were about three feet long, consisting of a thin strip of wood with irregular outlines, upon which were fastened

FIG. 324

twigs of a tree supporting little shelves. Figure 324 will give a better idea of their appearance than any description. The wood was browned by heat and looked old.

It is the custom with the Japanese when they go for a walk to bring back to the family some little present in the form of food of some kind, no matter how trifling. Takenaka says it is the universal custom. They have curious kinds of presents; a common one showing esteem is a box of a dozen eggs. This has come to me several times. On making a present of money there is written on the outside of the envelope, or wrapper, an inscription which reads, "Wherewithal to buy cake." Professor Parsons has received as a present from the family of Count Okubo a tall wooden tray of the purest white pine filled with candy of various shapes and colors. Every object has its significance. I could not resist sketching it (fig. 325). The little bunches of objects with bent ends represented the young sprouts of ferns which they eat. The large piece twisted so as to form an arch had on the top sprays of wistaria, colored, of course, and perfect imitations of the flower. The cakes had a stamp of the chrysanthemum on top; these were red and white and were made of bean paste and sugar. The Japanese are very fond of them, but they are rather insipid in taste. The tray was eighteen inches in height, so you can form an idea of the size of the candy. The whole conception was pure, simple, and artistic.

Fig. 325

Last week we had a severe earthquake. I was in the second story of the hotel in Yokohama. I record it, as it was one of the first earthquakes I had ever *heard*. The slight shocks we have in New England are accompanied by audible rumblings, while thus far the earthquakes in Japan are noticeable only for their vibrations; this one was preceded by a rumbling sound as if a heavy team were going along the road. Mrs. Hubbard, who has been here many years, told me it was the rumble of a heavy wagon going by and I thought nothing more about it. But the next instant a crashing, grinding, explosive thud made the whole building shake; it really seemed as if the building would fall in ruins if the shock were repeated. The lady nearly fainted with fright and other people in the hotel were hurrying about in an aimless, frightened way. It was the toughest one I had ever felt, and for the first time I got a little excited over it, probably because of the fright of others.

June 16. I was awakened by another earthquake which shook the house, made the doors rattle, and kept up for half a minute.

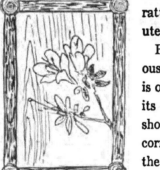

Figure 326 represents an ingenious way to teach botany. The panel is of the wood of a tree upon which its flowers are painted; the frame shows the bark of the tree; and the corners of the frame are sections of the branches

Fig. 326

Mrs. Takamine came to-day with the little Japanese boys who play with John. She brought with her three little devices in silk crape which look like pin cushions, but have pockets behind them to hold wooden toothpicks. Figure 327 represents two of them.

Coming from Yokohama the other day I saw from the car window a funny sight. It was a horse with a harrow attached, running away at a frantic gallop, with the farmer trying in vain to stop him. As the rice-paddies are now filled with water, the way the

FIG. 327

mud and water were flying, as the harrow bounced about dashing the stuff over the farmer, was ludicrous enough.

I came across a Japanese book in which were some remarkable studies of queues; also a series of sketches illustrating the various modes of dressing the hair for boys and men — old styles of a hundred years ago and the present styles. In

FIG. 328

figure 328 I have copied a few of the designs. Some of the styles are very often seen now, though there is no foreign idea that has been adopted so promptly as our style of dressing the hair; its common sense appealed to the people at once. Consider the bother of having the top of one's head shaved every two or three days and the queue waxed and firmly arranged on the bald ·spot. To keep it in place night and day must have been a burden. The fishermen, the farmers, and classes of that kind still adhere to the queue; also old scholars, antiquarians, and a few others. The students of the University have all adopted the foreign way of wearing the hair. Many of them find it difficult to have it smoothed down or parted in any way, and some of them have a perfect mop of hair radiating in all directions, but cut close. Shaving the top of the head since childhood has doubtless contributed to the difficulty of making the hair lie properly. I had a student living with me for some time, and one day I asked him if he suffered from rheumatism, as in walking he limped. He answered that his lameness was due to a sword cut received in a fight. My curiosity was excited, and finally I ventured to ask him if he got his wound in some battle. He smilingly told me that when he first saw a foreigner and realized the simple method of arranging the hair and meditated on the time saved in this style of hair-dressing, he surprised the school one day by appearing before his class shorn of his queue. One student in particular chided him for imitating the foreigner. Swords were drawn, with the result that my friend got a slash in the leg. Within six months the student who had chided him realized that the foreign way of wearing the hair was the only rational way and appeared at school shorn of his queue!

This afternoon we were invited by the Educational Department to a concert at the old Chinese college. The music was an old form known as *kibigaku*, two hundred years old, and came from the Province of Bizen. The hall in which the concert was given had carpets and chairs; the chairs being arranged in three rows on the two sides of the hall, leaving an open space in the middle. There were nearly two hundred people present, mostly Japanese, and among them were twenty teachers from the Female Normal School and Kindergarten. They were a fine-looking group of women. It was interesting to see how low and ceremoniously they

FIG. 329

bowed to one another as they met. In the middle of the floor were two *kotos*, or Japanese harps (fig. 329). The instrument is nearly five feet long and is an old form derived from China. After a while the performers came in, six in all,

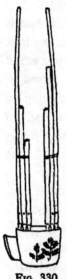

two for the harps, two singers, and two more, one playing the flute and one a curious instrument called the *sho* (fig. 330), often figured in the early Chinese books. It has a round base, like half a cocoanut, from which spring vertically a number of bamboo tubes of varying lengths; the mouthpiece is in the side of the base. The player holds it in his two hands as shown in the sketch (fig. 331). The leader was an old man, and he played the flute and at times a kind of short flageolet which had an extraordinary sound.

The performance began with the old man uttering a monotonous series of gruff howls. Had he been suffering from an overdose of cucumbers he could not have uttered more dismal sounds; it was really ludicrous, and one found

FIG. 330

it difficult to preserve one's gravity. While he was making these sounds another performer picked an accompaniment on

Fig. 331

the koto. This seemed to be a sort of prelude, for after a while one of the young men began to sing, and the old man played on the flute, and all the instruments started, the sho keeping up an accompaniment in one or two tones sounding not unlike a bagpipe. Each piece, though widely different in title, sounded very much alike to me. It was by no means unpleasant to hear, and yet from our standpoint I should not call it music. The title of one of the selections was, "Moon on a Spring Night"; another was named after a certain general; still another was dedicated to a celebrated river; another, which I thought would never end, was appropriately called "Time."

During a long interval I went outside, lit a cigar, and wandered up and down the grounds for a while. My cigar was unfinished when the orchestra began again, and so I laid it down carefully on the steps in a corner where if the wind blew it would not be disturbed. At the next interlude I came out again to find my cigar, and it had disappeared. Somewhat puzzled, I was looking about when a policeman came along and in a questioning manner soberly pointed to the place where I had left it. I answered 'yes' in Japanese, and then he pointed to some fire boxes, or hibachi, at the end of the corridor, and on going there I found my cigar carefully placed on the edge of a fire bowl, where if any coals fell from it they would fall into the ashes. Such is their great care in regard to fire.

A man performed one of the Japanese slow and dignified ceremonial dances; it was not exactly a dance, but a play in which a variety of gestures were made by stamping the foot, etc. It was interesting as illustrating an old style of play. The question constantly arose, "Is this music in our sense of the word?" It is, but widely unlike ours. The sober, passive countenances of the performers are never enlivened by a smile; there are no dilated nostrils nor sparkling eyes nor swings of the head as with our singers when inspired by the words. It seems impossible that they should feel any inspiration or thrill from the monotonous sounds. The nearest comparison I could make would be to an old man in our country, with no ear for music, alone in a woodshed, absent-mindedly trying to recall some slow-timed and rather dismal hymn tune. Now this impression is felt by one who frankly confesses that he knows nothing about it. We thought certain forms of Japanese pictorial art absurd: certain prints, for example, with startling violations of perspective; human figures whose femora would have the proportions of baseball bats, whose skeletons, if found, would be classed as new genera; and yet these pictures command the admiration of our artists. It may be that their music will ultimately prove to have merits of which we get no hint at present.

In return for a concert the Educational Department gave to the foreign professors, four of the University professors formed a quartette and practiced a number of songs. The quartette consisted of Professors Mendenhall, Fenollosa, Leland, and Morse. Among the selections we practiced were "Pilgrim's Chorus"; a few songs from the Arion collection; "Old Hundred"; "All honor to the soldier be"; and others. The Japanese teachers were assembled to the number of two hundred; every one was furnished with a pencil and paper, the selections were printed on a programme, and the teachers were requested to record their impressions. These were collected and are still in the hands of one of the singers, mostly untranslated. "All honor to the soldier be" we sang with great spirit, and were somewhat abashed to learn that the sentiments were offensive to the gentle Japanese. We were informed afterwards that the Japanese have neither in poetry nor in prose extolled the glories of battle.

I went to the theatre with the children this morning. The building is a new one and is the best and largest in Japan, and has a seating capacity of fifteen hundred. It is lighted by gas, well ventilated, and is altogether a fine exhibition hall. It is square in shape with galleries on the sides and ends of the hall, the gallery facing the stage being very deep; the gallery boxes are considered the choicest places. Instead of rows of seats as with us the hall was divided into bins, six feet square and a foot or more in depth, with a squatting capacity of four adults and two children. The aisles were on a level with the tops of these bins, the edges of the bins being four inches wide, so that one, on entering the theatre, walks up the aisles and then, balancing himself, walks along the rail of these bins to find his proper place. The building was finished in natural woods as are all the dwellings; not a touch of paint, oil, varnish, or wood filling is to be seen. The ceiling was apparently composed of planks three feet in width. There were two large gas chandeliers suspended from this, and gas was used for the foot-

FIG. 332

lights. Figure 332 is a very rough sketch of the theatre from the street; and hanging in front of it are bright-colored pictures of the actors.

The building, which must have cost many thousands of dollars, was of the most substantial character, constructed after the manner of the fireproof buildings, and it was imposing with its black polished walls and massive roofing tiles. As you enter the vestibule the ceiling is very low, made for Japanese height, and you knock your head on the rafters above. Your shoes are checked, a big wooden ticket being given you, and it is a curious sight to see the hundreds of pairs of wooden clogs arranged in little spaces on the walls. Ascending a steep flight of stairs you come to a narrow passageway from which by a number of doors the theatre is entered. The stage is very wide, but not deep. In the centre of the stage is a large turntable level with the floor, and while one act is being performed before a certain scene the stage carpenters are at work on another scene behind, and when the act is ended the turntable slowly rotates and a new scene comes into view. Looking down from the gallery it is very interesting to see the people in the depressed squares, — whole families, or a group of men and women. Having their hibachis they can heat the water for tea and bring out their lunches (or waiters from near-by restaurants bring in trays with a dinner or lunch), and lighting their pipes from the coals they have the happiest time imaginable.

The acting was exceedingly realistic, some of the scenes being shocking, as in the act of hara-kiri, where all the ceremonies lead up to the final catastrophe, when the head is carried away in a tray. All the details are shown: the baring of the abdomen, the cut from left to right with a short knife, the handle and blade held in the two hands; as the blade passes along, the cut appears as a blue line followed by a red fluid; the actor then throws his head forward and a friend starts to strike it off with a sword, but turning away in agony drops his weapon, which another quickly picks up, and terminates the sad tragedy. It is like a juggler's trick, for in the excitement you are not aware that some of the actors pass in front of the victim, so that the sword really seems to come down on the neck of the man, who has in the mean time, like a turtle, drawn his head within his loose robes. Be that as it may, a head with a bloody stump rolls out, which is gathered up, placed in a tray, and conveyed to the judge or daimyo, who, recognizing the features, knows that the act has been accomplished. The tragic sorrow of the friends is perfectly acted, and in the large audience many women are weeping. The play began at half-past six in the morning and continued in a series of acts until

nine o'clock at night. Some of the plays require two or three
days to perform and I was told that some plays in China require a month or two for a complete performance.

This play was fifteen hours long and recorded the history of
an early shogun, and I am sure if it were acted in America it
would attract a great deal of attention. The actors come up
the two main aisles from the rear of the theatre and act as

Fig. 333

they come up the aisle or retire to their rooms again. One
recognizes the theatrical stride and other tricks of acting that
one sees at home. In one scene there is an old house with a
boat drawn up in the midst of rushes; the boat is loaded with
fish and the vicinity looks like a swamp (fig. 333). The house
was large enough to hold twenty men who came in afterwards,
but for some time there was only an old woman, bent over
with age, who was fanning a few embers to make a smoke to
drive away imaginary mosquitoes. She would now and then

fan her neck and legs to drive them away; then she would
tenderly wipe her eyes inflamed from the smart of the smoke.
It was difficult to realize that this part was acted by a young
man; his behavior and every movement were those of a de-
crepit woman eighty years old. All the actors are men, the
female parts being represented by men, who speak in high,
falsetto voices.

A few conventional features of the old style of acting are still
retained and are grotesque to the last degree. It is impossible
to describe the acting; some parts of it are more like gymnas-
tic exercises, and unless it were explained to you it would be
impossible to interpret it. One man, a high samurai, will with
his fan overthrow a crowd of thirty men armed with swords
and spears, and it is a literal overthrow, as they leap in the air
and turn somersaults backward without touching the floor. In
one instance a man, who had repeatedly put to flight a crowd
of men who immediately returned to the conflict, becoming
hard-pressed, rushed up a short flight of steps and, making a
few desperate and heroic gestures, grasped the handle of his
sword, simply a threat to draw it, when the entire crowd fell
backward on the ground with their legs high in the air! It was
ridiculous to the last degree, and yet a certain power and
dominance over the peasant class were exhibited by the hero,
who, after having repelled the crowd, with his fan alone
showed what would be the result if he had been finally forced
to draw his dreadful sword. When night is supposed to come
on, the stage is not darkened, but a box is hung from the top
of the stage in which a crescent moon is cut out, illuminated by
a candle behind (fig. 334). A sign hung out saying, "It is now

night," would hardly be more absurd. In commenting on this feature to a Japanese who has lived in our country, he said they were accustomed to these conventions, — that there seemed nothing incongruous in them, — just as we are used to seeing an actor leaning against the side of a baronial castle causing it to sway back and forth. He recalled his amazement at the sight of it on our stage, and yet our people showed no concern.

FIG. 334

On the right of the stage is the orchestra shut in behind a black painted grating; from within came the sound of a big drum and a monotonous thrumming of a samisen as an accompaniment to the voices which followed the play, distressing or despairing according to the scene portrayed. On the left of the stage and even with the gallery was another barred enclosure, within which was a man possessed of a remarkable voice who wailed, cried, scolded, and shrieked, — making noises as of cats fighting, — and kept up this vocal accompaniment to the acting, going on hour after hour, tragic or otherwise. It really excites you or saddens you, as the case may be. At times the voice is ominous and prophetic and you anticipate some catastrophe which is sure to come.

The versatility of the Japanese servant is noticeable. Each one of the four I have is capable of performing the duties of the other three. The other day I allowed the boy and cook to go to the theatre, and the only woman servant got up a very nice dinner. Even the jinrikisha man can cook, can put up self-rolling curtains, or do anything of the sort, and when I have a big dinner he comes in barelegged and arranges the

flowers so beautifully that you wonder at his skill. He helps
about the garden and is ready to run errands, and he evidently believes it his duty to wash the dishes, which he does
every day and, I may say, without ever breaking them or
nicking them.

I have noticed how quickly my Japanese friends who come
to the house learn a game; they are mentally alert.

One of my Japanese special students, Matsura, of whom I
was very fond, died at the hospital last night of that mysterious disease called beri-beri. He had been ill for some time and
I had often been to the hospital to see him; he would inquire
how the work was getting along and kept up his interest to
the last moment. I learned that it would gratify the students
of his class if I would accompany them to the burial-place;
his mother, sister, and relatives lived five hundred miles south,
and could not come. About a hundred students gathered, and

Fig. 335

we waited some time for the coffin to appear. This was a long
plain box covered with white cloth and borne on the shoulders
of four men; a man in front carrying a long bamboo pole from
which was hanging a long, narrow strip of cloth (fig. 335). I
had noticed this flag on similar occasions, and learned that it

gave simply the name of the deceased and the province from which he came. In advance of all was a man carrying a long wooden post upon which was Matsura's name; this was a temporary grave-post. There was no organized procession. We followed the body in an irregular manner, but with sober and orderly demeanor. All the students were in native dress and resembled a class from a woman's college. Many of them wore our form of straw hat and their clogs made a curious clatter on the hard roadbed. A walk of nearly a mile and a half brought us to the cemetery, a very beautiful place with large trees, and flowers, and much natural scenery. The people we passed looked in curious wonder at seeing a foreigner in the procession. At the entrance to the cemetery was a sort of reception shed, where the bier with the coffin was placed resting on two wooden supports; the grave-post was rested against the coffin. Soon a Buddhist priest with clean-shaven head came out bearing sprigs of leaves which he leaned against the side of the coffin, one near each end; he then put on his rich brocade robes, lighted the candle, knelt down beside the coffin, and began mumbling a prayer, occasionally tapping a little bell which he had with him (fig. 336). The sound he made with his lips reminded one of the sound a huge bumblebee might make. I could not distinguish an articulate word, nor a pause in the mumbling. A few students stood near. Others were on the side of the road, some smoking their little Japanese pipes; they seemed to be utterly indifferent to the service, apparently regarding it as rather a bore, but one that had to be endured. Professor Yatabe, who was with me, told me that among the crowd of a hundred students there was

Fig. 336

probably not one who believed in the Buddhist or Shinto religion, but all would be buried in this way so that their mothers
and sisters would not feel hurt. Yet they were quiet and serious, talked in low tones, and were paying their last tribute to
their departed schoolmate with sobriety and dignity. The
grave was very deep, seven or eight feet, at least. After the
coffin had been lowered into it many of the students pushed
in a little earth with their umbrellas; others took up a handful of earth and tossed it in. It was a sad sight, these sober-
faced young men gathering about the grave and then quietly
dispersing.

I noticed many fine gravestones and monuments, some being made of natural slabs of rock with irregular contours just
as they were quarried from the ledge. Upon the smooth cleavage face of the rock were cut inscriptions; these, I was told,
were Shinto graves. Here were the signs of two widely differ-

ent cults side by side, and I thought of our own country, with its two branches of a single religion, each with its own cemetery, wider apart in death than they were in life

In discussing April Fools' day with Professor Yatabe, he said that the Japanese, dignified as they appear, were fond of playing mischievous tricks. One of these tricks was to fasten very lightly a sheet of red gossamer paper over the face of a sleeping person and then wake him by running through the room crying fire. The sleeper awakes, and seeing the red glare jumps up quickly, to realize that he has been made the victim of a joke. The Japanese samurai wear on the sleeves of their outer garment, as well as on the back, a beautiful design in white, left undyed when the silk is dyed black; this design is called a *mon*, and may be regarded as the coat of arms or crest of the family. These crests are often seen on porcelain, pottery, lacquer, and other objects which have been made for the use of the families owning them. A trick is sometimes played by cutting out of white paper a design of some crest representing some family under the ban. One side, being previously covered with paste, the design is concealed in the hand as a student approaches his friend and, placing his hand affectionately on his back, presses the mon to the coat, where it sticks to the amusement of the passers-by. As boys we used to play a similar trick by chalking some ridiculous figure in the palm of the hand and then slapping the back of another boy, who would go down the street unconcernedly parading this picture on his back.

It is interesting to watch carpenters at work, for they do many things so differently from what we should do and work with none of the appliances considered so essential by us. In drilling with an awl, the handle of which is short, we hold it in one hand and bore by turning the hand back and forth; the

FIG. 337

Japanese use a long-handled awl (fig. 337) and revolve the handle by pressing the open hands against the handle and moving them back and forth rapidly. As the hands gradually come down they instantly move them to the top of the handle, continually pressing down as they continue the movement. In this way they bore holes very quickly. They have no such device as a carpenter's bench, nor a vise like ours; the saws have long, straight handles, and with such a handle they can use both hands. Their contrivance for a vise is most clumsy and awkward.[1]

A boy in blowing bubbles uses a long bamboo tube, and instead of soap and water he uses a vegetable infusion. From the tube he will blow rapidly twenty to thirty bubbles, which float away giving the appearance of blowing bits of paper through the tube.

Many of the names of institutions are painted on long strips of wood. Writing as they do vertically, a sign, unless pictorial, takes little room except in a vertical direction. The Medical College, which is a large building having a bell tower on top and massive iron gates in foreign style, has a sign painted on a board, one foot wide and six feet long, and this is simply the name of the institution. The door-plates, or names of the

---

[1] We must, however, refer to the book on *Japanese Homes* for a more detailed description of carpenters' tools and their method of work.

occupants of a house, are painted on strips of wood and hung
at the side of the entrance
(fig. 338).

When Fourth of July came
my boy was greatly disap-
pointed at not being permitted to fire off crackers. As a
safeguard against conflagrations, not even in the yashiki
did the police permit the use
of fire-crackers, toy pistols,
and the like.

I must record my first public lecture in Japan before
an audience composed ex-

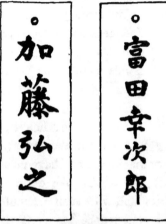

Fig. 338

clusively of Japanese. The young Japanese professors who
have returned from America admire our system of lecture
courses as a means of public instruction and have endeavored
to establish such an institution in Tokyo. They have met
with great difficulty in arousing an interest among the
people, as the whole idea was such an innovation. However they have gone ahead and hired a big room in a tea-
house. The people are so poor that the price of admission has
to be low. A few friends have started a journal to be devoted to
science, literature, antiquities, etc., in connection with the lecture course, and they honored me by asking me to give the
opening lecture of the course, Sunday, June 30. I selected as
a subject archæology. When I rode through a narrow alley to
the place I saw my name in Japanese on a large signboard with

other characters which I could not read. People were going in, and, meeting Mr. Agee, who was to act as interpreter, we entered the room which looked out over the river. It was a queer sight to see the floor entirely covered by Japanese sitting on the mats in the usual way, many of them with fans, some with their pipes, and others drinking tea. A blackboard had been provided. There was only one chair in the room and this I was to occupy. Mr. Enouye made a preliminary address, which I learned afterwards was a short sketch of me derived from some biographical article. Naturally passing unblushingly through this ordeal, for I did not understand a word of what he said, I was introduced. It was difficult to lecture through an interpreter. One can converse in that way without trouble, but in lecturing without notes you are compelled to wonder all the time how much your interpreter can remember, and that curbs all earnestness or impetuosity of speech. I went through the subject, literally step by step, giving a general sketch of archæology, and then telling them about the wide and unexplored field they had in Japan, describing the Omori shell mounds right at their doors and exhibiting some of the pottery. When I finished there was a hearty clapping of hands, which they had learned from the Japanese students who had been abroad. There were some intelligent-looking old men present, and all seemed to be interested. At the lecture sitting by the side of the stage was a policeman. The next day Mr. Agee came to the house and stated that the admission had been ten cents; students, half price; the hall was so much, the advertising so much, and the balance of ten dollars he insisted upon my taking. This, of course, was entirely unexpected and I tried to decline it. However, it was forced upon me and I resolved to buy some object and preserve it as a souvenir of the occasion, as I was told that this was the first time a foreigner had lectured under the conditions of an organized course of lectures. The organization has invited me to give a course of lectures, which I have offered to do in the autumn only on condition that there will be no honorarium. The subject will be Darwinism.

CHAPTER XII

July 13, 1878. I left Yokohama on the steamer this evening for Yezo. Our party consisted of Professor Yatabe, botanist, and his assistant and a servant; my assistant, Mr. Taneda, and a servant; and Mr. Sasaki. From the appropriation given me by the University I was able to have some assistance from Mr. Takamine and Mr. Fenton. The water was remarkably calm, and the voyage would have been delightful had not our steamer on a previous trip been filled with a cargo of fish and fish manure. The stench was simply intolerable; it permeated everything and the only spot on the vessel free from the stench was the extreme end of the bow. With this dreadful odor enhanced by a little seasickness the voyage was disagreeable enough. Leaving Saturday evening we had clear weather. Sunday was a clear day till the afternoon, when we ran into a dense fog and the whistle sounded at short intervals. Monday it cleared and we had a fine view of the northern coast of Japan. Sailing along at a distance of eight or ten miles the surface features could be plainly made out. The country is very mountainous with high peaks running into the clouds. The cloud effects were wonderful, bringing out the contour of the bold and craggy outlines of these volcanic ridges, for the whole range seems to be volcanic from Yezo to the southern part of Japan. There was one place along the coast that indicated a remarkable plateau, four or five hundred feet above the sea cut through in places by rivers (fig. 339).

Tuesday morning about four I heard the welcome sound of the bell tap to stop the engines, and looking out of my porthole I saw that we were near Hakodate, the high peak just back of the town looming up. The air outside the vessel was cool and

Fig. 339

delightful, for we were six hundred miles north of Tokyo and this makes a difference in temperature. Mr. Harris, the Consul, insisted that I should take breakfast with him, so engaging a boat among a number that surrounded the vessel after dropping anchor, we started off. The boat was like a logger's punt and oscillated fearfully as we sculled toward shore. This peculiar shaking-up before breakfast, with scarcely any food for three days, was anything but agreeable. However, the sun came up, tipping the mountains back of the town with its rays, and my spirits came up in proportion, though I must say that I felt rather discouraged when I critically examined the boats in the harbor, for not one of the many large and clumsy Japanese junks would answer my purpose for dredging. Mr. Harris was also perplexed, as he had become interested in the work I was to do, but he thought we might hire a rowboat from one of the few foreign vessels in the harbor. Landing in the midst of strange boats and the odor of fish, we went through the town to Mr. Harris's residence on higher land, from which the view of the town is delightful.

On my way I picked up a handful of snails (*Succinea*) which were crawling about the plants beside the road. Many of the plants were similar to our own. The white clover which has been introduced has larger blossoms than ours, with longer stems and a most fragrant perfume. The town is almost an

Fig. 340

island connected with the main island by a sand-neck (fig. 340), having a beautiful background in a mountain twelve hundred feet high, of volcanic origin. Most of the town is on low ground, but the better houses are built a little above on the slope of the mountain. The houses, instead of being covered with heavy tiles, have their shingled roofs closely covered with large beach-worn stones, giving a most curious appearance. Figure 341 is a rough outline of the town from a street which leads out to the sand-neck. I am continually reminded of Eastport, Maine. Not that there is the slightest resemblance between the two places, but the crisp, fresh air, the pure and cold salt water, the odor of fish, and the land beyond reminds one of Campobello, and the work I am doing, that of dredging, helps the illusion. After breakfast Professor Yatabe and I made a call on the Governor, a dignified Japanese

official. As soon as we had announced our names he said he
had received a letter from General Saigo, the Minister of Education, and a dispatch from the Vice-Minister of Education,
and he would be pleased to help us in any way. I told him
briefly our needs: first, a room for a laboratory, if possible on
some wharf where we could easily get salt water; and second,

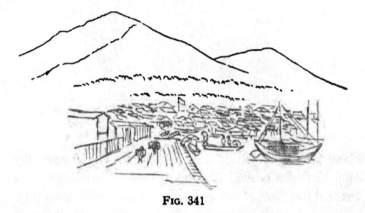

FIG. 341

a proper boat for dredging. He directed us to the old Japanese
custom house at the water's edge, and down we went escorted
by an official. I found two rooms, precisely what I needed for
a laboratory, and the occupants were immediately turned out
with polite protestations on my part and the sweetest accept-
ance of banishment on theirs. Then I modestly told him
that I wanted a running table along the rooms under the windows and some shelves, drawing a plan to illustrate. Within
an hour four carpenters were at work. I went to the place in
the evening at 9.30, and by the dim light of two candles the
four naked carpenters were still at it, and the next morning

everything was completed, the rooms thoroughly cleaned, and
the work ready. In the mean time the Governor had secured a fine steam launch with captain, engineers, and two
sailors, and this was placed at our disposal as long as we remained. Imagine the elation I felt. I had been in despair as
to a boat or room to work in, and in twelve hours I had a perfect outfit. I recalled my difficulties at Enoshima and the
weeks spent in getting any boat or accommodations for work,
and here in this short time I was amply provided with every
appliance necessary. The problem of lodging still remained
unsettled, as I could not subsist on Japanese food and there
was no hotel or boarding-house in the town. Two officials
were sent to canvass the town, and at three o'clock in the
afternoon they reported that they had got two rooms for us
with the Danish Consul, who lives in a foreign-built house.
So down I went and was presented to a charming old gentleman who spoke English perfectly, an old bachelor who expressed his delight that I should live with him. The Governor's official with two servants had, in the mean time, found
two chairs, a bureau, a table, bedstead, sheets, pillows, mosquito netting, and everything, even to a Brussels carpet; and
so without the slightest expense or trouble on my part I have
been most delightfully taken care of. A bottle of good beer
and a beefsteak for dinner every day, — what more could one
ask for?

A high wind came up on the next day with big rollers pounding on the beach, leading me to believe that a mass of stuff
would be thrown up. So getting the party together we started
off with high expectations, but, as is often the case, hardly a

thing was washed up. Among the refuse piles of the fishermen
I got a few interesting shells. The huts of the fishermen were
odd-looking objects, low, with heavy thatched roof, and a

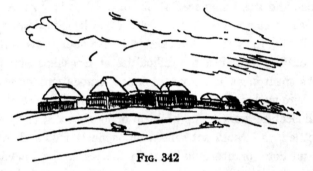

FIG. 342

bamboo wattled fence surrounding each one to break the
force of the wind, which often blows with hurricane violence
(fig. 342). The fishermen's huts at Beaufort, North Carolina,
under similar exposures resembled these Hakodate huts.
From the veranda of my house a fine view of the harbor is
obtained, and at a distance of twenty-five miles a volcano
named Komogatake looms up, its sharp peak in marked contrast to the gentle slopes about it. The volcano is now resting

FIG. 343

and having a quiet smoke, which can be seen like a white cloud hanging over the peak; but thirty years ago it was in eruption and threw cinders and stones into the bay (fig. 343).

The sailors in rowing their boats back and forth in the harbor have a peculiar song entirely unlike the sailors' songs farther south. It is musical and catchy.

The sailors are fine, muscular-looking fellows; wearing nothing but a breech-cloth, they are as brown as russet apples. In rowing the boat they push instead of pulling the oars, and consequently face the bow of the boat. The oar has a cross-piece of wood at the end of the handle. They row in pairs, and one is reminded of galley slaves. The rowlock is simply a loop of rope hanging on the side of the boat through which

FIG. 344

they put the oar. The sketch (fig. 344) is that of a boat loaded with rice. Some boats will have six or seven men on a side, and the curious chant from so many throats as it comes over the water is very pleasant.[1]

The harbor is now full of Japanese trading junks discharging loads of rice and loading with fish. Figure 345 is a fairly

[1] In the extreme southern part of Japan I heard the identical song sung by the sailors of Kagoshima Gulf, and on my return to America a Russian troupe which visited Salem sang a piece called a Volga sailor's song strongly suggesting the Hakodate song. Such an air might easily spread through northern Russia to Kamchatka and find its way to Yezo through the Kurile Islands.

FIG. 345

good sketch of one. The top of the mast is not broken; they all tip this way for some purpose. The vessel is entirely unpainted and is a picturesque-looking craft. It seems as if they were always at anchor, as one rarely sees them sailing. The vessel is literally flat-bottomed, — not the trace of a keel, — and so they can sail only before the wind. The rudder is of enormous proportions, and when not in use is tipped out of the water in a curious way (fig. 346). In their

FIG. 346

years of exclusion the Japanese Government would not permit the building of vessels on foreign models. It is said that the authorities recognized the unstable character of their vessels, and thus the natives were compelled to sail near shore, for in a storm their vessels were quite unmanageable. In their coasting trade they sail along the shore for two or three days, and on the slightest hint of a blow or storm they seek harbor and wait for the storm to come or to blow away. The Japanese promptly recognized the superiority of our models. Since the Revolution the law interdicting the building of vessels after foreign style has been repealed, and now they are building after foreign models. In this town there are six or seven schooners on the stocks, and good-looking models they are. The shipyards appear like our own and yet the workmen are all Japanese.

The earth used in repairing the streets or filling is conveyed in large straw bags hanging from a saddle (fig. 347). Five or

Fig. 347

six horses are tied together, and a woman, wearing a curious straw hat and an apron, leads them back and forth from the town to the hills. The bottom of the bag is gathered up in some way and tied. When the load is ready to dump, a twitch of the cord lets the earth rattle down to the ground. The bit is a curious device consisting of a large piece of wood on each side of the mouth. A rope, which for some purpose rests on the haunches of the horse, carries a number of wooden rollers so as to prevent galling. Another form of saddle is seen with hooks of wood on each side

made out of the crotch of a tree (fig. 348). This is designed
for carrying wood or long timbers. Everything is transported on the backs of horses. I have seen
no wheeled vehicles except the jinrikisha and
there are very few of these. It is a relief to
get away from the continual solicitations of
Tokyo jinrikisha men.

FIG. 348

On the sand beach there was a curious
device for a sound signal, used by watch-
men to strike the hour, or to indicate the time of patrol, or
to bang furiously in case of fire. It consisted of a square oak
board, two feet long by one foot high, suspended from a

post as seen in figure 349, with a wooden
mallet hung by a cord to strike it. It was
astonishing to hear the clear, ringing sound
it gave out. Farmers and others could adopt
the idea with advantage. The Japanese use
wooden devices of this nature for various
purposes: at the theatre two square pieces
of hard wood are struck together to signal
the rising of the curtain; at the college, at
the close of the lecture a man goes through

FIG. 349

the corridor clapping two pieces of wood together; the watchman strikes two clappers; and in the garden is hung a wooden
device, sometimes in the shape of a fish, which is struck with
a wooden mallet as a summons to go to the tea ceremony
in a little house in the garden. In our country, wood is used
in this manner only as a musical instrument, as in the xylo-
phone, or as a time measure in the clappers and castanets.

The other evening at the tea-house, where the rest of the party are staying, I heard a little child in the next room reading in the usual high-toned, sing-song manner. On inquiring as to what she was reading, Professor Yatabe listened for a moment and then said it was a sad classic which was as follows: "When parents die the sweetest food tastes bitter and lovely flowers lose their fragrance"; and more of the same nature.

Friday, July 19. Had my first dredging experience. The steam launch was ready to take us out into the straits known as Tsugaru Straits, which separate Yezo from the main island of Japan. The launch was so neat and clean that I explained that the operation of dredging was very dirty, with its mud and water, and got a boat towed behind from which we dredged. Figure 350 gives a rough idea of the old Japanese custom house. We have half the building on the right, and the five windows close together give us a flood of light. The roof

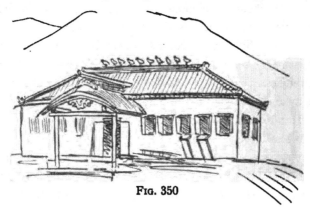

Fig. 350

is heavily tiled, and when I made my sketch a number of gulls were roosting on the ridge, their heads all pointing in the same direction. Figure 351 represents the steam launch, with native boat towed behind into which the dredge is pulled and the contents sifted, after which we take the buckets of shells, starfish, and the like into the launch and pick over the material we wish to preserve. I never had more convenient and luxuri-

FIG. 351

ous arrangements for the work. On our first excursion it rained very hard and I got wet to the skin. The material brought up was very different from that of the more southern region; the shells were more like northern forms, yet with certain southern forms mixed; beautiful Brachiopods, one a *Terebratulina*, light red in color and heavily ribbed; and other forms which I shall keep alive for study. Yesterday we tore our dredge bag, and so we visited a fishing village about five miles away. The walk led first through a long muddy street, and after that along the beach, where we picked up many curious shells. At the village we found a public place, where, if it had not been for a ravenous appetite, little would have been eaten. After this rest we started for the hills, which gave us a tough pull for nearly a mile through a kind of swamp with the water most of the time up to our knees. It had its attractions, however, with the tall grass, the beautiful purple iris and other flowers, a few interesting little shells, and curiously enough a little polished land shell which is circumpolar in its distribution; it is found all over northern Europe and America, and here it is in Yezo! I also found a large fresh-water snail resembling *Lymnæa auriculata* of Europe. When we finally reached high land we had a grand view of Hakodate and the bay. On our way back we had to tackle the swamp again, and

FIG. 352

we got to Hakodate tired out. I have been wet to the skin, or nearly so, for four days, and yet I never felt better in my life. On our way back we passed a monument erected over the graves of three Japanese who had been beheaded for attempting to incite a rebellion (fig. 352). The simple fragment of dark-gray stone, with the inscription cut on a cleavage surface, might be adopted in our country in place of some of the monuments one sees in our cemeteries.

The other day, on a new way to the beach, I sketched a series of stone images, three feet in height, on a base of rough and finished stones. These were evidently Buddhas, and at right angles to them was a row of square wooden posts each capped with a little roof. These posts had inscriptions upon them. In every post was an iron wheel that could be revolved by hand; tied to the wheels were a number of iron rings which jangled as you gave the wheel a twirl. These are called

FIG. 353

"praying-posts," and the jangle of the iron rings calls the attention of the gods to the supplicants. This was told me by one of my men, and I recalled the praying-wheels of Tibetan Buddhists. In their case every turn is a prayer and by vigorous turning of the wheel you can pour in a volume of sup-plications. I have not yet seen the device in Japan proper, though it may exist. Figure 353 is a sketch of the images and posts, and figure 354 a sketch of the wheel with its jangling rings.

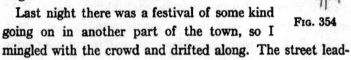

FIG. 354

Last night there was a festival of some kind going on in another part of the town, so I mingled with the crowd and drifted along. The street leading to the temple was illuminated on each side with a double row of lanterns extending for a quarter of a mile. In one of the rows on each side every lantern had an offhand, comic sketch upon it, most of them funny and all of them different. I could not but admire the diversity and ingenuity of the artists, and yet they had all been dashed off in the greatest hurry, as one could see. At the temple an immense crowd had gathered, and the people were pitching their coins into a big box on the veranda, clapping their hands and praying earnestly. The priests were evidently holding high mass and granting dispensations, or at least selling bits of paper to paste over the door to guard against the entrance of evil spirits. The beggars of the town — perhaps a dozen men — were sitting in a row at the side of the avenue and striking bells which they held in their hands in a slow, monotonous bang, keeping time.

It was an odd sight, and it seemed strange to me to be elbowing my way through crowds of these good natured, smiling people. Elbowing is the wrong word for Japan, for no matter how dense the crowd, you never touch those surrounding you: simply say, "Go men na sai" and the crowd parts. Furthermore, I felt perfectly at home, and the many curious objects and incidents which, when I first saw them, kept me busy recording, now no longer arrest my attention, which shows the importance of a journalist instantly jotting down his first impressions.

Figure 355 is of an old house diagonally across from where I live. It is a typical form which one often sees: a fireproof building with a house-like structure built around it. In case of

FIG. 355

fire everything is rushed into the fireproof part and the windows plastered with mud.

July 25. We started for Otaru, on the west coast of Yezo, in a little wooden steamer, the size of a towboat, owned, commanded, and worked by Japanese. I was the only foreigner aboard, and as I watched the way the crew shipped some cows and the lack of efficient directions, I felt some fear of the voyage of three hundred miles we were to undertake along a rocky coast where there were no lighthouses. Moreover, no survey or sailing charts had been made. When we started at ten o'clock at night, it was dark, threatening weather, and I must confess to a little anxiety as we pitched into the darkness of Tsugaru Straits. There was certainly no danger of collision, as there would be no vessel to collide with, but there was danger of the helmsman losing his bearings on a dark and stormy night. Soon after leaving Hakodate we ran into a dense fog, and at midnight a storm came up with heavy rain squalls, and we pitched into it in grand style and were all more or less sick.

In the cabin was a long stack of Spencer repeating rifles, two small steel cannon, and a Gatling gun. This precaution against pirates added a certain excitement to the voyage. All night it stormed and the little vessel pitched fearfully; dishes were smashing in the cuddy, and the cows were stumbling about below. The food served for breakfast was Japanese and simply awful. When we came out of the harbor of Hakodate, a French ironclad had just come in from Yokohama to avoid the excessive heat of the south. She resembled a floating turtle; the bow looked like a plough, and she was tough-looking. Certainly a hundred junks were in the harbor, many with sails spread to dry.

I must remark in passing that never before have I seen a crew of sailors who did not swear or a set of officers who did not peremptorily order. There was no swearing, and every order was given in a quiet manner; even this perilous life did not seem to change the manner of the people.

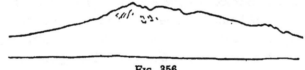

FIG. 356

This morning we awoke to a bright, sunshiny day and in the distance saw a mountain over fifty-five hundred feet high with large patches of snow on its slopes (fig. 356). It is known as Okamui and is thirty miles south of Otaru. It was interesting to realize that we were nearly a thousand miles north of Tokyo and nearer Kamchatka and the Kurile Islands. There was a freshness of air and odor of the north temperate zone, and yet, according to parallels of latitude, not so far north as middle Maine. No one appreciates the sight of land more than one who has been on a rocking ship even for a short voyage: all apprehensions disappear, and no matter at what impossible distance he may be from it, his spirits rise. As we neared our port we sailed round a great point and for a time

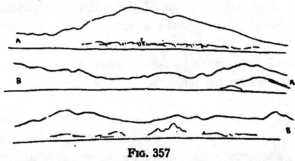

Fig. 357

went due south by the compass. On both sides of the great bay which we entered were ranges of mountains, densely wooded and untrodden by white man; none but Ainus had ever penetrated their ravines, and many regions had not been visited by them. The woods are frequented by savage bears, and the Government offers a high bounty for their destruction. Last winter a Japanese was devoured by bears, and from all the stories told me the creature must be a dangerous one to encounter.

As we approached Otaru I made a sketch of the range of mountains from Okamui to beyond Otaru (fig. 357). To represent them on a single sheet of paper as they looked, one must join A to A, and B to B. The outlines were very interesting and varied from the lower mountain lines I had

seen farther south. As we approached the harbor of Otaru
the shore-line became more distinct, and we then realized
how far inland were the beautiful mountains and how craggy
and precipitous were the low hills which immediately fringed
the coast.

Figure 358 is a rough sketch of the headland just before

FIG. 358

entering the port of Otaru. Some of these cliffs are six to
seven hundred feet in height and rise almost vertically. The
headlands, just before rounding into the harbor of Otaru, are
very striking (fig. 359). I resolved to study them during my
stay at Otaru, but the objects of our expedition were too en-
grossing to permit the time. The whole coast shows evidences
of great elevation and extensive erosion and to the geologist
would furnish material of much interest. The rocks appear
volcanic so far as I could judge, yet near Otaru are signs of
distinct stratification with a sharp northern dip. Extensive
fields of coal are found in the interior of the island. The village
of Otaru is seen straggling along the shore for two miles.

We landed at about ten o'clock, and the way people stared
at us showed that foreigners were yet a novelty. We found our
way to the only tea-house in the town, and the very first thing
that greeted my eye was a little lot of broken pottery in a
basket which I recognized at once as typical shell-heap pottery.
On inquiry I learned that a foreign teacher from Sapporo, in

the interior, had collected it from a shell heap near the village, and had left it for his students to bring back with other specimens which they hoped to get. I at once had some digging implements made by a blacksmith, and in the afternoon we visited the deposits, which were quite extensive, and found quite a number of fragments and a few stone implements

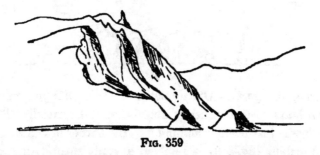

Fig. 359

which I intended giving to the teacher if he was making a study of them.

We were barely settled when an officer came to tell me he had brought some horses from Sapporo for our use, as a telegram had come from Hakodate stating that we were on our way to Sapporo by way of Otaru. On landing I had noticed a little steam launch, and had wondered if it would be possible to secure it for dredging. Yatabe and I made a visit to the head official of the place, to whom we presented our cards, stating our mission, and the fact that we were making collections for the Imperial University. We then gently hinted that our work would be greatly facilitated if we could secure the use of the launch for a few days, adding, furthermore, that the Governor of Hakodate had given us the use of a steam launch at that

place. After these broad suggestions he could not refuse, and
we were offered the use of the launch for two days. Such luck!
We were greatly elated.

The harbor and shore are very picturesque. Curious peaks
of rock stand up from the water like monuments. Figure 360
is a view of some of these remarkable rocks. The lines of
stratification are sharply defined and the uplift excessive.

FIG. 360

Great erosion must have taken place to have left these pin-
nacles of rock. I had no chance to study them and do not
know whether the region has been examined by a geologist.
Most of the work of that nature in Yezo has been done from
an economic standpoint.

Figure 361 is a view from the stone pier at Otaru. It would
make an interesting picture in color. The distant mountains,
the craggy rocks, picturesque boats and houses, the rich color
and contrasts of the vegetation, the pure blue water and rich
brown seaweed would delight the heart of an artist.

I notice a marked difference in the Japanese here as com-

pared with those of middle Japan: the people have more
color in their faces and the women are much taller than those
farther south. There are curious types of fish-women who
come from some northern province of Japan, crossing Tsugaru Straits and settling along the coast during the summer

FIG. 361

months, to trade in fish and peddle through the towns. They
are short in stature, stunted in growth, and very plain. One
little old woman with inflamed eyes, and looking seventy at
least, though she was probably not over fifty, came along the
road with the carrying-stick across her shoulders, and from
either end was suspended a huge basket of a large scallop
which she was peddling. I called her in and bought a number
of her shells and endeavored to lift the load as she did, but
found it impossible to start more than one basket from the
ground. My Japanese companions, in turn, made the attempt,
but the weight was altogether too much for them. The old
woman seemed greatly amused, and when we had given up
trying to raise even one basket, she, although it may seem incredible, quietly lifted this load, and with a polite "sayonara"
went gayly swinging out of the yard and up the street at an

absolute trot. Though this little, dried-up old woman had
already carried the load for a mile or more, she had breath
enough left repeatedly to cry out her market stuff.

Being settled in our tea-house we sought accommodations
for a laboratory. An officer went with us in search of a place,
and we finally found a room in an abandoned inn near the
water, the old post for the sign still standing. The place was

Fig. 362

dirty enough, full of old dried fish in bundles of matting, or
rolls, and from numerous signs the place had also been used
as a tea-house. However, in a short time two coolies cleaned
things after a fashion. A table and a few chairs were brought,
and we unpacked two boxes containing our dredges, jars, alcohol, etc.

Figure 362 shows the building, and our room is indicated
by the door and the opening through which a number of
people are rapturously gazing. Every movement we made and

each bottle we unpacked furnished a theme for conversation, judging from the way their tongues rattled, for never before had they seen such a thing as a zoölogical collecting crowd with an "outside barbarian" thrown in for good measure.

Finally their continual staring annoyed me, and I endeavored to drive them away by deliberately sketching them.

FIG. 363

This, however, had no effect, but I got a sketch, which is shown in figure 363. Our working-room is represented in figure 364.

Our dredging has been very successful, and we have bought many interesting specimens from the fishermen who peddle their products through the village. The natives seem to eat anything and everything that comes from the sea. I am over one hundred miles from Hakodate and from bread-and-butter, and having no meat or other articles of food which I had at Hakodate I have finally resigned myself to the Japanese food of this region and to consider my stomach as a dietetic labo-

ratory which will assimilate the necessary nutritive elements
from the material offered. And of all places to start such an
experiment is this village! It required some courage and a
good stomach to eat for dinner the following: fish soup, very
poor; bean paste, which was not so bad; eggs of sea urchin,
which were served raw and were fairly good-tasting; and holo-

Fig. 364

thurian, or sea cucumber, tough as rubber, doubtless nutritious, but by no means agreeable. It was eaten with Japanese
sauce, *shoyu*, which renders everything more or less palatable.

I had for supper marine worms, — actual worms, resembling our angleworms, only slightly larger, and judging from
the tufts about one end they probably belonged to the genus
Sabella. They were eaten raw and the taste was precisely
as seaweed smells at low tide. I ate a large plateful and slept
soundly. I have also had served and have eaten a gigantic
ascidian belonging to the genus *Cynthia*. I often eat *Haliotis*,

the abalone of California. The scallop is very good. I have
mentioned in this enumeration articles of food the names of
which I know. I am also eating things that I do not know
and cannot even guess what they are. On the whole, I am
keeping body and its animating principle together, but long
for a cup of coffee and a slice of bread-and-butter. I am the
only outside barbarian in town. The children crowd around
me and stare, but the slightest attempt at making friends with
them sends them screaming away in terror.

END OF VOLUME I